MW00697411

PRAISE FOR

OPTION SPREAD STRATEGIES
Trading Up, Down, and Sideways Markets

by Anthony J. Saliba

with Joseph C. Corona and Karen E. Johnson

"Must reading for any professional who wants to learn directly from one of the top leaders in the options industry."

—LARRY CONNORS
CEO, TradingMarkets.com

"An excellent guide for learning how to trade option spreads. Saliba offers in-depth discussions on how and when to employ these advanced strategies and how to manage the risk of each position."

—PETER LIPSKI
Trader, Pan Capital

"*Option Spread Strategies: Trading Up, Down, and Sideways Markets* is an invaluable addition to any market resource collection. The book concisely walks through the dynamics of spread strategies and helps guide the reader though the return and risk metrics of the trades. . . . This is a must-have book for anyone seriously undertaking options investing."

—CHIP NORTON
Managing Director of Research, Fortigent

OPTION SPREAD
STRATEGIES

Also by
ANTHONY J. SALIBA
with Joseph C. Corona and Karen E. Johnson

Option Strategies for Directionless Markets:
Trading with Butterflies, Iron Butterflies, and Condors

Related titles also available from Bloomberg Press

BLOOMBERG MARKET ESSENTIALS: TECHNICAL ANALYSIS

Fibonacci Analysis
by Constance Brown

DeMark Indicators
by Jason Perl

Breakthroughs in Technical Analysis:
New Thinking from the World's Top Minds
edited by David Keller

New Insights on Covered Call Writing:
The Powerful Technique That Enhances Return
and Lowers Risk in Stock Investing
by Richard Lehman and Lawrence G. McMillan

New Thinking in Technical Analysis:
Trading Models from the Masters
edited by Rick Bensignor

Trading ETFs:
Gaining an Edge with Technical Analysis
by Deron Wagner

Trading Option Greeks:
How Timing, Volatility, and Other Pricing Factors Drive Profit
by Dan Passarelli

A complete list of our titles is available at
www.bloomberg.com/books

ATTENTION CORPORATIONS

This book is available for bulk purchase at special discounts. Special editions or chapter reprints can also be customized to specifications. For information, please e-mail Bloomberg Press, press@bloomberg.com, Attention: Director of Special Markets or phone 212-617-7966.

OPTION SPREAD STRATEGIES

Trading Up, Down,
and Sideways Markets

ANTHONY J.
SALIBA with Joseph C. Corona
and Karen E. Johnson

BLOOMBERG PRESS
NEW YORK

© 2009 by International Trading Institute, Ltd. All rights reserved. Protected under the Berne Convention. Printed in Canada. No part of this book may be reproduced, stored in a retrieval system, or transmitted, in any form or by any means, electronic, mechanical, photocopying, recording, or otherwise, without the prior written permission of the publisher except in the case of brief quotations embodied in critical articles and reviews. For information, please write: Permissions Department, Bloomberg Press, 731 Lexington Avenue, New York, NY 10022 or send an e-mail to press@bloomberg.com.

BLOOMBERG, BLOOMBERG ANYWHERE, BLOOMBERG.COM, BLOOMBERG MARKET ESSENTIALS, *Bloomberg Markets*, BLOOMBERG NEWS, BLOOMBERG PRESS, BLOOMBERG PROFESSIONAL, BLOOMBERG RADIO, BLOOMBERG TELEVISION, and BLOOMBERG TRADEBOOK are trademarks and service marks of Bloomberg Finance L.P. ("BFLP"), a Delaware limited partnership, or its subsidiaries. The BLOOMBERG PROFESSIONAL service (the "BPS") is owned and distributed locally by BFLP and its subsidiaries in all jurisdictions other than Argentina, Bermuda, China, India, Japan, and Korea (the "BLP Countries"). BFLP is a wholly-owned subsidiary of Bloomberg L.P. ("BLP"). BLP provides BFLP with all global marketing and operational support and service for these products and distributes the BPS either directly or through a non-BFLP subsidiary in the BLP Countries. All rights reserved.

This publication contains the authors' opinions and is designed to provide accurate and authoritative information. It is sold with the understanding that the authors, publisher, and Bloomberg L.P. are not engaged in rendering legal, accounting, investment-planning, or other professional advice. The reader should seek the services of a qualified professional for such advice; the authors, publisher, and Bloomberg L.P. cannot be held responsible for any loss incurred as a result of specific investments or planning decisions made by the reader.

First edition published 2009

1 3 5 7 9 10 8 6 4 2

Library of Congress Cataloging-in-Publication Data

Saliba, Anthony J.
    Option spread strategies : trading up, down, and sideways markets / Anthony J. Saliba with Joseph C. Corona and Karen E. Johnson. — 1st ed.
        p. cm.
    Includes index.
    Summary: "Proven author Anthony Saliba provides step-by-step instructions for spread trading techniques for options traders. Saliba helps readers understand the nuances of each technique, when to employ each spread strategy, and how to adjust when market conditions change. This hands-on guide includes quizzes and a final exam to help readers test their comprehension"—Provided by publisher.
    ISBN 978-1-57660-260-7 (alk. paper)
    1. Stock options. 2. Options (Finance) I. Corona, Joseph C., 1957- II. Johnson, Karen E., 1967- III. Title.

HG6042.S245 2009
332.64'53—dc22

2008040986

Important Disclosures

Following are several important disclosures we are required to make according to the rules of the Chicago Board Options Exchange (CBOE), by which we are governed. We encourage you to read them.

- Prior to buying or selling an option, one must receive a copy of the booklet "Characteristics and Risks of Standardized Options." Copies of this document are available at www.theocc.com/publications/risks/riskchap1.jsp or from International Trading Institute, Ltd., 311 South Wacker Dr., Suite 4700, Chicago, IL 60606.

- Options involve risk and are not suitable for all investors.

- In order to trade strategies discussed in this book, an individual must first have his account approved by a broker/dealer for that specific trading level.

- No statement in this book should be construed as a recommendation to purchase or sell a security or as an attempt to provide investment advice.

- Writers of uncovered calls or puts will be obligated to meet applicable margin requirements for certain option strategies discussed in this book.

- For transactions that involve buying and writing multiple options in combination, it may be impossible at times to simultaneously execute transactions in all of the options involved in the combination.

- There is increased risk exposure when you exercise or close out of one side of a combination while the other side of the trade remains outstanding.

- Because all option transactions have important tax considerations, you should consult a tax adviser as to how taxes will affect the outcome of contemplated options transactions.

- The examples in this book do not include commissions and other costs. Transaction costs may be significant, especially in option strategies calling for multiple purchases and sales of options, such as spreads and straddles.

- Most spread transactions must be done in a margin account.

- Supporting documentation for any claims and statistical information is available upon request by contacting International Trading Institute, Ltd., 311 South Wacker Dr., Suite 4700, Chicago, IL 60606.

Contents

Acknowledgments

Our goal with this book was to take a basic approach to teaching the intricacies of advanced option strategies so investors could successfully put them to use in their own portfolios. I wish to thank my coauthors, Karen Johnson and Joe Corona, for their diligent efforts on this project.

In addition, I wish to express my gratitude to several of our staff, including David Schmueck, Christopher Hausman, and Scott Mollner, for their proofreading and edits of the manuscript.

I would like to extend a special thank you to the staff at Bloomberg Press, including Stephen Isaacs, JoAnne Kanaval, and Judith Sjo-Gaber, and to Kelli Christiansen at bibliobibuli, all of whom were very helpful and patient throughout the process.

Lastly, I wish to thank my agent, Cynthia Zigmund, for presenting me with this opportunity.

 Anthony J. Saliba
Founder
International Trading Institute

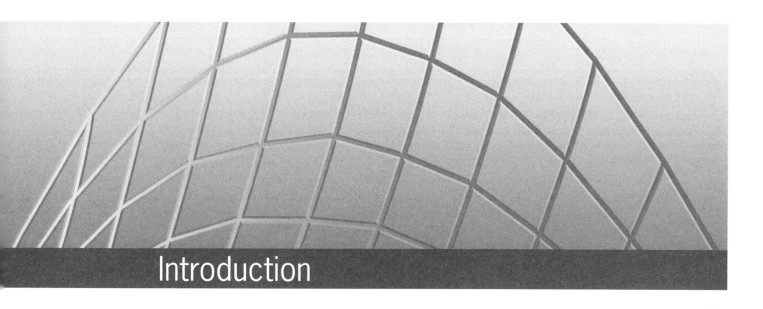

Introduction

The fact that listed option trading volumes are exploding is not news. As of May 1, 2008, volume is up approximately 41 percent over 2007, which was also a record year. Option volumes have grown at a rate of approximately 30 percent per year for the last four years, and have more than tripled since 2000.

The forces driving option growth are much larger than recent market volatility and the need to hedge risk—after all, much of the double-digit growth took place during the low-volatility years of 2003 through early 2007. Several forces have combined to give the individual investor greater access to the options markets and to help level the playing field for the individual and the professional options traders:

Technology—All exchanges are now fully or partially electronic. This has opened up access to the individual options trader, as brokers now supply front-end systems that offer direct connections to every exchange and tools to help analyze, execute, and manage position risk.

Commissions—Commission rates continue to plummet as brokers leverage technology and compete for business.

Number of viable exchanges—The number of options exchanges continues to defy predictions and grow. With the recent addition of the Nasdaq Options Market (NOM), the number has now reached seven. These exchanges are in competition for the business of individual investors, and fee reductions and other incentives are the result.

Educational resources—The number of entities dedicated to options education and training continues to increase, along with the number of investors utilizing their services. The exchanges, the Options Industry Council, brokers, and other private entities offer robust programs at low cost.

Tighter bid-ask spreads—Although it is having a large negative impact on institutional options traders, the penny pilot program is very beneficial to the smaller individual investor because it has tightened spreads in many popular names.

The bigger news in the U.S.-listed options market is the growth in the electronic trading of spreads. Behind the scenes the volume of trading of complex option structures has outpaced overall growth in options trading. This book is dedicated to the art (and science) of spread trading. A number of factors have contributed to the explosion in spread trading:

Electronic spread books—Currently the Chicago Board Options Exchange (CBOE) and the International Securities Exchange (ISE) offer electronic spread books (the Philadelphia Stock Exchange [PHLX] is not far behind). These electronic "complex order books" allow traders the potential to electronically enter and trade multileg spread orders of various strategies—all of which are covered in this book—without the risk of being "legged" (missing one side of the spread). Spreads also can be traded in penny increments even if their underlying options cannot.

Ease of entry and exit—These same electronic spread books are accessible through the same front-end systems offered by most brokers. (If a broker doesn't offer direct access to the spread books, it is time to switch brokers.)

Portfolio-based margining—In the past, the margining of spreads sometimes made them economically unrealistic for many investors. The availability of portfolio-based margining at many brokers has made spread margining more realistic and affordable for many investors.

Limited-risk strategies—Spreads offer investors different ways to participate in market scenarios in a limited-risk fashion. Vertical spreads, butterflies, condors, and time spreads are all limited-risk strategies that the investor can use to address different market scenarios. (After the recent subprime meltdown, limiting risk has once again become fashionable.)

Spread trading is the new frontier for the individual options trader, and this frontier is opening up rapidly. This book is dedicated to spread strategies, both of the limited-risk and unlimited-risk varieties, and to how and when to use them.

OPTION SPREAD
STRATEGIES

1

The Covered-Write

CONCEPT REVIEW

Intrinsic value: The amount by which an option is "in-the-money."

Extrinsic value: The portion of an option price that cannot be attributed to intrinsic value.

Implied volatility: The volatility component of an option's theoretical pricing model determined by using current prices along with other known variables. It may be viewed as the market's forecast of what the average volatility of the underlying instrument might be during the time remaining before its expiration.

Delta: The sensitivity (rate of change) of an option's theoretical value (assessed value) to a $1 move of the underlying instrument.

Gamma: The sensitivity (rate of change) of an option's delta with respect to a $1 change in the price of the underlying instrument.

Theta: The sensitivity (rate of change) of theoretical option prices to the passage of small periods of time. Theta measures the rate of decay in the time value of options. Theta may be expressed as the amount of erosion of an option's theoretical value over one day in time.

Vega: The sensitivity (rate of change) of an option's theoretical value to a change in implied volatility. Vega may be expressed as the number of points of theoretical value gained or lost from a 1-percent rise or fall in implied volatility.

Synthetic: Two or more trading vehicles (for example, call, put, and underlying) packaged together to emulate another trading vehicle or spread. Some examples:

(long call = long put + long underlying) (short call = short put + short underlying)

(long put = long call + short underlying) (short put = short call + long underlying)

(long underlying = long call + short put) (short underlying = short call + long put)

Conversion: A position that consists of a long underlying, a short call, and a long put with the same strike price, which is considered a market neutral position.

Vertical spread: The simultaneous purchase and sale of options of the same class and with the same expiration times but with different strike prices. Depending on which strike is bought and which strike is sold, vertical spreads can be either bullish or bearish. For example, with XYZ July 100/105 call vertical spread, a bullish trader would buy the 100 call and sell the 105 call, whereas a bearish trader would buy the 105 call and sell the 100 call.

STRATEGY OVERVIEW

A *covered-write* is a strategy that combines a long stock position and a short call (**Figure 1.1**). In options parlance a *written* option is an option that is sold, in this case a call, and a short call is *covered* by a long stock

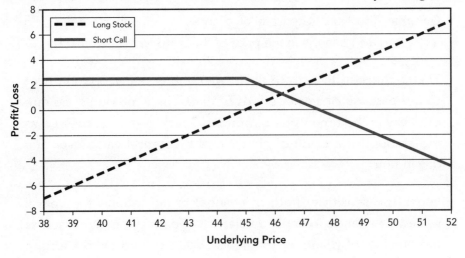

Figure 1.1 Components of a Covered-Write P&L Diagram

position, hence the name *covered-write*. The calls are sold in equal amounts against the long underlying shares. In the United States, the contract size of a stock option is usually 100 shares; therefore, one call would be sold against 100 shares, five calls against 500 shares, and so on. The strike price and expiration date of the call(s) chosen can vary depending on the investment objective, market view, and risk appetite of the investor, as well as the pricing of the calls themselves.

STRATEGY COMPOSITION

Components: Sell one 45 call at $2.25
Purchase 100 shares of XYZ stock at $45.00

Maximum Profit: Limited to the premium received for the sale of the call, plus any increase in value of the underlying up to the strike price of the short call ($2.25)

Maximum Loss: Substantial loss on the downside for the long underlying position (limited by zero), less the premium received for the sale of the call

Breakeven: Price paid for the underlying minus the premium received for the sale of the call ($42.75)

The writing of a call against a long stock position serves two purposes: It generates potential income and provides some downside protection. However, in return, the investor gives away any upside price appreciation in the stock above the strike price.

• Income Generation

The price of an option has two components, intrinsic value and extrinsic value. Intrinsic value is the amount, if any, that the option is "in the money." A call option is in-the-money if the stock price is higher than the strike price. Any remaining value is extrinsic value. Extrinsic value is the additional premium carried by an option based on many factors including, but not limited to, interest rate levels, dividend flows, time to expiration, and implied volatility levels. The extrinsic value of an option declines as time passes, and upon expiration it is gone entirely. This phenomenon is known as *time decay* (see **Figure 1.2**). Sellers of options benefit from time decay (which is referred to as the Greek "theta") as the extrinsic value in an option declines over time. This provides income for the investor in a covered-write strategy, as over time the extrinsic value of the written (sold) call will decline.

• Downside Protection

Writing a call also offers some downside protection for the long stock position, as the premium(s) collected from selling the call can partially

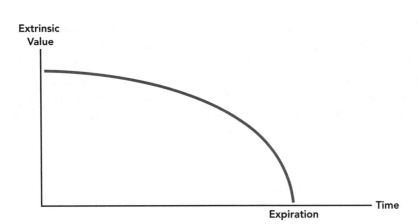

Figure 1.2 Extrinsic Value Diagram

offset a decline in the stock price. However, this protection is only equal to the amount of the premium collected when the call was written. Once the magnitude of the stock decline exceeds the premium collected, the protection ends.

- **Upside Limitations**

A covered-write is a neutral to mildly bullish strategy. The reason it is only a mildly bullish strategy is that the profit potential of the position to the upside is limited by the short call. If the stock price rises above the strike price, the short call becomes in-the-money and begins to accumulate intrinsic value as the stock price rises, eventually offsetting any gains in the stock with losses in the short call. Also, if the stock rises above the strike price and the investor takes no action, it is likely for the stock to be "called away" by the owner of the call. This may have unpleasant tax consequences that should be considered.

Modifications

In the event that the underlying stock falls too far, or rises too high, modifications to the position will have to be made to either limit risk, as in the case of the former, or extend the range of profitability, as in the case of the latter. We will discuss modifications later in the chapter. These modifications may increase execution costs, affecting profitability.

RISK MANAGEMENT: THE GREEKS OF THE COVERED-WRITE

The "Greeks" are metrics used to quantify the sensitivity of option prices to changes in underlying market conditions. They can be effective risk management tools and are especially helpful for understanding and managing the risk of positions. They can also be applied to positions that are combinations of options and underlying positions, such as a covered-write. To evaluate the sensitivity of a position to changing market conditions, the Greeks of the various components of the position are simply summed, giving an aggregate exposure for the position. It must be understood, however, that as market conditions change, the Greeks themselves also change, so the Greeks of any position are in a constant state of flux.

Basic pricing models calculate the theoretical price of an option based on six inputs used to describe market conditions:

- Underlying price

- Strike price

- Time to expiration

- Interest rates

- Dividends (if any)

- Implied volatility

Since a covered-write position is part option and part stock, it is the Greeks of the option component of the position that will change; the Greeks of the stock component of the position will remain constant. A brief review of the basic Greeks follows, to help the reader understand how a covered-write position behaves as market conditions change.

THE GREEKS

Delta

Delta describes the sensitivity (rate of change) of an option's price with respect to changes in the underlying price. Expressed as a percentage, it represents an equivalent amount of the underlying at a given moment in time. Calls are assigned a positive delta (call option prices are positively correlated with the underlying price); puts are assigned a negative delta (put option prices are negatively correlated with the underlying price). The delta of a call option can range between 0.00 (0 percent) and 1.00 (100 percent), while the delta of a put option can range between 0.00 (0 percent) and −1.00 (−100 percent). (See **Figures 1.3** and **1.4**.) A short position in any of the above call or put options reverses the delta; for example, a short call will have a negative delta and a short put will have a positive delta.

Examples

By what amount can one expect the price of a call with a delta of 0.50 (50 percent) to change if the stock price rises by 1.00?

$$1.00 \times 0.50 = 0.50$$

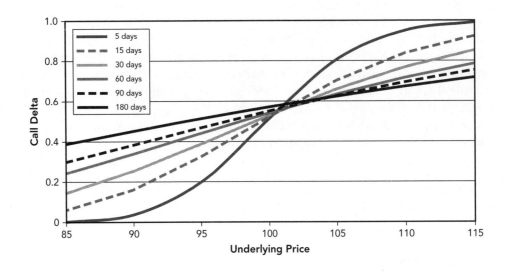

Figure 1.3 100 Call Delta vs. Underlying Price

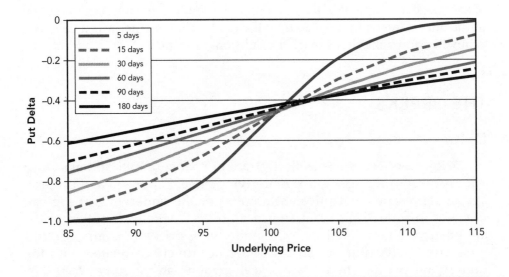

Figure 1.4 100 Put Delta vs. Underlying Price

A long call with a delta of 0.50 (50 percent) represents what equivalent amount of the underlying stock?

$$+100 \times 0.50 = +50 \text{ shares}$$

The delta of an underlying position is constant, and is represented by the actual amount and position in the shares; for example, long 100 shares is a delta of +100, and short 100 shares is a delta of −100.

• **Delta of a Covered-Write**

The delta of a covered-write position is simply the sum of the deltas of the components.

Example

What is the delta of a covered-write consisting of 100 shares of long stock and short 1 call with a .50 delta?

$$100 + (100 \times -.50) = 100 + (-50) = 50 \text{ shares}$$

Note that the delta of the call is reversed because it is a short call.

Gamma

The delta of an option does not remain constant because it is sensitive to changes in market conditions, one of these being changes in underlying price. Gamma describes the sensitivity (rate of change) of an option's delta with respect to changes in the underlying price. The convention is to express gamma in terms of the change in delta produced by a one-point move in the underlying. For example, if the delta of a 100 call changed from 0.50 to 0.60 as the underlying moved from 100.00 to 101.00, the call would be said to have a gamma of .10 because the delta changed by .10 as the underlying price rose. If the underlying price declined from 100.00 to 99.00, the delta of the call would fall from 0.50 to 0.40. This would have an impact on the delta of a covered-write position because as the underlying price changed, the delta of the short call would change, affecting the delta of the overall position.

Example

An investor has a covered-write position consisting of 100 shares of long stock and short one .50 delta call. The call has a gamma of .10. What is the delta of the overall position if:

The stock rises 1.00 . . .

$$+100 + (100 \times -(0.50 + 0.10)) = +40 \text{ shares}$$

The stock falls 1.00 . . .

$$+100 + (100 \times -(0.50 - 0.10)) = +60 \text{ shares}$$

Note that the gamma simply increases or decreases the delta of the option as the underlying price changes; it does not change whether the delta is positive or negative.

The gamma of an option is not linear and is also sensitive to market conditions. It is highly dependent on the location of the strike price relative to the underlying price (sometimes called *moneyness*) and the time left until expiration. **Figure 1.5** shows the relationship between the gamma of an option, moneyness, and time until expiration.

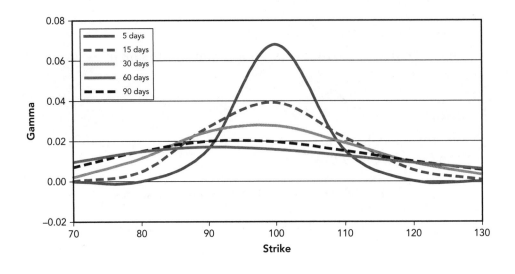

Figure 1.5 Gamma vs. Strike

Gamma is highest when an option is at-the-money, and the rate of change of gamma itself increases as expiration approaches. For the covered-write, this means that the delta of the position will change the most as the underlying crosses the strike of the short call, and that this effect will be greater as time to expiration decreases.

Vega

Vega describes the sensitivity of an option's theoretical value to a 1 percent change in implied volatility. It is usually expressed as the change in value that would be gained or lost from a 1 percent rise or fall in implied volatility. Long option positions have a positive vega, and short option positions have a negative vega. Because a covered-write has a short call as its option component, it will always have a negative vega.

Rising implied volatility causes the extrinsic value of options to rise, and falling implied volatility causes the extrinsic value of options to fall. Furthermore, longer-dated options are more sensitive to changes in implied volatility, since a rise or fall of implied volatility over a longer period is extrapolated to a much larger (in the case of rising volatility) or much smaller (in the case of falling volatility) universe of possible price outcomes at expiration. This is illustrated in **Figure 1.6**.

Because a covered-write has a negative vega, rising implied volatility will cause the value of the structure to fall as the short call component of the strategy rises in price. Conversely, falling implied volatility will cause the value of the covered-write to rise, as the short call component of the strategy falls in price. In addition, the value of a covered-write with a longer-dated short call component will be more sensitive to fluctuations in implied volatility than a covered-write with a shorter-dated short call component.

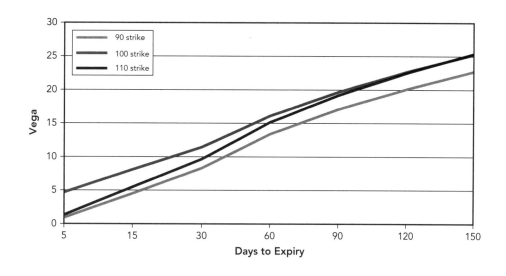

Figure 1.6 Vega vs. Time to Expiration

Example

An investor has a covered-write position consisting of 100 shares of long stock at $100.00 and short one 100 strike call at $5.00. The call has a vega of 0.10. With the stock unchanged, what is the change in value of the overall position if:

Implied volatility rises 5 percent . . .

The price of the call will change from $5.00 to $5.50 ($5.00 + 5 × 0.10), so the value of the position will change accordingly:

Initial Position Value ➤ **New Position Value**

Stock price	$100.00		Stock price	$100.00
− Call price	$5.00		− Call price	$5.50
Position value	$95.00		Position value	$94.50

Implied volatility falls 5 percent . . .

The price of the call will change from $5.00 to $4.50 ($5.00 − 5 × 0.10), so the value of the position will change accordingly:

Initial Position Value ➤ **New Position Value**

Stock price	$100.00		Stock price	$100.00
− Call price	$5.00		− Call price	$4.50
Position value	$95.00		Position value	$95.50

As these examples show, rising implied volatility works against a covered-write, while falling implied volatility works in favor of a covered-write.

Theta

Theta is used to describe the sensitivity of an option's theoretical value to the passage of time. It is usually expressed as the number of points that are lost from one day's time decay. Long option positions have a negative theta, and short option positions have a positive theta. Because a covered-write has a short call as its option component, it will always have a positive theta.

As mentioned above in "Strategy Overview," all options are composed of intrinsic value and extrinsic value, and as time passes, the extrinsic value begins to decay. At expiration, the extrinsic value is gone, and an option is either in-the-money and has intrinsic value, or it expires worthless. This means that, all else being equal, the theoretical value of an option should fall by some amount every day. However, this amount varies because the rate at which extrinsic value decays is not linear and is itself dependent on other market factors, especially time to expiration and moneyness, as can be seen in **Figure 1.7**:

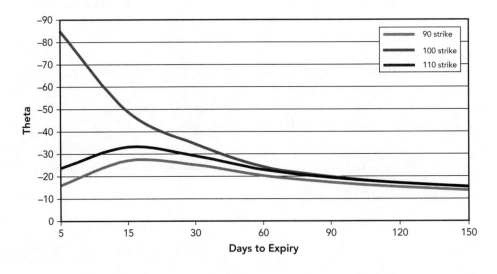

Figure 1.7 Theta vs. Time to Expiration

We can see in the figure that the theta of all long-dated options is low and is very similar for the 90, 100, and 110 strike calls. As time moves forward toward expiration, time decay begins to accelerate and the theta for all of the options begins to rise. Then, as expiration approaches, the in- and out-of-the-money calls (the 90 and 110 strike calls) lose their extrinsic value early, and their thetas begin to decline. Notice, however, that the theta of the 100 strike call, which is the at-the-money option, begins to accelerate. Heading into expiration, when the surrounding in- and out-of-the-money options no longer have extrinsic value to lose, the decay of the at-the-money option will continue to accelerate.

Example

An investor has a covered-write position consisting of 100 shares of long stock at $100.00 and short one 100 strike call at $5.00. The call has a theta of 0.02. With the stock unchanged and implied volatility unchanged, what is the change in value of the overall position if:

Five trading days pass . . .

The price of the call will change from $5.00 to $4.90 ($5.00 − 5 × 0.02), so the value of the position will change accordingly:

Initial Position Value	⟶	New Position Value
Stock price	$100.00	Stock price	$100.00
− Call price	$5.00	− Call price	$4.90
Position value	$95.00	Position value	$95.10

As this example shows, time decay works in favor of a covered-write.

INVESTMENT OBJECTIVES

As mentioned earlier in "Strategy Overview," the covered-write strategy is a neutral to mildly bullish strategy. The main objectives of a covered-write are the generation of income and limited downside protection. Every covered-write is a mixture of both and, depending on how the investor structures the trade, that is, which strike price and expiration cycle are chosen, the trade will be more of one and less of the other. It is also *extremely* important to distinguish between the covered-write as a long-term, systematic strategy, and the covered-write as a short-term trade.

Covered-Write as a Long-Term Strategy

Investors who use the covered-write as a long-term strategy usually have a core portfolio of stocks that—up or down, better or worse—they will hold. They systematically write calls against the stocks in the portfolio to help generate income, and, over time, lower the cost basis of the portfolio. Even though the written calls provide some downside protection for the portfolio, these investors are not as sensitive to downside risk because they will be holding the portfolio regardless of whether the market rises or falls in the short-term.

Covered-Write as a Short-Term Trading Strategy

The investor who uses the covered-write as a short-term trading strategy usually purchases the stock specifically for the purpose of writing a call against it and creating a strategy. Many times this trade is executed as a spread on an exchange known as a *buy-write*. The stock is not part of a long-term core portfolio, and, therefore, the short-term covered-write investor is usually much more sensitive to downside risk than the long-term covered-write investor is and requires a stronger, bullish market view.

Rates of Return

Regardless of whether one is a short-term or long-term covered writer, the best outcome is a slow rise that allows the stock to appreciate in price while the option slowly decays, and, hopefully, expires worthless. This allows the investor to capture both the price appreciation in the stock and the time decay in the option, generating a profit on the overall position. The exact amount of profit depends on how the covered-write was constructed, the stock price, the option price, and the strike price. Usually covered-write strategies are analyzed in terms of rates of return at various points:

- **Return to Call**

This is the rate of return generated on the position if the stock price is at the strike price or higher at expiration, a price at which the stock would be called away by the holder of the written call. The stock price at or higher than the strike price is the best-case scenario for a covered-write:

$$\text{Return to call} = \left(\frac{K}{(S_1 - C)} - 1 \right) \times 100\%$$

Where:
  C = Call price
  K = Strike price
  S_1 = Beginning stock price

Example

An investor buys stock at a price of \$100.00 and sells a 105 strike call against it for \$5.00. There are thirty days until expiration. What would be the rate of return if the stock were called?

$$\left(\frac{105}{(100 - 5)} - 1 \right) \times 100\% = 10.53\%$$

- **Return to Unchanged**

This is the rate of return generated on the position if the stock is unchanged but is still lower than the strike price at expiration, meaning an out-of-the-money call was written. This is the rate of return if the written call expires worthless while the stock remains unchanged:

$$\text{Return to unchanged} = \left(\frac{S_2}{(S_1 - C)} - 1 \right) \times 100\%$$

Where:
  C = Call price
  S_1 = Beginning stock price
  S_2 = Ending stock price

Example

An investor buys stock at a price of $100.00 and sells a 105 strike call against it for $5.00. There are thirty days until expiration. What would be the rate of return if the stock were unchanged at expiration?

$$\left(\frac{100}{(100 - 5)} - 1 \right) \times 100\% = 5.26\%$$

Return to call and *Return to unchanged* are variations of the same formula with the numerator representing the selling price for the stock at the end of expiration. In the case of *Return to call,* the numerator is represented by the strike price, because that is the price an investor would receive for his stock if it were called. In *Return to unchanged* it is represented by the current stock price, because that is the price an investor would receive for his stock if he wished to sell it in the open market.

Break-Even Point

The break-even point is the point at which the decline in stock price equals the amount of premium collected on the written call. At this point all of the protection furnished by the written call is "used up" and the investor is exposed to losses if the stock continues lower:

$$\text{Break-even point} = S_1 - C$$

Where:
  C = Call price
  S_1 = Beginning stock price

Example

You buy stock at a price of $100.00 and sell a 105 strike call against it for $5.00. There are thirty days until expiration. What is the break-even point?

$$\textit{Break-even point} = \$100.00 - \$5.00 = \$95.00$$

STRATEGY COMPONENT SELECTION

So how does one structure a good covered-write strategy? The answer to this question depends on many of the variables we have discussed in previous sections:

- What is one's current market forecast?

  — Neutral

  — Mildly bullish

  — Moderately bullish

- What is one's risk appetite?
    - Is covered-writing part of a long-term strategy against a portfolio?
    - Is covered-writing part of a short-term trading strategy?
- What is the goal of one's covered-write?
    - Income generation?
    - Downside protection?
    - Some of each?
- What is the current state of implied volatility in the market?
    - High volatility?
    - Low volatility?
    - What are the potential rates of return?

What Is One's Current Market Forecast?

As we have mentioned several times, the covered-write is a neutral to moderately bullish strategy, so, first and foremost, it is mandatory to have a neutral to moderately bullish outlook on the stock or portfolio one is considering as a candidate for a covered-write program. An extremely bullish strategy is inappropriate because the upside is limited, and a bearish approach is also inappropriate because the long stock portion of the position will lose money, which is only partially offset by the premium received when writing the call. A sharp or sustained move lower in a stock or portfolio is disastrous for covered-writes.

Whatever methodology one chooses to use for forecasting market behavior—fundamental analysis, technical analysis, broker forecasts and research, or other methods—one should consider a covered-write strategy only if confident in a market forecast of neutral to moderately bullish. Where the forecast falls within that range will help determine strike selection. It is always desirable to have the stock price greater than or equal to the strike price at expiration, to achieve maximum returns, so the strike selected for writing should be where one expects the stock to be at expiration.

• Neutral to Bullish

With a neutral outlook one is likely forecasting little change in the underlying price through expiration. In this case, one would want to write a call that is at-the-money to potentially achieve maximum returns.

• Mildly Bullish

With a mildly bullish outlook, one is most likely forecasting a slight rise in the underlying price through expiration. In this case, one would want to write a call that is out-of-the-money in the expected target zone to potentially achieve maximum returns.

- **Moderately Bullish**

With a moderately bullish outlook, one is likely forecasting a more substantial rise in the underlying price through expiration. In this case, one would want to write a call that is further out-of-the-money in the expected target zone to attempt to achieve maximum returns.

What Is One's Risk Appetite?

The risk appetite of an investor interested in pursuing a covered-write strategy is usually determined by the category into which he falls in terms of time frame. Risk appetite determines strike selection and duration. The risk in a covered-write is determined by the premium received for the written call, which provides some downside protection for the stock position. This premium, in turn, is determined by the location of the strike price relative to the stock price (moneyness) and the time until expiration (duration).

- **Long-Term (High Risk Appetite)**

The long-term covered writer usually has a portfolio of stocks that he or she has selected to hold. These investors have purchased the stocks in their portfolios because they like their long-term prospects and because they intend to hold them no matter what the market chooses to do in the short-term. They are pursuing a covered-write strategy against the stocks in their portfolio in order to help generate income and lower the overall cost basis of the portfolio. They are not particularly interested in the downside protection aspect of the covered-write since they are going to hold their portfolio regardless of what the market might do; therefore, they are less sensitive to risk.

High Risk Appetite: Investors with high risk appetites can afford to collect less premium for downside protection; this allows them to write calls that are further out-of-the-money or of shorter duration. Writing calls that are further out-of-the-money creates a covered-write that has a stronger bullish stance, allowing for more potential appreciation in the stock price. Writing calls of shorter duration generates a larger time decay (theta) for faster income generation.

- **Short-Term (Low Risk Appetite)**

The short-term covered writer usually enters the position as a trade. In other words, he has no particular long-term view for the stock that he is buying; he is more interested in the potential return of the covered-write itself, and is attracted to situations where high volatility (higher call premiums) are throwing off high potential rates of return. Because, for these investors, the covered-write is a short-term strategy or trade, they are very sensitive to risk because a loss in the position cannot be recouped over time as it might be with a long-term covered-write. Indeed, because short-term covered writers tend to be more the "trader" type than the "investor" type, they tend to keep their trades on a short leash, may only be in the trade a few days, and will exit at the first sign of trouble.

Low Risk Appetite: The investor with a low risk appetite needs to collect more premium for downside protection; this forces him to write calls that are at- or even in-the-money or of longer duration. Writing calls that are at- or in-the-money creates a covered-write that has a defensive stance of neutral to slightly bearish, and this removes any chance for upside appreciation in the stock price. Writing calls of longer duration will generate a smaller time decay (theta), slowing potential income generation.

What Is the Purpose of the Covered-Write?

• Income Generation

Time decay is the key to income generation, and, as we noted in the earlier discussion of theta in "Strategy Composition," shorter-dated options have a higher rate of time decay (a larger theta) than longer-dated options, and at-the-money options have a higher rate of time decay than in- or out-of-the-money options. This pushes the investor interested in income generation into the short-dated options. Of course, this has to be balanced with market view and risk appetite, which require some give and take, but, in general, covered writers interested in quick income generation need to be operating in the shorter-dated (forty-five days to expiry and less) options that are near-the-money. This produces maximum time decay.

• Downside Protection

The investor interested in protecting his portfolio needs to generate larger premiums when writing calls against his holdings. Calls that are in-the-money, or of longer duration, generally carry larger premiums. Writing calls that are in-the-money creates a covered-write that has more of a defensive stance, which offers greater downside protection. However, structuring a covered-write in this fashion eliminates most if not all of the potential for upside appreciation in the stock price. In addition, writing calls of longer duration will result in a smaller time decay (theta), thus slowing income generation and increasing the holding period for the trade.

What Is the Current State of Implied Volatility in the Market?

Implied volatility is determined by the current pricing of options in the marketplace. By using the current option price and an option pricing model, investors are able to solve for the volatility implied by the option price. An option calculator such as the one on the Chicago Board Options Exchange (CBOE) website can make this calculation easier (www.cboe.com).

Implied volatility reflects the consensus opinion of options market participants about what the expected volatility of the underlying will be through expiration. High implied volatility means that market participants are expecting high volatility in the price of the underlying through that particular expiration cycle. Low implied volatility means that market participants are expecting low volatility in the price of the underlying through that particular expiration cycle. Implied volatility is in a constant state of flux as new information influences the market and alters the expectations of the participants. It is a "market" in and of itself.

As we discussed in "Strategy Composition," when we examined vega, rising implied volatility causes option prices to rise, while falling implied volatility causes option prices to fall. This has a direct impact on the covered-write because it is the premium generated by the sale of the call option(s) that determines the risk, reward, break-even point, and potential rate of return of the strategy.

• High Implied Volatility

As mentioned previously, high implied volatility means that market participants are expecting high volatility (that is, a lot of movement) in the price of the underlying through that particular expiration cycle. That means three things to the potential covered writer:

- Market participants see risk in the price of the underlying.

- Premiums may be elevated to reflect this risk.

- Rates of return may be higher than normal to reflect this risk.

Remember that the first and most important determining factor for a covered-write strategy is a neutral to moderately bullish forecast for the underlying price. High implied volatility is an indication that market participants have built in the possibility of greater than usual movement in the underlying price both to the upside and downside. In other words, they see risk and, because of that, option prices and rates of return on a covered-write are elevated to reflect this perceived risk. The investor who is confident of a neutral to bullish forecast for the stock and who has a view opposite the marketplace may be rewarded, if correct, by a higher than usual rate of return. But remember: It is the neutral to bullish price forecast that should be the first determining factor for a covered-write, never the rate of return! The rate of return is simply an indicator of the risk level perceived by market participants at that time. Using rate of return to determine covered-write strategies is a trap.

• Low Implied Volatility

Low implied volatility means that market participants are expecting low volatility (that is, a lack of movement) in the price of the underlying through that particular expiration cycle. That means three things to the potential covered writer:

- Market participants may see low risk in the price of the underlying.

- Premiums may be depressed to reflect this lack of risk.

- Rates of return may be lower than normal to reflect this lack of risk.

Once again remember that the first and most important determining factor for a covered-write strategy is a neutral to mildly bullish forecast for the underlying price. Low implied volatility is an indication that market participants may have built in the possibility of less than usual movement in the underlying price both to the upside and downside. In other words, they see potentially less risk, and because of that, option prices and rates of return on a covered-write are somewhat lower to reflect this perceived relatively reduced risk.

TRADE MANAGEMENT

Regardless of whether one falls into the short-term or long-term, high-risk or low-risk category, one thing is for sure: After the trade is selected and executed, it will have to be managed. As time passes and the underlying moves up or down, adjustments will have to be made. As we have mentioned time and again in the preceding pages, the covered-write is a neutral to moderately bullish strategy. If the behavior of the underlying deviates from that scenario, that is, moves too far to the upside or too far to the downside, action will need to be taken. When expiration approaches and the written call loses all of its extrinsic value, action will need to be taken, and, of course, if one's market view changes or if one wishes to lock in profits or reduce losses, action will need to be taken. The covered-write is not the "forget about it and watch the money roll in" strategy as seen on late-night television.

Adjustments

- **Situation 1: Change in Market View**

Once again, the covered-write is a strategy to be applied in a neutral to moderately bullish environment. If one's market view suddenly shifts away from neutral to moderately bullish (that is, becomes bearish or rampantly bullish) then the covered-write is an inappropriate strategy and should be liquidated. There are actually two ways to exit a covered-write quickly. One is to liquidate the original position as:

Example 1: Liquidation of a Covered-Write Consisting of Long 100 Shares of XYZ and Short 1 XYZ June 100 Call

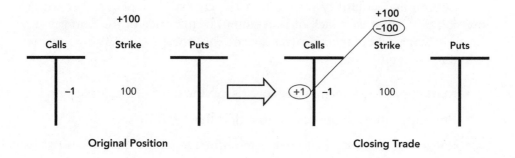

The second method is to utilize a synthetic relationship that exists between a covered-write position and the put of the same strike and expiration. A covered-write is actually the synthetic equivalent of a short put of the same strike and expiration of the short call component of the covered-write. This means that the covered-write behaves exactly as a short put in terms of the risk, reward, and break-even points of the position. So a quick way to cauterize a covered-write position is to purchase the put of the same strike and expiration cycle as the short call in the covered-write position.

Example 2: Liquidation of a Covered-Write Consisting of Long 100 Shares of XYZ and Short 1 XYZ June 100 Call Using the Synthetically Equivalent Position

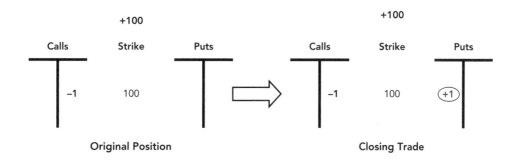

Using this technique leaves a residual arbitrage position known as a *conversion*. The conversion has very little risk but still may require some capital to hold, and it may or may not have to be managed at expiration regarding the exercise of the long put. This liquidation option is meant for an emergency situation in which one has to bail out of the position quickly.

• Situation 2: Underlying Moves Up Through the Strike

Once the underlying stock or index moves up through the strike, the upside profit potential of the covered-write is capped. In order to give the position some more upside potential, the short call has to be "rolled up" to a higher strike. This can be accomplished by buying a vertical call spread, covering the short call, and selling a higher strike call in the same expiration month. Or it can be accomplished by executing a diagonal call spread known as an *up and out*—covering the short call and selling a higher strike call in a further deferred expiration month. Which method is chosen usually depends on the cost of the "roll." The purchase of a long call spread will cost the investor some money, thus adding to the cost basis of the position, whereas the up and out diagonal call spread will usually cost less, or depending on the time to expiration of the call to be sold, could even be executed for no cost or a credit. For this reason, many covered writers opt for the diagonal up and out adjustment.

Example 1: Rolling the Covered-Write Up Using a Long Call Spread

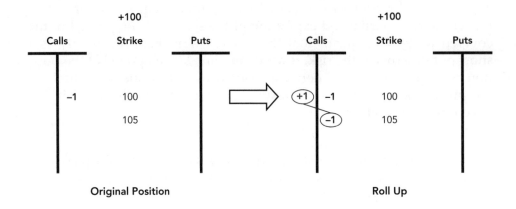

In the preceding example, the 100/105 call spread is purchased, closing out the short call position at the 100 strike and establishing a new short call position at the 105 strike. This gives the position 5.00 more points of "room to run" to the upside, but the cost of the strategy is increased by the cost of the call spread.

Example 2: Rolling the Covered-Write Up and Out with a Diagonal Call Spread

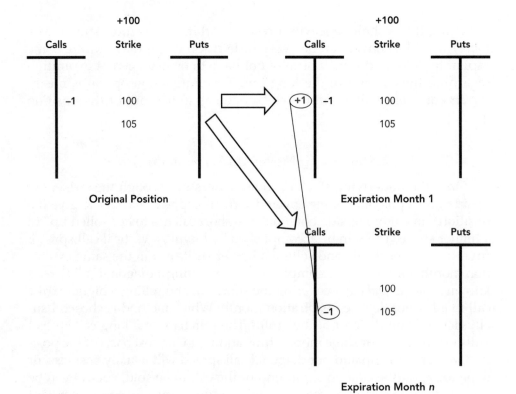

In the preceding example, the 100/105 diagonal call spread is purchased, closing out the short call position at 100 strike in the original expiration month and establishing a new short call position at the 105 strike in expiration month *n*. This gives the position 5.00 more points of "room to run" to the upside, and the cost of the strategy is increased or decreased by the debit or credit, respectively, of the diagonal call spread.

- **Situation 3: The Underlying Weakens or Moves Lower; More Protection Is Desired**

The covered-write does offer a modest amount of downside protection for long underlying positions. The amount of this protection is equal to the premium collected when the investor writes the call. If he wants additional protection, additional premiums must be collected. This can be accomplished by "rolling down" the short call to a lower strike by selling a vertical call spread in the same expiration month. Or, it can be accomplished by executing a diagonal call spread known as a *down and out*—covering the short call and selling a lower strike call in a deferred expiration. Both strategies should generate a credit that will provide further downside protection for the underlying position. Which method is chosen usually depends on the amount of protection wanted and the size of the credit that can be generated.

Example 1: Rolling the Covered-Write Down Using a Short Vertical Call Spread

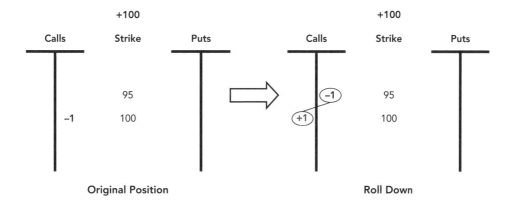

In the preceding example, the 95/100 call spread is sold, closing out the short call position at 100 strike and establishing a new short call position at the 95 strike. Depending on the credit generated, this gives additional downside protection to the underlying position.

Example 2: Rolling the Covered-Write Using a Down and Out Diagonal
            Call Spread

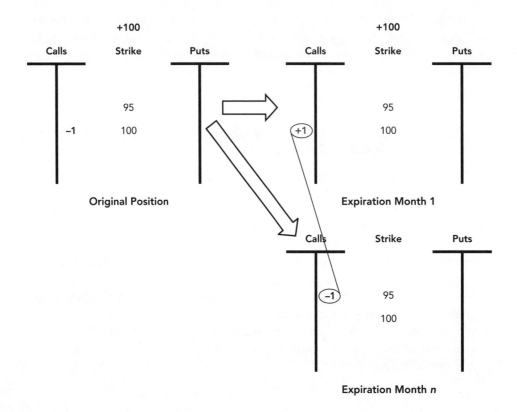

In the preceding example, the 100/95 diagonal call spread is sold, closing out the short call position at 100 strike in the original expiration month and establishing a new short call position at the 95 strike in expiration month n. Depending on the credit generated, this gives additional downside protection to the underlying position.

COVERED-WRITES are not "fire and forget" trades. They require attention, and multiple adjustments may have to be made to maintain one's risk profile as the market moves up, down, or sideways, and as the clock ticks.

The covered-write can be an excellent strategy for generating income against a portfolio of stocks that will be held for the long term. Covered-writes also offer modest (limited) downside protection for a portfolio, and they may be an excellent trading strategy for very specific market conditions discussed in this chapter: steady to rising underlying prices and/or steady to falling implied volatility levels.

A word of caution, however, covered-writes are not the "instant cash machines" or the "fire and forget" strategies as advertised on late night television and Internet sites. Covered-writes require hard work, discipline, and attention to detail. Underlying price and implied volatility levels need to be monitored closely for possible entry opportunities. After the position has been entered, the analysis of both underlying price and implied volatility levels must continue. Adjustments to the position must be made as price swings, changes in implied volatility levels, and the passage of time shifts risk/reward ratios either for or against the trader.

It cannot be forgotten that covered-writes are risky positions, with a risk profile identical to that of a short put. This means there can be large risk to the downside with limited upside potential—not a great risk/reward profile except for very specific market conditions as discussed. The downside risk must be managed ruthlessly so that when the forecast of conditions benevolent to a covered-write position—steady to rising underlying price, steady to falling implied volatility—is proven wrong, the trader must exit or neutralize the position immediately.

CHAPTER 1 EXERCISE

1. A conversion consists of a long underlying position, a short call, and a long put. True or false?

2. An increase in volatility will have a negative effect on the covered-write position since an option with a higher volatility may have a better chance of ending up in-the-money. True or false?

3. A short call will always have a positive theta. True or false?

4. Will falling implied volatility cause the value of the covered-write to rise or fall?

5. A covered-write will always have a positive vega. True or false?

6. What is the synthetic equivalent of a covered-write?

7. To allow for increased upside potential for the covered-write, an investor could purchase a vertical call spread. True or false?

8. What is the delta of a covered-write consisting of 100 shares of long stock and short a delta call of 40?

9. Does time decay have a positive or a negative effect on the covered-write position?

10. If an investor's opinion is neutral to bullish and he expects little change in the underlying price through expiration, would the investor want to sell a call that is at-the-money or out-of-the-money?

Chapter 1 Exercise Answer Key

1. True
2. True
3. True

4. Rise
5. False
6. Short put having the same strike and same expiration as the short call
7. True
8. 60 [100 + (100 × −40) = 100 + (−40) = 60 shares]
9. Positive (time decay works for the position)
10. At-the-money

CHAPTER 1 QUIZ

1. The profit for a covered-write strategy is limited to the premium received for the sale of the call. True or false?

2. How is the break-even point of the covered-write strategy calculated?

3. With a covered-write strategy, is the gamma at the highest or the lowest when the option is at-the-money?

4. An investor purchases stock at $100.00 and sells a 100 strike call against it for $8.00. Calculate the rate of return for the covered-write at expiration if the stock remains unchanged (assume expiration is thirty days away).

5. If an investor purchases stock at $105.00 and sells a 100 call against it for $7.00, what is the break-even point? (Assume thirty days to expiration.)

6. If an investor is bullish, anticipating a substantial rise in the underlying, and is considering a covered-write strategy, would he want to write a call that is at-the-money or out-of-the-money?

7. Relative to longer-dated options, do shorter-dated options have a higher or a lower rate of time decay?

8. Once the underlying breaks through the strike of the covered-write, the profit on the upside is capped. True or false?

9. To allow a covered-write to have more upside potential, would an investor buy or sell a vertical call spread?

10. A covered-write behaves like as a short put in terms of risk, reward, and break-even points. True or false?

Chapter 1 Quiz Answer Key

1. False (plus any increase in value in the underlying)
2. Price paid for the underlying minus the premium received for the sale of the call
3. Highest

4. 8.69% $\{[100 \div (100 - 8)] - 1\} \times 100\%$
5. $98.00 ($105.00 − $7.00)
6. Out-of-the-money
7. Higher
8. True
9. Buy
10. True

2

Verticals

CONCEPT REVIEW

Implied volatility: The determination of the volatility component of an option theoretical pricing model by using current prices along with other known variables rather than historical prices and variables.

Synthetics: Two or more trading instruments packaged to emulate another trading instrument or vehicle. For example:

synthetic long call = long stock + long put

synthetic short call = short stock + short put

synthetic long put = short stock + long call

synthetic short put = long stock + short call

synthetic long stock = long call + short put

synthetic short stock = short call + long put

Butterfly spread: A strategy that combines four option contracts of the same type that span three strike prices. For example: Buy one call at the lowest strike price, sell two calls at the next higher strike price, and buy one call at the third highest strike price.

STRATEGY OVERVIEW

A vertical spread is the simultaneous purchase and sale of options of the same class (calls or puts) and expiration, but with different strike prices. Vertical spreads are directional strategies typically employed under the following circumstances:

- To capture moderate underlying moves to the upside or downside
- To implement limited-risk bullish or bearish positions when implied volatility levels are high and the outright purchase of a call or put is too expensive
- To help lower the overall risk of a bullish or bearish position
- To combine a directional view with an implied volatility view
- To help generate short-premium income in a limited-risk fashion

STRATEGY COMPOSITION

Depending on which strike is bought and which strike is sold, the vertical spread can have either a bullish or a bearish bias. For example, if the trader were bullish, he could purchase the bull call spread or the bull put spread. Let's look first at the components of a bull call spread and examine the risk/reward profile (**Figure 2.1**).

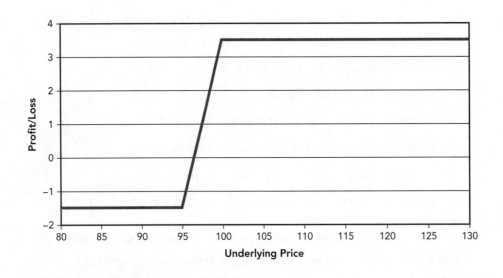

Figure 2.1 Bull Call Spread P&L Diagram

Bull Call Spread

Components:	Buy Sept. 95 call at $5.00
	Sell Sept. 100 call at $3.50
Debit Incurred:	$1.50
Breakeven:	$96.50 (lower strike plus price paid for the spread)

| Maximum Loss: | $1.50 (price paid for the spread) |
| Maximum Profit: | $3.50 (difference between strikes minus price paid for the spread) |

Or, the bullish trader could choose to employ puts. Let's look at the components of the bull put spread and examine the risk/reward profile (**Figure 2.2**):

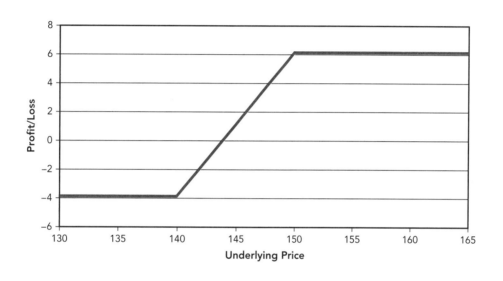

Figure 2.2 Bull Put Spread P&L Diagram

Bull Put Spread

Components:	Buy Sept. 140 put at $3.50 Sell Sept. 150 put at $9.60
Credit Received:	$6.10
Breakeven:	$143.90 (higher strike minus credit)
Maximum Loss:	$3.90 (difference between strikes minus credit)
Maximum Profit:	$6.10 (credit received)

Alternatively, if the trader were bearish, he could purchase the bear call spread or the bear put spread. Let's look at the components of both and examine the risk/reward profiles (**Figures 2.3** and **2.4**):

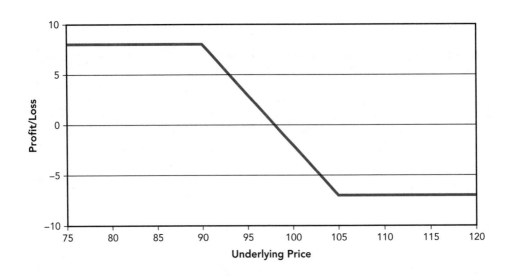

Figure 2.3 Bear Call Spread P&L Diagram

Bear Call Spread

Components: Buy Sept. 105 call at $2.10
                     Sell Sept. 90 call at $10.10

Credit Received: $8.00

Breakeven: $98.00 (lower strike plus credit received)

Maximum Loss: $7.00 (difference between strikes minus credit)

Maximum Profit: $8.00 (credit received)

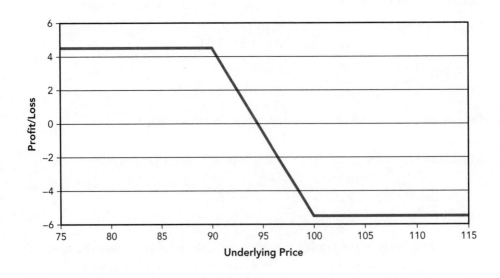

Figure 2.4 Bear Put Spread P&L Diagram

Bear Put Spread

Components:	Buy Sept. 100 put at $7.10
	Sell Sept. 90 put at $1.60
Debit Incurred:	$5.50
Breakeven:	$94.50 (higher strike minus debit)
Maximum Loss:	$5.50 (price paid for spread)
Maximum Profit:	$4.50 (difference between strikes minus debit)

Naming Conventions

Vertical spreads are basic spreads, but somehow there always seems to be a great deal of confusion surrounding them. Most of this confusion comes from terminology, and most of the confusion surrounding the terminology comes from the cash flow aspect of the positions. Bullish or bearish vertical spreads can be constructed using either calls or puts, but choosing calls over puts or vice versa reverses the cash flow of the position. Thus, with vertical spreads, *bull and bear* and *long and short* are constantly commingled and confused. We will attempt to clarify this in the discussion that follows.

• Bull Vertical Spreads

Bull vertical spreads, or *bull spreads*, are a class of vertical spreads that should profit when the underlying moves higher. Any vertical spread in which a lower strike option is purchased and a higher strike option is sold (with the same class and same expiration) is a bull spread, regardless of cash flow or whether the investor is using calls or puts.

Bull Call Spread: In the case of calls, because a lower strike call is being purchased and a higher strike call is being sold, the result is a negative cash flow, or a *debit*. For this reason, a *bull call spread* is often referred to as a *long call spread* and sometimes is called a *debit call spread* because the investor has to pay for it. All three are the exact same position; hence, the confusion. So, *bull call spread* equals *long call spread* equals *debit call spread*. It's all the same thing.

Figure 2.5 illustrates the structure of a bull call spread (or long call spread). In this case the 100 strike call is purchased, and the 105 strike call is sold. Because the 100 strike call will be more expensive than the 105 strike call, this spread will result in a debit.

Bull Put Spread: When constructing a bull spread using puts, purchasing the lower strike put and selling the higher strike put results in a positive initial cash flow, or a *credit*. For this reason, a *bull put spread* is often referred to as a *short put spread* and sometimes as a *credit put spread*, because the investor collects money for it. Once again, all three are the exact same position.

Calls	Strike	Puts
+1	100	
−1	105	

Figure 2.5   Bull Call Spread (Also Called Long Call Spread or Debit Call Spread)

Figure 2.6 illustrates the structure of a bull put spread or short put spread. In this case the 100 strike put is purchased, and the 105 strike put is sold. Because the 100 strike put will be less expensive than the 105 strike put, this spread will result in an initial credit.

Calls	Strike	Puts
	100	+1
	105	−1

Figure 2.6   Bull Put Spread (Also Called Short Put Spread or Credit Put Spread)

• Bear Vertical Spreads

Bear vertical spreads, or *bear spreads,* are a class of vertical spreads that could profit when the underlying moves lower. Any vertical spread in which a higher strike option is purchased and a lower strike option is sold (with the same class and same expiration) is a bear spread, regardless of cash flow and regardless of whether the investor is working with calls or puts.

Bear Call Spread: In the case of calls, because a higher strike call is being purchased and a lower strike call is being sold, the result is a positive initial cash flow, or a *credit.* For this reason, a *bear call spread* is often referred to as a *short call spread* and sometimes as a *credit call spread* because the investor receives money for it. All three terms refer to the exact same position.

Figure 2.7 illustrates the structure of a bear call spread (or *short call spread*). In this case the 105 strike call is purchased, and the 100 strike call is sold. Because the 105 strike call will be less expensive than the 100 strike call, this spread will result in an initial *credit.*

Bear Put Spread: When constructing a bear spread using puts, purchasing the higher strike put and selling the lower strike put results in a negative cash flow, or a *debit.* For this reason, a *bear put spread* is often referred to as a *long put spread* and sometimes as a *debit put spread*

Calls	Strike	Puts
−1	100	
+1	105	

Figure 2.7 Bear Call Spread (Also Called Short Call Spread or Credit Call Spread)

because the investor has to pay for it. Once again, all three are the exact same position.

Calls	Strike	Puts
	100	−1
	105	+1

Figure 2.8 Bear Put Spread (Also Called Long Put Spread or Debit Put Spread)

Figure 2.8 illustrates the structure of a bear put spread or long put spread. In this case the 105 strike put is purchased, and the 100 strike put is sold. Because the 105 strike put typically will be more expensive than the 100 strike put, this spread will result in a *debit*.

Limited Risk, Limited Return

Because vertical spreads consist of an equal number of calls or puts purchased and sold (that is, the ratio is always one long call and one short call or one long put and one short put), the structures have both limited risk and limited return. This is why they may be appropriate for specific market views, which we will explore later.

THE GREEKS OF THE VERTICAL SPREAD

The "Greeks" of a spread position are equal to the sum of the Greeks of the component parts of the spread. It may be helpful to review the definitions, characteristics, and sensitivities of the Greeks from Chapter 1.

Bull Spreads

• **Delta**

The delta of a bull spread is the difference in delta of the lower strike option and the higher strike option. For example, the delta of the 100/105 bull call spread discussed earlier (and illustrated in Figure 2.1) would be calculated as follows:

$$100 \text{ strike call delta} = 0.75$$

$$105 \text{ strike call delta} = 0.25$$

$$100/105 \text{ bull call spread delta} = 0.75 - 0.25 \text{ or } 0.50$$

Remember that puts have a negative delta, so the calculation of the delta of the 100/105 bull put spread would be as follows:

$$100 \text{ strike put delta} = -0.25$$

$$105 \text{ strike put delta} = -0.75$$

$$100/105 \text{ bull put spread delta} = -0.25 - (-0.75) \text{ or } 0.50$$

The delta of a bull vertical spread can range between zero and 100 depending on the location of the underlying relative to strike prices, time left until expiration, implied volatility levels, and other factors. Because it is bullish, the delta of a bull spread will be either zero or a positive number, but it will never be negative.

As can be seen in **Figure 2.9**, the delta of the bull spread is greatly dependent on the location of the underlying and time until expiration. When expiration is near and the deltas of the component options are very sensitive to "moneyness" (whether they are in- or out-of-the-money), the delta of the bull spread also is sensitive to changes in underlying price, particularly when the underlying is between the upper and lower strikes and one option is in-the-money and one option is out-of-the-money. Notice that moving further away from expiration decreases the sensitivity of the bull

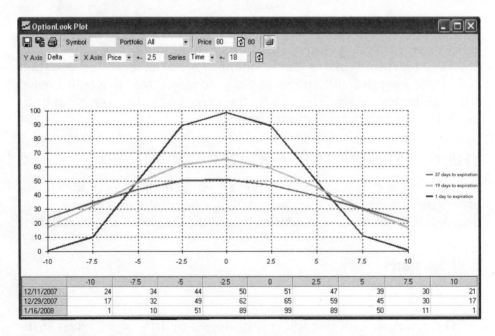

Figure 2.9 Delta vs. Time to Expiration *Source: LiquidPoint, LLC*

vertical spread. It is also important to note that the delta of the structure always returns to zero at the extremes, illustrating the limited-risk, limited-reward characteristics of this type of position.

• **Gamma**

The gamma (rate of change of the delta) of a bull spread is the sum of the gamma of the lower strike option and the higher strike option positions. Recall from Chapter 1 that a long option position will have a positive gamma while a short option position will have a negative gamma. Therefore, in the case of the bull vertical spread the lower strike option will generate positive gamma while the upper strike option will generate negative gamma.

For example, the gamma of the 100/105 bull call spread would be calculated as follows:

$$100 \text{ strike call gamma} = 0.15$$

$$105 \text{ strike call gamma} = -0.05$$

$$100/105 \text{ bull call spread gamma} = +0.15 + (-0.05) \text{ or } +0.10$$

Calls and puts of the same strike and expiration have the same gamma, so the calculation of the gamma of the 100/105 bull put spread would be calculated as follows:

$$100 \text{ strike put gamma} = 0.15$$

$$105 \text{ strike put gamma} = -0.05$$

$$100/105 \text{ bull put spread gamma} = 0.15 + (-0.05) \text{ or } +0.10$$

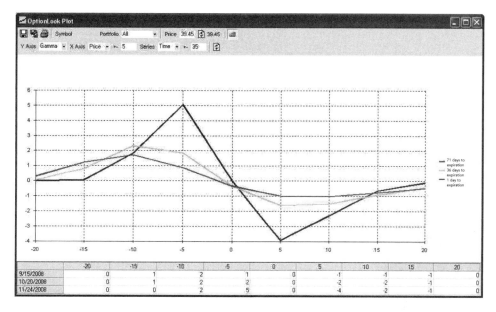

Figure 2.10 Gamma vs. Time to Expiration *Source: LiquidPoint, LLC*

The gamma of a bull vertical spread can range between zero and +1.00 or zero and −1.00, depending on location of the underlying relative to strike prices, time left until expiration, implied volatility levels, and other factors.

As can be seen in **Figure 2.10**, the gamma of the bull spread is greatly dependent on location of the underlying and time until expiration. When expiration is near and the gammas of the component options are very sensitive to moneyness (whether they are in- or out-of-the-money), the gamma of the bull spread also is sensitive to changes in underlying price, particularly when the underlying is near one of the strikes. Notice that the gamma of the position is positive when the underlying is near the lower strike long option, negative when the underlying is near the upper strike short option, and neutral when the underlying is exactly between the strikes or on the extremes. As with delta, notice that moving further away from expiration decreases the sensitivity of the gamma of the bull vertical spread and that the gamma of the structure always returns to zero at the extremes.

• **Vega**

The vega (sensitivity to changes in implied volatility) of a bull spread is the sum of the vega of the lower strike option and the higher strike option positions. Recall from Chapter 1 that a long option position will have a positive vega while a short option position will have a negative vega. So, in the case of the bull spread, the lower strike option will generate positive vega while the upper strike option will generate negative vega.

For example, the vega of the 100/105 bull call spread would be calculated as follows:

$$100 \text{ strike call vega} = 0.28$$

$$105 \text{ strike call vega} = -0.12$$

$$100/105 \text{ bull call spread vega} = 0.28 + (-0.12) \text{ or } +0.16$$

Calls and puts of the same strike and expiration have the same vega, so the vega of the 100/105 bull put spread would be calculated as follows:

$$100 \text{ strike put vega} = 0.28$$

$$105 \text{ strike put vega} = -0.12$$

$$100/105 \text{ bull call spread vega} = 0.28 + (-0.12) \text{ or } +0.16$$

The range of the vega of a bull vertical spread cannot be defined (mathematically). It is also dependent on the location of the underlying relative to strike prices, time left until expiration, implied volatility levels, and other factors.

As can be seen in **Figure 2.11**, the vega of the bull spread, like the other Greeks, is greatly dependent on the location of the underlying and time until expiration. Notice that the vega of the position is positive when the underlying is near the lower strike long option, negative when the underlying is near the upper strike short option, and neutral when the underlying is

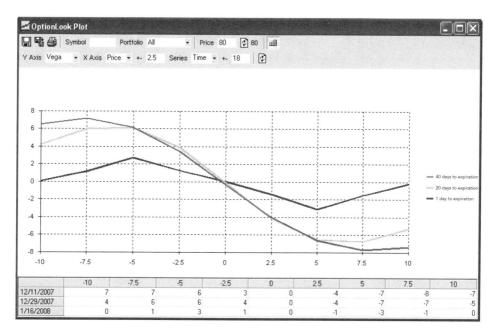

Figure 2.11 Vega vs. Time to Expiration *Source: LiquidPoint, LLC*

exactly between the strikes or on the extremes. However, because vega increases with time to expiration, notice that moving further away from expiration increases the sensitivity of the vega of the bull vertical position as the vega of the individual options increases with greater time to expiration.

• Theta

The theta (sensitivity to the passage of time) of a bull spread is the sum of the theta of the lower strike option and the higher strike option positions. Recall from Chapter 1 that a long option position will have a negative theta while a short option position will have a positive theta. So, in the case of the bull spread, the lower strike option will generate negative theta while the upper strike option will generate positive theta.

For example, the theta of the 100/105 bull call spread would be calculated as follows:

$$100 \text{ strike call theta} = -0.11$$

$$105 \text{ strike call theta} = +0.03$$

$$100/105 \text{ bull call spread theta} = -0.11 + 0.03 \text{ or } -0.08$$

Calls and puts of the same strike and expiration have the same theta, so the theta of the 100/105 bull put spread would be calculated as follows:

$$100 \text{ strike put theta} = -0.11$$

$$105 \text{ strike put theta} = +0.03$$

$$100/105 \text{ bull put spread theta} = -0.11 + 0.03 \text{ or } -0.08$$

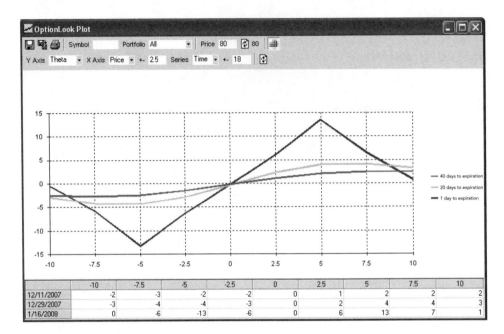

Figure 2.12 Theta vs. Time to Expiration *Source: LiquidPoint, LLC*

The theta of the bull spread also is dependent on location of the under-lying relative to strike prices, time left until expiration, implied volatility levels, and other factors.

As can be seen in **Figure 2.12**, the theta of the bull spread, like the other Greeks, is greatly dependent on the location of the underlying and time until expiration. Notice that the theta of the position is negative when the underlying is near the lower strike long option, positive when the underlying is near the upper strike short option, and neutral when the underlying is exactly between the strikes or on the extremes. Once again, notice that moving further away from expiration decreases the sensitivity of the theta of the bull vertical position.

Bear Spreads

• Delta

The delta of a bear spread is the sum of the deltas of the lower strike option and the higher strike option.

For example, the delta of the 100/105 bear call spread would be calcu-lated as follows:

$$100 \text{ strike call delta} = -0.75$$

$$105 \text{ strike call delta} = +0.25$$

$$100/105 \text{ bear call spread delta} = -0.75 + 0.25 \text{ or } -0.50$$

Remember that puts have a negative delta, so the calculation of the delta of the 100/105 bear put spread would be as follows:

$$100 \text{ strike put delta} = -(-0.25)$$

$$105 \text{ strike put delta} = -0.75$$

$$100/105 \text{ bear put spread delta} = -(-0.25) + (-.075) \text{ or } -0.50$$

The delta of a bear vertical spread can range between zero and -100 depending on location of the underlying relative to strike prices, time left until expiration, implied volatility levels, and other factors. Because it is bearish, the delta will either be zero or a negative number, but it will never be positive.

As can be seen in **Figure 2.13**, the delta of the bear spread is greatly dependent on the location of the underlying and time until expiration. When expiration is near and the deltas of the component options are very sensitive to moneyness, the delta of the bear spread also is sensitive to changes in underlying price, particularly when the underlying is between the upper and lower strikes and one option is in-the-money and one option is out-of-the-money. Notice that moving further away from expiration decreases the sensitivity of the bear vertical spread. It also is important to notice that the delta of the structure always returns to zero at the extremes, illustrating the limited-risk, limited-reward characteristics of this type of position.

- **Gamma**

The gamma (rate of change of the delta) of a bear spread is the sum of the gamma of the lower strike option and the higher strike option positions.

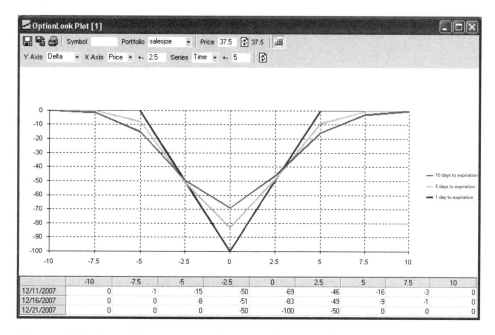

Figure 2.13 Bear Put Spread—Delta vs. Time to Expiration
Source: LiquidPoint, LLC

Recall from Chapter 1 that a long option position will have a positive gamma while a short option position will have a negative gamma. So, in the case of the bear spread, the lower strike option will generate negative gamma while the upper strike option will generate positive gamma.

For example, the gamma of the 100/105 bear call spread would be calculated as follows:

$$100 \text{ strike call gamma} = -0.15$$

$$105 \text{ strike call gamma} = +0.05$$

$$100/105 \text{ bear call spread gamma} = -0.15 + 0.05 \text{ or } -0.10$$

Calls and puts of the same strike and expiration have the same gamma, so the calculation of the gamma of the 100/105 bull put spread would be as follows:

$$100 \text{ strike put gamma} = -0.15$$

$$105 \text{ strike put gamma} = +0.05$$

$$100/105 \text{ bull put spread gamma} = -0.15 + 0.05 \text{ or } -0.10$$

The gamma of a bear vertical spread can range between +1.00 and −1.00 depending on location of the underlying relative to strike prices, time left until expiration, implied volatility levels, and other factors.

As can be seen in **Figure 2.14**, the gamma of the bear spread is greatly dependent on the location of the underlying and time until expiration. When expiration is near and the gammas of the component options are very sensitive to moneyness, the gamma of the bear spread also is sensitive to changes in underlying price, particularly when the underlying is

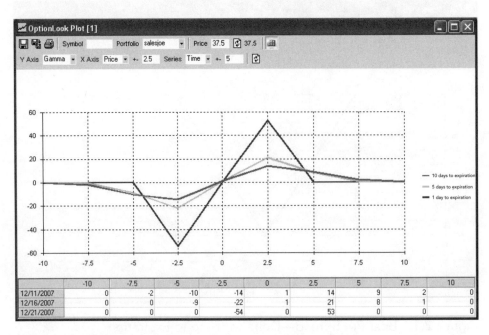

	-10	-7.5	-5	-2.5	0	2.5	5	7.5	10
12/11/2007	0	-2	-10	-14	1	14	9	2	0
12/16/2007	0	0	-9	-22	1	21	8	1	0
12/21/2007	0	0	0	-54	0	53	0	0	0

Figure 2.14 Bear Spread Gamma vs. Time to Expiration
Source: LiquidPoint, LLC

near one of the strikes. Notice that the gamma of the position is positive when the underlying is near the upper strike long option, negative when the underlying is near the lower strike short option, and neutral when the underlying is exactly between the strikes or on the extremes. Once again, notice that moving further away from expiration decreases the sensitivity of the gamma of the bear vertical spread and that the gamma of the structure returns to zero at the extremes.

- ## Vega

The vega (sensitivity to changes in implied volatility) of a bear spread is the sum of the vega of the lower strike option and the higher strike option positions. Recall from Chapter 1 that a long option position will have a positive vega while a short option position will have a negative vega. So, in the case of the bear spread, the lower strike option will generate negative vega while the upper strike option will generate positive vega.

For example, the vega of the 100/105 bear call spread would be calculated as follows:

$$100 \text{ strike call vega} = -0.28$$

$$105 \text{ strike call vega} = +0.12$$

$$100/105 \text{ bear call spread vega} = -0.28 + 0.12 \text{ or } -0.16$$

Calls and puts of the same strike and expiration have the same vega, so the vega of the 100/105 bear put spread would be calculated as follows:

$$100 \text{ strike put vega} = -0.28$$

$$105 \text{ strike put vega} = +0.12$$

$$100/105 \text{ bear put spread vega} = -0.28 + 0.12 \text{ or } -0.16$$

The range of the vega of a bear vertical spread cannot be defined (mathematically), but it is also dependent on the location of the underlying relative to strike prices, time left until expiration, implied volatility levels, and other factors.

As can be seen from **Figure 2.15**, the vega of the bear spread, like the other Greeks, is greatly dependent on the location of the underlying and time until expiration. Notice that the vega of the position is positive when the underlying is near the upper strike long option, negative when the underlying is near the lower strike short option, and neutral when the underlying is exactly between the strikes or on the extremes. Once again, notice that moving further away from expiration decreases the sensitivity of the vega of the bear vertical position even though the vega of the individual options increases with greater time to expiration.

- ## Theta

The theta (sensitivity to the passage of time) of a bear spread is the sum of the theta of the lower strike option and the higher strike option positions. Recall from Chapter 1 that a long option position will have a negative theta

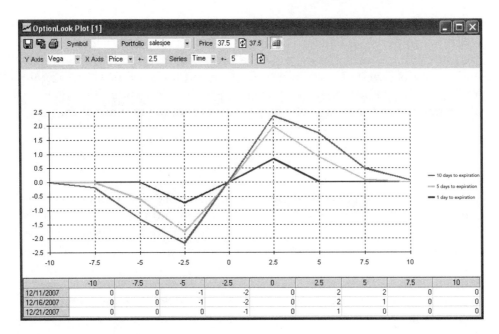

Figure 2.15 Bear Spread—Vega vs. Time to Expiration
Source: LiquidPoint, LLC

while a short option position will have a positive theta. So, in the case of the bear spread, the lower strike option will generate positive theta while the upper strike option will generate negative theta.

For example, the theta of the 100/105 bear call spread would be calculated as follows:

$$100 \text{ strike call theta} = +0.11$$

$$105 \text{ strike call theta} = -0.03$$

$$100/105 \text{ bear call spread theta} = +0.11 + (-0.03) \text{ or } +0.08$$

Calls and puts of the same strike and expiration have the same theta, so the theta of the 100/105 bear put spread would be calculated as follows:

$$100 \text{ strike put theta} = +0.11$$

$$105 \text{ strike put theta} = -0.03$$

$$100/105 \text{ bear put spread theta} = +0.11 + (-0.03) \text{ or } +0.08$$

The theta of the bear spread also is dependent on the location of the underlying relative to strike prices, time left until expiration, implied volatility levels, and other factors.

As can be seen in **Figure 2.16**, the theta of the bear spread, like the other Greeks, is greatly dependent on the location of the underlying and time until expiration. Notice that the theta of the position is positive when the underlying is near the lower strike short option, negative when the underlying is near the upper strike long option, and neutral when the underlying

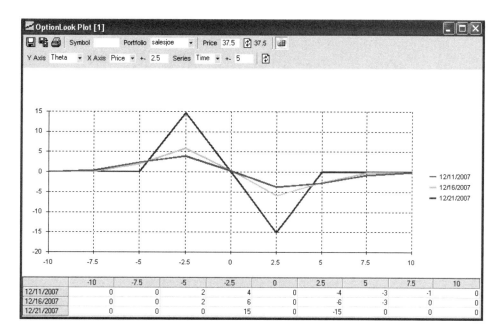

Figure 2.16 Bear Spread—Theta vs. Time to Expiration
Source: LiquidPoint, LLC

is exactly between the strikes or on the extremes. Once again, notice that moving further away from expiration decreases the sensitivity of the theta of the bear vertical position.

Call Spreads vs. Put Spreads

As is evident in this discussion, the Greeks of call and put bull spreads and call and put bear spreads (same strikes, same expiration) are similar. They should be: They share exactly the same sensitivities, and in fact, exactly the same characteristics. In fact, call and put bull spreads and call and put bear spreads are synthetically equivalent to one other and may be used interchangeably to accomplish the same task. Deciding which one is best to use depends on the pricing at the point of execution. We will cover that later in this chapter.

INVESTMENT OBJECTIVES

As mentioned in "Strategy Overview," vertical spreads are directional strategies. Because both risk and reward are limited by the offsetting purchase and sale of a call or a put, they may be employed to target specific market situations.

Moderate Directional Underlying Movement

In the "moderate move" scenario, the investor is expecting a directional move, either up or down, of moderate magnitude. A vertical spread is well

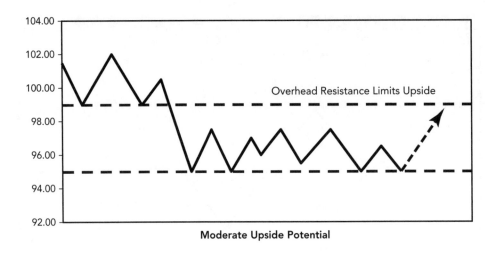

Figure 2.17 Moderate Upside Potential

suited to this type of scenario because its structure allows it to participate in a directional move in the amount equal to the strike differential. So, if the investor is looking for a rally to a certain point or a sell-off to a certain point, the bull or bear vertical spread may allow him or her to target that type of move. An investor would not use a vertical spread, for example, if he were forecasting an up or down move of a large magnitude, because a vertical spread would only capture a portion of such a move.

In **Figure 2.17** the market has declined into support near the 95.00 level, but the upside rally potential is limited by overhead resistance near the 99.00 level.

In **Figure 2.18** the market has rallied into resistance near the 102.00 level, but potential for a downside correction is limited by underlying support near the 98.00 level.

In **Figure 2.19** the market is confined to a trading range by underlying support near the 95.00 level and overhead resistance near the 102.00 level.

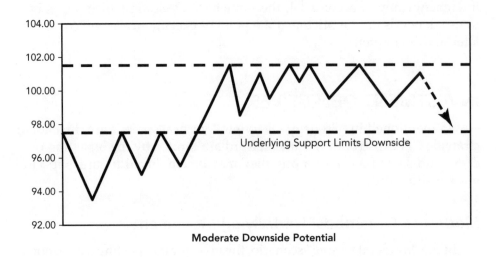

Figure 2.18 Moderate Downside Potential

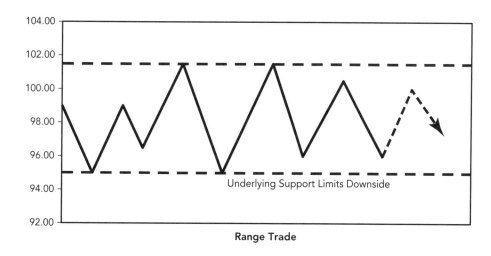

Figure 2.19 Range Trade

High Implied Volatility Levels

As discussed in Chapter 1, high implied volatility levels mean that the option market is forecasting volatile movement in the underlying through that particular expiration cycle, and option prices are marked up to reflect this perception. This means that a bullish or bearish position consisting of a long call or a long put can become exceedingly expensive and leave a trader exposed to a great deal of implied volatility (vega) risk. Because the vertical spread is composed of both a long and a short option, the price and volatility risks are substantially less, allowing one to enter a limited-risk bullish or bearish position without having to pay too high a price or having too much exposure to implied volatility levels.

Lowering Directional Risk

In "Strategy Composition" it was demonstrated that the ultimate risk of a vertical spread strategy is limited to either the cost of the structure, in the case of a bull call spread (long call spread) or a bear put spread (long put spread), or to the strike differential minus the sale price of the structure, in the case of the bear call spread (short call spread) or bull put spread (short put spread). Because of this, the vertical spread may be a good strategy for countertrend trades (**Figures 2.20** and **2.21**) when the market or an underlying becomes oversold or overbought and the trader is forecasting a bounce or a correction against the trend. The danger in this type of trade is that if the forecast of a bounce or a correction is incorrect, the trend usually continues and sometimes accelerates in its original direction. This makes the practice of bottom picking and top picking for a bounce or a correction quite risky. Using vertical spreads in this situation may allow the trader to capture the bounce or correction if his or her forecast is correct, but reduces the risk if the forecast is incorrect.

In Figure 2.20 the trader is anticipating a bounce from the 95.00 support level, but realizes that if he is incorrect and support is broken, the downside risk will be large, so the situation calls for a limited-risk bullish strategy.

In Figure 2.21 the trader is anticipating a correction from the 100.00 resistance level, but realizes that if he is incorrect and resistance is penetrated,

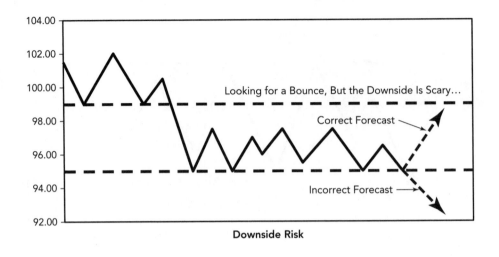

Figure 2.20 Looking for a Bounce

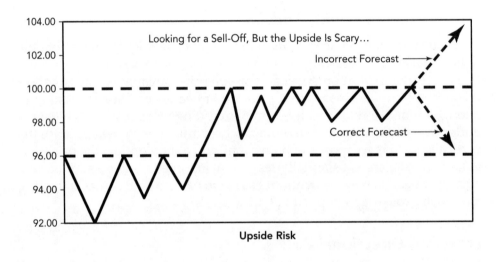

Figure 2.21 Looking for a Sell-Off

the upside risk will be large, so the situation calls for a limited-risk bearish strategy.

Combining Directional and Implied Volatility Views

Because vertical spreads have both a long option (long vega) and a short option (short vega) component, bullish and bearish trades can be constructed with a rising or declining implied volatility bias included in the position. This allows the investor to express a multidimensional market view that includes both market direction and the direction of implied volatility. As noted in "The 'Greeks' of the Vertical Spread," the overall vega of a vertical spread position is dependent on many things, but chief among them is the location of the underlying price relative to the strike prices of the structure. If the underlying price is near the strike price containing the long option component of the vertical spread, the spread will have a positive vega. If it is near the short option component of the vertical spread, the spread will have a negative vega. This allows the investor to tweak the positioning of a bullish or a bearish position to include a long or short volatility bias, should he wish to include one.

Income Generation in a Limited-Risk Fashion

Selling out-of-the-money options to collect premiums and help generate income through time decay has long been a desirable strategy. The problem with that strategy is that it is very risky, as the naked selling of calls and puts leaves the investor open to unlimited risk should some sort of unforeseen event take place. Obviously this is highly undesirable—and downright scary. Vertical spreads can offer a way around this. By selling limited-risk out-of-the-money credit spreads (bull or short put spreads, bear or short call spreads), investors can still sell premium and help generate income through time decay. The advantage gained by using vertical spreads is that should the unforeseen event take place, the investor's risk is limited rather than open-ended. The investor will lose money, but the amount of loss may be limited, hopefully allowing him or her to stay in the ballgame.

STRATEGY COMPONENT SELECTION

So, how should one structure a vertical spread strategy? The answer to that question depends on many of the variables we have discussed in previous sections:

- What is one's current market forecast?
  - Bullish
  - Bearish
- What is the magnitude of the forecast move?
  - Choose a target price.
- What is the time horizon of the forecast move?
  - Determine when one expects the target price to be reached.
- What is one's risk appetite?
- What is the purpose of the vertical spread?
  - Capture market movement
  - Capture volatility movement
  - Income generation

What Is One's Current Market Forecast?

One could theoretically make money with vertical spreads without having a directional bias, for example selling credit spreads. However, typically one will have a directional bias, bullish or bearish, which is the basis of the strategy selection. Remember that the bullish or bearish forecast should be moderate for the vertical spread strategy to be appropriate.

What Is the Magnitude of the Forecast Move?

For structuring purposes, it is important for the investor to have an idea of target price—where he thinks the underlying is likely to go if his bullish or bearish forecast is correct. This is important because, as we saw in "Strategy Composition," the point of maximum profitability of a vertical spread is at or beyond the short strike (at or above the short strike for a bull spread, at or below the short strike for a bear spread). Ideally, the investor would like the underlying to move to the short strike at or near expiration to capture the majority of the move with the spread.

Example

The investor believes ABC is set to move from the 100.00 level to the 110.00 level. What strikes should he incorporate into a bull spread strategy to make an optimal return on this move?

- **Answer**

Long the 100 strike option, short the 110 strike option (either calls or puts, depending on pricing at the point of execution).

What Is the Time Horizon of the Forecast Move?

Again, for structuring purposes, it is important to incorporate a time horizon into the forecast. This will allow the investor to choose the correct option expiration for his bull or bear spread.

Example

The investor believes XYZ will move down from 90.00 to the 70.00 area and that it will take two months for this to occur. What expiration cycle should he choose for his bear spread strategy, to make an optimal return on this move?

- **Answer**

The expiration cycle that most closely corresponds to his time horizon forecast.

What Is One's Risk Appetite?

Obviously the answer to this question plays a large part in strategy selection. Because the risk in a vertical spread is limited, the investor can choose the amount he or she wishes to risk before the trade is put in place. By choosing which available spread to buy or sell and in what amounts, the investor can tailor the risk of a bull or bear spread to his or her risk appetite.

Example

The investor believes that GHF is about to move from 100.00 to 110.00 and would like to capture this move with a bull call spread. The 100/110 call spread is offered at $5.00 while the 105/110 call spread is offered at $2.50. The investor can only risk $250.00 per trade. Which bull spread can he buy?

• Answer

The investor can only afford to buy one 105/110 call spread at 2.50. $2.50 (per call spread) × $100/contract = $250.00 investment (not counting exchange fees, commissions, and so on).

What Is the Purpose of the Vertical Spread?

Usually the purpose of a bull or bear spread is to capture a bullish or bearish move, but other times there may be a volatility view involved or the vertical spread position might be simply for income generation purposes (credit spreads).

• Volatility View

If there is a volatility view involved, it is important to incorporate the ultimate vega exposure of the vertical spread (the vega exposure at the time and target zone) into the strike and expiration selection.

Example

The investor believes HIJ is going to go up from 120.00 to 130.00 in the next thirty days and that implied volatility will decline sharply on this move. How should he structure a bull spread strategy to take advantage of this view?

• Answer

The vega exposure of a vertical spread is dependent on the location of the underlying relative to the long and short strikes. When the underlying is near the long strike, the position will have a positive vega. When the underlying is near the short strike, the position will have a negative vega. Because the investor is forecasting a rally from 120.00 up to a target price of 130.00 along with a sharp volatility decline, it will be important that the position have a negative vega when the underlying arrives at 130.00. This means the investor will want his bull spread's short strike to be the 130.00 strike and the long strike to be either the 120.00 strike or a 125.00 strike, depending on his risk appetite.

• Income Generation

If the purpose of the trade is to help generate income by selling premium and collecting time decay, it is important that the investor believes that it is unlikely that the underlying will move to the area of the short strike(s) of his credit spread(s). How the investor determines this is subjective, however. Technical analysis, fundamental analysis, statistical analysis, and so forth all can play a part in this type of strategy.

Example

EFGH announces spectacular earnings results and gaps from 30.00 to 37.00 the next day. The investor believes it is highly unlikely the stock will trade down to 30.00 again in the next six months. The investor would like to generate some income based on this view by selling credit spreads. Which strikes should he select for this purpose?

• Answer

If the investor believes the stock will not trade down to 30.00, then he could initiate bull put spreads (short put spreads) within his six-month time frame using 30.00 as the short strike and a lower strike (depending on his risk appetite) as the long strike.

At the Point of Execution: Call Spread or Put Spread?

As mentioned earlier in our examination of the Greeks in "The Greeks of the Vertical Spread," bull call and put vertical spreads (long call spreads and short put spreads) and bear call and put vertical spreads (short call spreads and long put spreads) are synthetically equivalent to one another. They have identical sensitivities and risk reward character-istics; the only difference is price and cash flow. When executing a bull spread—buying the lower strike option and selling the higher strike op-tion—the bull call spread will result in a negative cash flow (a debit), while the bull put spread will result in positive cash flow (a credit). Con-versely, when executing a bear spread—buying the higher strike option and selling the lower strike option—the bear put spread will result in negative cash flow (a debit), while the bear call spread will result in posi-tive initial cash flow (a credit).

Pricing Anomalies

It would seem to make sense that a particular spread executed for a credit would be superior to a synthetically equivalent spread executed for a debit. After all, one can collect interest on a credit balance, whereas one must pay interest on a debit balance. Unfortunately, it is a bit more compli-cated than that, and the fact of the matter is that this advantage is usually a mirage.

Pricing models build interest costs, no matter how trivial, into the price of each option. This means that options prices are discounted to com-pensate for the cost of financing the position. The buyer of an option or a spread will pay slightly less premium to compensate for the fact that he will incur financing costs for his debit balance, while the seller of an option or a spread will receive slightly less premium to compensate for the fact that he will receive interest on his or her credit balance. This discounting tends to remove any advantage associated with a credit versus debit trade of synthetically equivalent positions.

• The Box

The best way to illustrate this is to break out the interest-rate component that accounts for the difference in pricing between a bull call spread and a bull put spread or a bear call spread and a bear put spread. The structure that contains the interest rate component and links bull and bear call and put vertical spreads is a structure called a *box*. A box is composed of a bull spread and a bear spread (same strikes, same expiration). **Figures 2.22** and **2.23**, next, illustrate the structure of a box spread:

Calls	Strike	Puts
+1	100	−1
−1	105	+1

Figure 2.22 The Long Box

Calls	Strike	Puts
−1	100	+1
+1	105	−1

Figure 2.23 The Short Box

Combining two debit spreads (a bull call spread and a bear put spread with the same strikes and the same expiration) creates a long box spread. A bear call spread and a bull put spread (same strikes, same expiration) creates a short box spread.

• Box Value

The box is a neutral structure with an interest rate component. It has no delta, no gamma, no theta, no vega—it can't because it is composed of offsetting positions in two synthetically equivalent spreads (bull spread + bear spread = neutral). It does, however, have an interest-rate component, and it is this component that explains the difference in pricing between bull and bear call and put spreads.

At expiration, the value of a box spread will always be the difference between its strike prices ($K_2 - K_1$). This is the *maturity value* of the box. Any time before expiration, it will trade at a discount to compensate for carrying costs. The discounted value, or the *present value*, of the difference between the strike prices yields the fair value of the box spread, as shown in the equation below:

$$\text{BOX} = \frac{(K_2 - K_1)}{(1 + r)^t}$$

For example, what is the fair value of the 95/100 box spread with ninety days until expiration at an interest rate of 4.04 percent?

$$\text{BOX} = \frac{(100 - 95)}{(1 + 0.0404)^{.25}}$$

$$\text{BOX} = 4.95$$

This means that the present value of the box spread carries a 0.05 discount to compensate for carrying costs. Now we will apply this to the relationship between the bull and bear call and put spreads to explain pricing differences (**Figures 2.24** and **2.25**).

Calls	Strike	Puts
0	100	+1
0	105	−1

Figure 2.24 Bull Call Spread − Box = Bull Put Spread

Note that the equation in Figure 2.24 can also be rearranged to read Bull Put Spread + Box = Bull Call Spread.

Calls	Strike	Puts
0	100	−1
0	105	+1

Figure 2.25 Bear Call Spread + Box = Bear Put Spread

Note that the equation in Figure 2.25 can be rearranged to read Bear Put Spread − Box = Bear Call Spread.

Practical Uses

When it comes time to pull the trigger on a bull or bear vertical position, whether at the point of entry or exit, we can evaluate which structure is a better trade by incorporating the box formula into the evaluation process.

Remember that call spread value + put spread value = box value. If the equation does not balance, there is a relative advantage available.

Example

An investor's "system" has given a buy signal on ABC stock and the investor would like to initiate a 5-point bull vertical. He has two choices, buying the 50/55 call spread or selling the 50/55 put spread. The value of the 50/55 box is 4.95, and the quotes the investor is seeing are 2.50 bid − 2.60 ask, for the call spread, and 2.45 bid − 2.55 ask, for the put spread. Should he buy the call spread or sell the put spread?

• Answer

If we use the formula call spread value + put spread value = box value, we can compare the relative value of the call spread offer and the put spread bid to see which, if any, has a relative advantage:

$$CS + PS = BOX$$

$$2.60 + PS = 4.95$$

$$PS = 4.95 - 2.60 = 2.35$$

With the call spread offered at 2.60 and a box value of 4.95, the put spread bid should theoretically be 2.35, but in the open market it is actually 2.45. So selling the put spread to initiate a bull spread is a trade that is superior to buying the call spread. Here are some easier and faster shortcuts for determining whether the call spread or the put spread represents the better trade.

Bull Spread Rules

- If call spread ask + put spread bid > box value, sell put spread
- If call spread ask + put spread bid < box value, buy call spread

Bear Spread Rules

- If call spread bid + put spread ask > box value, sell call spread
- If call spread bid + put spread ask < box value, buy put spread

---

Example

An investor wants to initiate a 5-point bear spread. The quote on the 45/50 call spread is 1.40 − 1.50, and the put spread is 3.55 − 3.65. The box is valued at 4.95. Should the investor sell the call spread or buy the put spread?

• **Answer**

Call spread bid + Put spread ask = 1.40 + 3.65, or 5.05

This is greater than the box value, so the investor should sell the call spread.

Note: These techniques for identifying relative pricing advantages can also be used when exiting a trade.

TRADE MANAGEMENT

Even though vertical spreads are pretty tame from a risk standpoint (they are generally low-cost and have limited risk), it is still a good idea to have a plan, regardless of whether one's market forecast is correct or incorrect. Good traders have their exits planned before they enter the trade. These questions need to be addressed before the trade:

- What is the most efficient way to take profits? Losses?
- What does one do if the underlying reaches the target ahead of schedule?
- What does one do if he or she is completely wrong on direction?
- What does one do if he or she underestimated the magnitude of the move?
- What if volatility behavior or any of the other assumptions that went into one's forecast turn out to be incorrect?

One mistake that is consistently made by options traders (probably because they tend to fancy themselves as chess masters) is staying too long in a position or making too many modifications when their market view changes from the initial forecast. The simplest and most effective rule in risk management is this: If the trader is wrong, he should get out!

This means that if any of the assumptions that went into a market forecast turn out to be wrong, the investor should get out of the position. There is no room for hoping or praying . . .

Sample Adjustments

• When to Exit

There are two reasons to exit a trade: when one's market forecast has been met or when it has changed. The vertical spread is a directional strategy meant to be applied when one is forecasting a moderate directional move. If one's view of the market suddenly shifts away from this forecast, then the trade will need to be modified or liquidated, depending on the shift in market view. In the case of liquidation there are two ways to exit a vertical spread. One is to liquidate the original position, and (recalling the section "Strategy Component Selection") the other is to liquidate via the synthetic equivalent.

• How to Exit

The decision whether to liquidate using the original position versus the synthetic equivalent depends on two factors: price and liquidity. Price is simple enough if one remembers to apply the pricing rules from "Strategy Component Selection" and use the most advantageously priced bull or bear spread to liquidate the position. Additionally, execution costs will affect the overall price.

The other factor is liquidity, and liquidity issues usually have to do with the moneyness of the individual options that compose the vertical spread. As options move in-the-money, they acquire a larger delta, and this makes hedging them riskier for market makers. Accordingly, market makers will widen the bid-ask spread of in-the-money options to compensate for this risk. Conversely, out-of-the-money options have a lower delta, making hedging them less risky for market makers. This usually results in out-of-the-money options having a narrower bid-ask spread than their in-the-money counterparts. The net effect on vertical spreads is that a spread consisting of in-the-money options usually will have a wider bid-ask spread than a vertical spread consisting of out-of-the-money options. This is because an in-the-money call vertical has a synthetically equivalent out-of-the-money put vertical and an in-the-money put vertical has a synthetically equivalent out-of-the-money call vertical. This moneyness effect (especially on profitable trades) can make using synthetically equivalent positions to exit a trade even more appealing.

Example 1: Liquidation of a Bull Call Spread

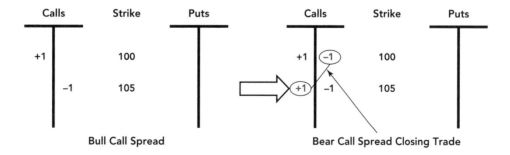

In this example, the original position is simply liquidated by executing the reverse position; in this case a bear call spread liquidates an existing bull call spread. Sometimes liquidity or pricing issues arise in liquidating the original spread. When these occur, the synthetically equivalent spread may be used to close the position.

Example 2: Liquidation of a Bull Call Spread via a Synthetically
            Equivalent Put Spread

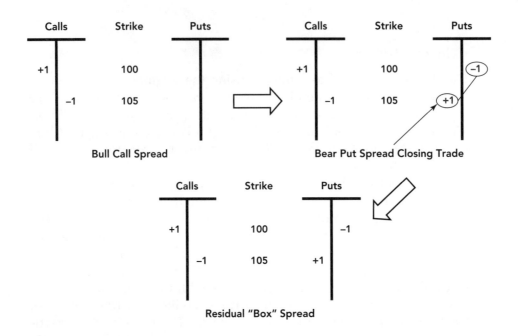

Bull Call Spread

Bear Put Spread Closing Trade

Residual "Box" Spread

This is an example of the dilemma that sometimes occurs when one is correct and the vertical spread is profitable. In this example, a bull call spread is now composed of in-the-money calls, leading to a wide bid-ask spread on the vertical spread and making liquidation difficult. One choice would be to employ the synthetically equivalent bear put spread to close the trade.

Modifying the Trade

• "Rolling" Vertical Spreads

Occasionally the magnitude of a directional movement might be underestimated and the trader may want to "roll" the spread into a different set of strikes so that it can continue to participate in the further price movement of the stock. When one's price target is reached prematurely, or when the underlying looks as though it might make a stronger move in the anticipated direction, "rolling" the spread up or down can allow one to continue to participate in the move. Rolling a vertical spread is accomplished by using another spread, the butterfly. Selling a butterfly that overlaps to the upside rolls a bull spread up:

Example 3: "Rolling Up" a Bull Call Spread

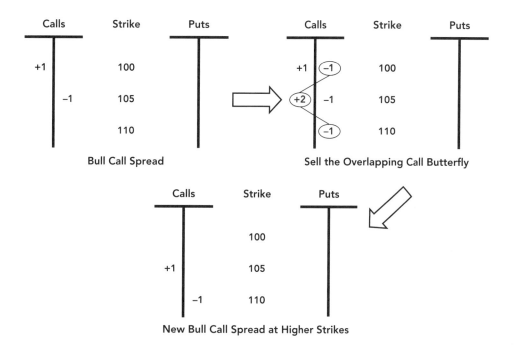

Example 4: "Rolling Up" a Bull Put Spread

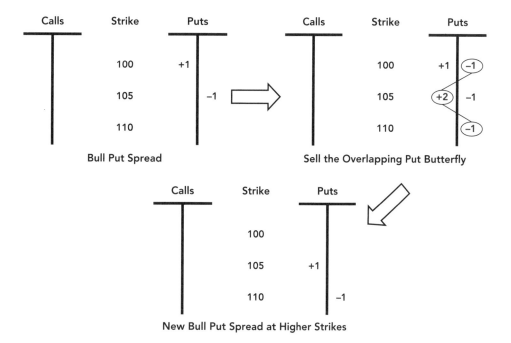

A benefit of rolling vertical spreads by selling butterflies is that it takes a little money off the table and allows the trader to stick with the trade idea and participate in the extended directional move. Selling a butterfly that overlaps to the downside rolls a bear spread down:

Example 5: "Rolling-Down" a Bear Call Spread

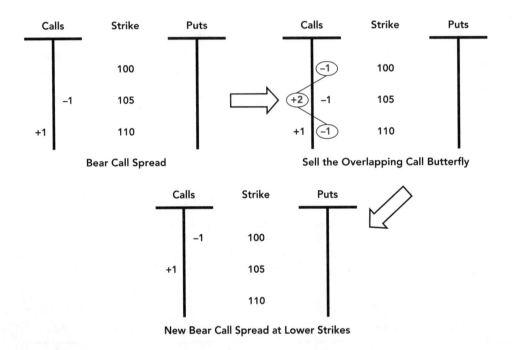

Example 6: "Rolling-Down" a Bear Put Spread

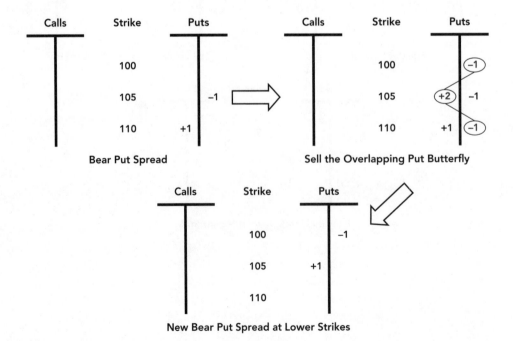

Using this technique the trader is able to buy time should the underlying reach the target price prematurely, or participate in movement of a greater magnitude should it appear that the underlying is set to continue its directional move in a magnitude greater than originally forecast.

CHAPTER 2 EXERCISE

Figure 2.26 Data for Exercises *Source: LiquidPoint, LLC*

Refer to **Figure 2.26** to answer the following questions:

1. What are the components of the XYZ 110/115 bear credit spread?

2. What is the delta value of the XYZ 105/115 bear put vertical?

3. What will be the delta value of the put vertical above if the underlying stock drops by $1.00?

4. An investor is long the XYZ Jan. 100/110 call vertical, with the stock at 110.00. Is the vega on the spread positive or negative?

5. A debit spread takes advantage of theta decay over time. True or false?

6. What is the maximum risk of the XYZ 105/115 put vertical if sold at $4.10?

7. What should be the fair value of the 100/105 box with ninety days until expiration at an interest rate of 6.00?

8. An investor bought the XYZ 105/110 call spread for $1.00 months ago and now the stock has rallied up. With the stock now above 110.00, he wants to take profits. Which is the best way to unwind the position, selling the 105/110 call spread out or legging into the market neutral 105/110 box spread? The carrying cost on the 105/110 box is $0.05. (Assume buying on the offer and selling on the bid.)

9. An investor anticipates that XYZ has a bit higher to go and sees major resistance at the 115.00 level. He wants to play the move from 110.00 to 115.00. What is the best way to play it? A credit spread or a debit spread? (Assume buying on the offer and selling on the bid.)

10. An investor is long the 105/110 call spread and would like to take advantage of a move up to 115.00. How can he roll the call spread to the 110/115 call spread?

Chapter 2 Exercise Answer Key

1. −1 XYZ Jan. 110 call/+1 XYZ Jan. 115 call
2. −0.69 − (−0.20) = −0.49
3. The gamma of the spread is 0.047 + (−0.037) = 0.010; therefore, XYZ dropping 1.00 point will change the delta from −0.49 to −0.50.
4. Negative
5. False. An out-of-the-money debit spread has negative time decay and will theoretically lose money over time.
6. Maximum loss is the difference between strikes ($115.00 − $105.00 = $10.00) less the premium collected by selling the spread; therefore, $10.00 − $4.10 = $5.90.
7. The fair value of the 100/105 box is $4.93.
8. He can sell out the 105/110 call spread at $3.30 ($7.30 − $4.00 = $3.30), which makes a profit of $2.30. He can buy the 105/110 put spread for $1.55 ($2.70 − $1.15 = $1.55). The box value is $5.00 − $0.05 = $4.95. If he legs into the box for $1.00 (the price at which he bought the call spread) plus $1.55 (the price at which he bought the put spread), the total cost is $2.55. Therefore, his profit is $4.95 − $2.55 = $2.40. Legging into the market neutral box gives the investor an extra $0.10 of profit over outright selling of the call spread. This is a good example of what happens when an investor's original position goes in-the-money and the bid-offer spreads widen out.
9. The 110/115 call spread could be bought for $2.35, giving the investor a profit potential of $2.65. The 115/110 put spread could be sold for $2.60, which is the same as his maximum profit. Therefore, buying the 110/115 call spread gives him $0.05 more potential profit and represents the best spread to play the move up to 115.
10. By selling the 105/110/115 call butterfly

CHAPTER 2 QUIZ

Refer to Figure 2.26 to answer the following questions:

1. What are the components of a 110/120 bull credit spread in XYZ?

2. What is the delta value of the XYZ Jan. 110/115 call vertical?

3. What is the rate of change in the deltas for the XYZ Jan. 110/115 call vertical?

4. In the case of a bull call spread, is the vega of the spread positive or negative if the underlying is at the short strike option?

5. Which spread, credit or debit, takes advantage of theta decay if the underlying stays the same till expiration?

6. What is the maximum risk of the XYZ 105/110 call spread that was sold for a $3.30 credit?

7. Calculate the carrying cost of the 100/110 box spread with 180 days till expiration at an interest rate of 4.25.

8. With the XYZ 55/60 box value at $4.85 and the XYZ 55/60 call spread value at $2.35, what should the XYZ 55/60 put spread value be?

9. An investor is long the XYZ 75/85 call spread, and the underlying is approaching 85.00. What two trades can he make to take profits on the trade and get into a neutral position in the stock?

10. An investor is long the XYZ 55/60 call spread and would like to roll it up to the 60/65 call vertical. What is the most efficient way to accomplish the roll?

Chapter 2 Quiz Answer Key

1. +1 Jan. 110 put/−1 Jan. 120 put
2. $0.57 - 0.31 = 0.26$
3. $0.053 + -0.047 = 0.006$
4. Negative
5. Credit spread
6. Maximum loss is the difference between strikes ($110.00 - $105.00 = $5.00) less the premium collected by selling the spread; therefore, $5.00 - $3.30 = $1.70.
7. Box = ($110.00 - $100.00) ÷ $(1 + 0.425)^{.50}$ = $9.794. Therefore, the carrying cost is $0.205.
8. $2.50
9. He can sell the XYZ 75/85 call spread to offset the position or buy the XYZ 75/85 put spread to leg into the XYZ 75/85 box.
10. Sell the 55/60/65 call butterfly

3

Collars and
Reverse-Collars

CONCEPT REVIEW

Implied volatility skew: Implied volatilities of the lower strike option increase as the strike prices fall, and implied volatilities of the higher strike option fall as the strike prices rise.

Stop-loss order: A buy or a sell order placed in the market that is triggered if certain price conditions are met, at which point it is turned into a market order.

Support: The price level at which a stock historically has had difficulty falling below.

Resistance: The price at which a stock historically has had difficulty rising above.

STRATEGY OVERVIEW

Collar and reverse-collar strategies can be used as bullish (reverse-collar) or bearish (collar) stand-alone speculative strategies, or they can be used to hedge or modify the risk in an existing bullish or bearish position in the underlying market. We will explore both categories in this chapter.

The Collar and Reverse-Collar as Directional Strategies

When used as options spread strategies, the collar and reverse-collar usually are employed for very specific market scenarios:

- To help capture strong directional moves to the upside or downside
- To play contingent "if/then" types of scenarios
- To play specific breakout or breakdown scenarios

STRATEGY COMPOSITION

Collar

Components:	Stock = 100
	Buy 1 March 95 put at $5.00
	Sell 1 March 105 call at $4.75
	Initiated for a $0.25 debit
Maximum Profit:	Put strike +/− credit/debit
	($95.00 − $0.25 = $94.75)
Maximum Loss:	Unlimited above short call (105)
	If between strikes, then = debit
	(if any). ($0.25)
Breakeven(s):	Put strike − debit, if initiated for a debit
	($95.00 − $0.25 = $94.75)
	Call strike + credit (if initiated for a credit)

The collar (**Figure 3.1**) is a bearish spread strategy in which the purchase of an out-of-the-money put is financed by the simultaneous sale of an out-of-the-money call of the same expiration cycle. Usually this trade

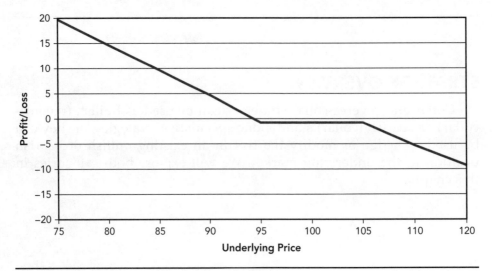

Figure 3.1 Collar (Unhedged) P&L Diagram

is structured so that the total cost of the spread is near zero, meaning that the purchase price of the put is close to the sale price of the call. For this to occur, the two options need to be approximately equidistant from the current underlying price so that they carry approximately the same premium. This structure gives the collar its name. (The premium carried by the two options also is dependent on many factors, including interest rates, dividends, implied volatility skews, and other factors.)

Figure 3.2 illustrates the typical structure of a collar. At the point of initiation, the underlying price would be approximately 105.00 for the cost of the collar to be near zero.

Calls	Strike	Puts
	100	+1
	105	
−1	110	

Figure 3.2 The Collar

Reverse-Collar

Components:	Stock = 100
	Buy 105 call at $5.00
	Sell 95 put @ $5.25
	Initiated for a $0.25 credit
Maximum Profit:	Unlimited above call (105)
	If between strikes, then = credit (if any)
Maximum Loss:	Below put strike, then put strike −/+ credit/debit ($95.00 − $0.25 = $94.75)
	If between strikes, then debit (if any)
Breakeven(s):	Put strike − credit (if any) ($95.00 − $0.25 = $94.75)
	Call strike + debit (if any)

The reverse-collar (**Figure 3.3**) is a bullish spread strategy in which the purchase of an out-of-the-money call is financed by the simultaneous sale of an out-of-the-money put of the same expiration cycle. The reverse-collar usually is structured so that the total cost of the spread is near zero, meaning that the purchase price of the call is close to the sale price of the put. For this to occur, the two options need to be approximately equidistant from the current underlying price so that they carry approximately the same premium.

Figure 3.4 illustrates the typical structure of a reverse-collar. At the point of initiation, the underlying price would be approximately 105.00 for the cost of the reverse collar to be near zero.

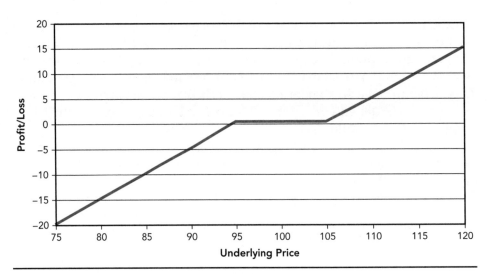

Figure 3.3 Reverse-Collar P&L Diagram

Calls	Strike	Puts
	100	−1
	105	
+1	110	

Figure 3.4 The Reverse-Collar

THE VOLATILITY COMPONENT OF A COLLAR OR REVERSE-COLLAR

The reason a collar or reverse-collar might be chosen for a particular market scenario over another strategy, and one of the reasons for the popularity of these trades, is that it is deliberately structured to minimize implied volatility risk and time decay risk. As we will see when we examine the Greeks, the structure of a collar or a reverse-collar—one long option, one short option, equidistant from the current price of the underlying—minimizes the exposure to implied volatility risk and time decay, so that the timing of a forecasted bullish or bearish move need not be precise. In addition, collars and reverse-collars can be used to address any anomalies in the existing structure of implied volatility at the time of the trade.

THE COLLAR AND REVERSE-COLLAR AS HEDGING VEHICLES

Collars and reverse-collars can also make excellent hedging vehicles. Wrapping a collar around an existing long underlying position will convert the risk/reward of such a position into that of a limited-risk bull vertical spread. Wrapping a reverse-collar around an existing short underlying position will convert the risk/reward of such a position into that of a limited-risk bear vertical spread. Traders can use collars and reverse-collars to modify the risk of outright long and short underlying positions as market conditions evolve, jumping from unlimited-risk/reward to limited-risk/reward positions as they see fit.

Role of Synthetic Options Positions

The reason the risk/reward profile changes from that of an outright position to that of a bull or bear vertical spread when a collar or reverse-collar hedge is applied to an outright long or short underlying position is that the combination of an underlying position with an option position creates a *synthetic option position*. Combining a long underlying position with a collar creates a *synthetic bull vertical spread*; combining a short underlying position with a reverse-collar creates a *synthetic bear vertical spread*.

- **Collar-Hedged Long Underlying Position**

As mentioned, combining a long underlying position with a collar creates a synthetic bull vertical spread. **Figures 3.5** and **3.6** illustrate the synthesis of a collar-hedged long underlying position into a bull vertical spread.

	+100 Shares	
Calls	Strike	Puts
	100	+1
	105	
−1	110	

Figure 3.5 Collar Hedge of a Long Underlying Position

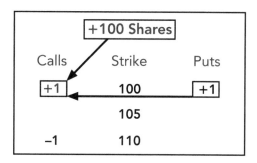

Figure 3.6 Synthesis of a Collar-Hedged Underlying into a Bull Spread

In Figure 3.6, the combination of one long 100 put with 100 shares of long stock creates one synthetic long 100 call, effectively transforming the position into a 100/110 bull call spread. An alternate way to view the synthesis would be to combine the short 110 call with the long stock position, creating a synthetic short 110 put. This would transform the position into a 100/110 bull put spread, which, as we learned in Chapter 2, has the same risk/reward properties as the 100/110 bull call spread.

- **Reverse-Collar-Hedged Short Underlying Position**

As mentioned above, combining a short underlying position with a reverse-collar creates a synthetic bear vertical spread. **Figures 3.7** and **3.8** illustrate the synthesis of a reverse-collar-hedged short underlying position into a bear vertical spread.

	−100 Shares	
Calls	Strike	Puts
	100	−1
	105	
+1	110	

Figure 3.7 Reverse-Collar Hedge of a Short Underlying Position

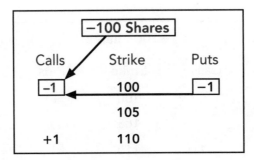

Figure 3.8 Synthesis of a Reverse-Collar-Hedged Underlying into a Bear Spread

Figure 3.8 illustrates how the combination of one short 100 put with 100 shares of short stock creates a *synthetic* short 100 call, effectively transforming the position into a 100/110 bear call spread. An alternate way to view the synthesis would be to combine the long 110 call with the short stock position, creating a synthetic long 110 put. This would transform the position into a 100/110 bear put spread—which has the same risk reward properties as the 100/110 bear call spread.

THE GREEKS OF COLLAR AND REVERSE-COLLAR SPREADS

The Collar

The collar ultimately is a long out-of-the-money put coupled with a short out-of-the-money call, and, on the extremes, it behaves as such. On the far downside, it is a long put; on the far upside, it is a short call. However, the behavior of the Greeks in between the strikes and over time and ranges of implied volatility makes this position interesting.

- **Delta**

The delta of a collar is the sum of the position-adjusted deltas of its component options. For example, the delta of the 100/110 collar would be calculated as follows:

$$100 \text{ put delta} = -0.25$$

$$110 \text{ call delta} = 0.25$$

$$\text{Collar delta} = (-0.25 \times 1) + (0.25 \times -1) \text{ or } -0.50$$

Remember that the 100 put has a negative delta but a positive position (long), yielding a negative position-adjusted delta. The 110 call has a positive delta but a negative position (short), also yielding a negative position-adjusted delta. The delta of the collar can range between zero and −100 depending on the price of the underlying relative to the strike prices involved, time left until expiration, implied volatility levels, and other factors. Because it is a bearish position, the delta will be either zero or a negative number, never positive. **Figure 3.9** shows the delta of the March 47.50/57.50 collar with the stock price at 52.50.

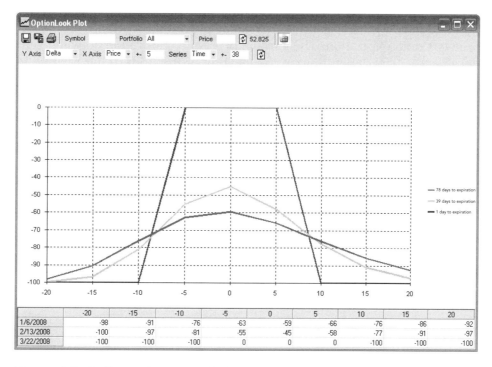

Figure 3.9 Collar Delta vs. Underlying Price and Time to Expiration
Source: LiquidPoint, LLC

As can be seen in the preceding figure, the delta of the collar, while always negative, becomes increasingly negative as the underlying moves below the lower strike, the long put moves in-the-money (or above the upper strike), and the short call moves in-the-money. The sensitivity of the delta of the collar to the underlying price increases as expiration approaches. Notice, in the figure, the difference in the delta generated at various times until expiration. At expiration the sensitivity becomes severe, with the delta of the collar being zero anywhere between the two strikes and –100 anywhere outside the two strikes. The sensitivity is less severe with greater amounts of time until expiration.

• **Gamma**

The gamma of a collar is the sum of the position-adjusted gammas of its component options. For example, the gamma of the 100/110 collar would be calculated as follows:

$$100 \text{ strike put gamma} = 0.05$$

$$110 \text{ strike call gamma} = 0.05$$

$$\text{Collar gamma} = (0.05 \times 1) + (0.05 \times -1) \text{ or } 0.00$$

Recall that long options have positive gamma while short options have negative gamma, and that the gamma of an option is greatly dependent on the moneyness of the option, with at-the-money options having the greatest gamma. Also recall that gamma is very sensitive to the time to expiration. All things being equal, an at-the-money option near expiration will have a greater gamma than an at-the-money option with greater time left until expiration. The gamma of a collar can range between zero +0.50 and −0.50 depending on the location of the underlying relative to strike prices, time left until expiration, implied volatility levels, and other factors. **Figure 3.10** shows the gamma of the March 47.50/57.50 collar with the underlying at 52.50.

The following figure clearly shows how the gamma of the collar depends on the location of the underlying and time until expiration. When expiration is near and the underlying price is near the strike price of the long put, the position will have a large positive gamma. When expiration is near and the underlying price is near the strike price of the short call, the position will have a large negative gamma. When the underlying is exactly between the two strikes, the gamma will approach zero. Note that moving further away from expiration (back in time) decreases the sensitivity of the gamma of the collar, as illustrated by the flattening of the curve in this chart. Also note that the gamma of the collar always returns to zero at the extremes.

• **Vega**

Remember that vega is the sensitivity of option prices to fluctuations in implied volatility. The vega of a collar is the sum of the position-adjusted

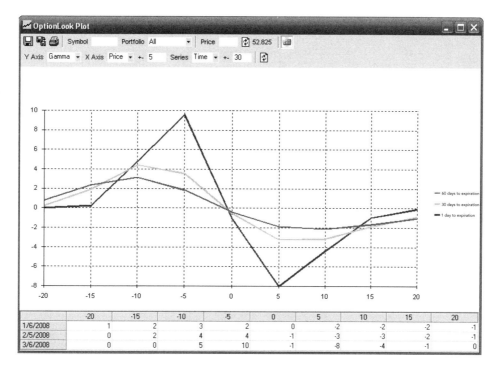

Figure 3.10 Collar Gamma vs. Underlying Price and Time to Expiration
Source: LiquidPoint, LLC

vegas of its component options. For example, the vega of the 100/110 collar would be calculated as follows:

$$100 \text{ strike put vega} = 0.28$$

$$110 \text{ strike call vega} = 0.25$$

$$\text{Collar vega} = (0.28 \times 1) + (0.25 \times -1) \text{ or } +0.03$$

Recall that long options have a positive vega while short options have a negative vega. So, in the case of the collar, the lower strike option will generate a positive vega while the upper strike option will generate a negative vega. This means that the vega of the collar position will be positive when the underlying price is near the lower strike long put, and it will be negative when the underlying price is near the upper strike short call. As with gamma, vega also is dependent on moneyness, with at-the-money options having a greater vega than in- or out-of-the-money options of the same expiration. Vega *increases* with the time to expiration so that, all things being equal, the vega of an option with a larger amount of time left until expiration will be greater than the vega of an option with a smaller amount of time left until expiration. **Figure 3.11** illustrates the vega of the March 47.50/57.50 collar.

The following figure clearly shows that the vega of the collar depends on the location of the underlying price and time until expiration. Vega is positive when the underlying price is near the lower strike long put, and it is negative when the underlying is near the upper strike short call. Vega increases as the time to expiration increases, as can be clearly seen in the graph. The vega of the collar, whether positive or negative, is greater in absolute

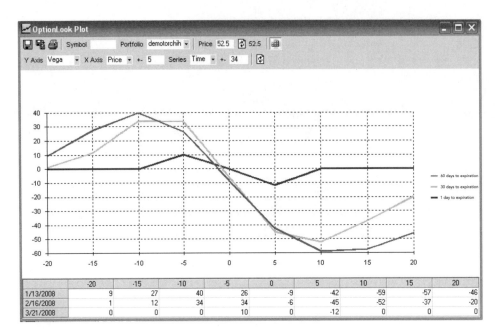

Figure 3.11 Collar Vega vs. Underlying Price and Time to Expiration
Source: LiquidPoint, LLC

terms when there is a larger amount of time left until expiration. When the underlying is between the two strikes, the vega will approach zero.

- ### Theta

The theta of a collar is the sum of the position-adjusted thetas of its component options. For example, the theta of the 100/110 collar would be calculated as follows:

$$100 \text{ strike put theta} = -0.02$$

$$110 \text{ strike call theta} = -0.03$$

$$\text{Collar theta} = (-0.02 \times 1) + (-0.03 \times -1) \text{ or } +0.01$$

Because theta (time decay) is negative, a long option position will have a negative theta (negative time decay) while a short option position will have a positive theta (positive time decay). In the case of the collar, the lower strike long put will generate negative theta while the upper strike short call will generate positive theta. This means that the theta of the collar position will be negative when the underlying price is near the lower strike long put, and will be positive when the underlying price is near the upper strike short call. As with gamma and vega, theta also is dependent on moneyness, with at-the-money options having greater theta than in- or out-of-the-money options of the same expiration. The theta of an at-the-money option *increases* as the time to expiration decreases, so that, all things being equal, the theta of an at-the-money option with a lesser amount of time left until expiration will be greater than the theta of an at-the-money option with a greater amount of time left until expiration. **Figure 3.12** shows the theta of the March 47.50/57.50 collar.

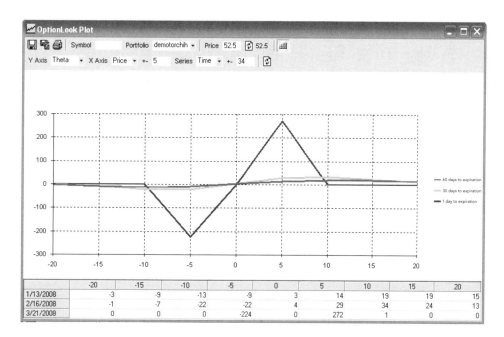

Figure 3.12 Collar Theta vs. Underlying Price and Time to Expiration
Source: LiquidPoint, LLC

As can be seen in the preceding figure, the theta of the collar, as with the other Greeks, is greatly dependent on the location of the underlying and time until expiration. Notice that the theta of the position is negative when the underlying is near the lower strike long put, positive when the underlying is near the upper strike short call, and neutral when the underlying is between the strikes or on the extremes. The theta of the collar, in absolute terms, reaches its peak when the underlying is at the upper or the lower strike price at expiration, as, for example, with the March 21, 2008, data series in Figure 3.12. The relationship softens as the time to expiration increases, as with the January 13, 2008, and February 16, 2008, data series shown in the same figure.

The Reverse-Collar

The reverse-collar, being a long out-of-the money call and a short out-of-the-money put of the same expiration, is the exact opposite of the collar, and will, of course, have Greeks exactly opposite those of the collar. The calculation methodology remains the same.

- **Delta**

As can be seen in **Figure 3.13**, the delta of the reverse-collar, although always positive, becomes increasingly positive as the underlying moves below the lower strike (the short put moves in-the-money); or above the upper strike (the long call moves in-the-money). The sensitivity of the delta of the reverse-collar to the underlying price increases as expiration approaches. Notice, in the figure, the difference in the delta generated at various times until expiration. At expiration, the sensitivity becomes severe, with the delta of the reverse-collar being zero anywhere between the two strikes as both options are out-of-the-money and on the verge of expiring worthless. The

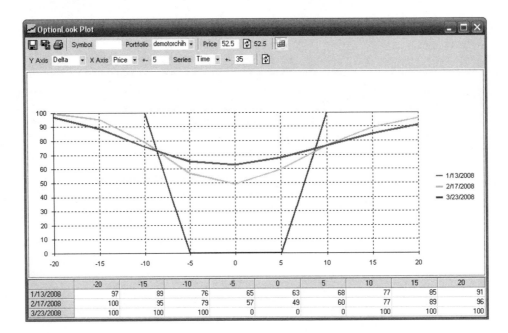

Figure 3.13 Reverse-Collar Delta vs. Underlying Price and Time to Expiration *Source: LiquidPoint, LLC*

delta is +100 anywhere outside the two strikes where both options are in-the-money and on the verge of either being exercised or assigned, resulting in a +100-share stock position. The sensitivity is less severe with greater amounts of time until expiration.

- **Gamma**

Figure 3.14 clearly shows how the gamma of the reverse-collar depends on the location of the underlying and the time until expiration. With the option positioning now reversed, the position has a negative gamma when the underlying is near the lower strike short put and a positive gamma when the underlying price is near the upper strike long call.

When expiration is near and the underlying price is close to the strike price of the long call, the position will have a large positive gamma; when expiration is near and the underlying price is close to the strike price of the short put, the position will have a large negative gamma; and when the underlying is exactly between the two strikes, the gamma will approach zero. Once again notice that moving further away from expiration (back in time) decreases the sensitivity of the gamma of the position.

- **Vega**

Figure 3.15 shows how the vega of the collar depends on the location of the underlying price and the time until expiration. The vega is positive when the underlying price is near the upper strike long call, and it is negative when the underlying is near the lower strike short put. As with the collar, the vega of a reverse-collar, whether positive or negative, is greater in absolute terms when there is a larger amount of time left until expiration. When the underlying is between the two strikes, the vega will approach zero.

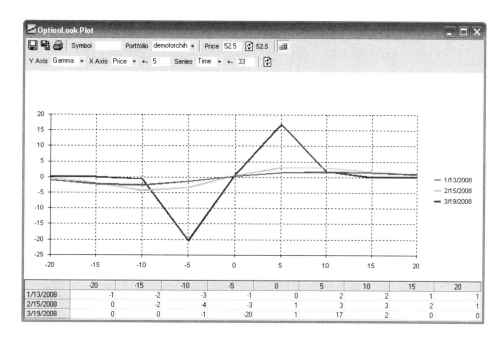

	-20	-15	-10	-5	0	5	10	15	20
1/13/2008	-1	-2	-3	-1	0	2	2	1	1
2/15/2008	0	-2	-4	-3	1	3	3	2	1
3/19/2008	0	0	-1	-20	1	17	2	0	0

Figure 3.14 Reverse-Collar Gamma vs. Underlying Price and Time to Expiration *Source: LiquidPoint, LLC*

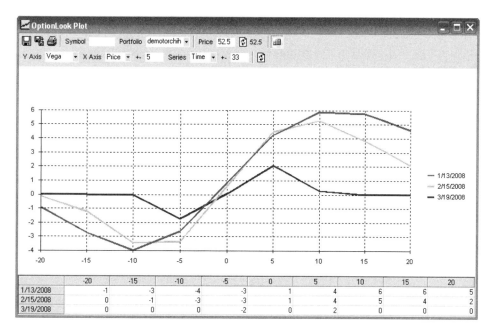

	-20	-15	-10	-5	0	5	10	15	20
1/13/2008	-1	-3	-4	-3	1	4	6	6	5
2/15/2008	0	-1	-3	-3	1	4	5	4	2
3/19/2008	0	0	0	-2	0	2	0	0	0

Figure 3.15 Reverse-Collar Vega vs. Underlying Price and Time to Expiration *Source: LiquidPoint, LLC*

- **Theta**

As can be seen in **Figure 3.16**, the theta of the reverse-collar, as with the other Greeks, is dependent on the location of the underlying price and time until expiration. Notice that the theta of the position is positive when the underlying is near the lower strike short put, negative when the underlying price is near the upper strike long call, and neutral when the underlying

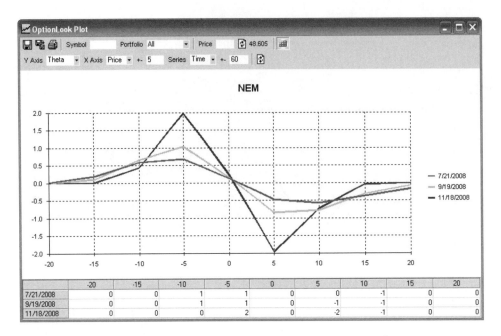

Figure 3.16 Reverse-Collar Theta vs. Underlying Price and Time
to Expiration *Source: LiquidPoint, LLC*

price is more or less between the strikes, or on the extremes. As with the collar, the theta of the reverse-collar, in absolute terms, reaches its peak when the underlying is at the upper or lower strike price at expiration, and the relationship softens as the time to expiration increases.

COLLARS AND REVERSE-COLLARS (HEDGED AGAINST UNDERLYING POSITIONS)

Collar-Hedged Stock

With the exception of delta, the Greek exposure of a hedged collar position—long stock with a collar wrap—will amount to exactly the same strategy as the collar (**Figure 3.17**). The stock position only contributes to the delta portion of the Greeks, so the gamma, theta, and vega of the positions will be identical to their positions in a traditional collar.

Note that this is the same profile as the delta of the bull spread from Chapter 2 because a long stock position hedged with a collar on a 1-to-1 basis is synthetically equivalent to a bull spread.

Reverse-Collar-Hedged Stock

Once again, note (**Figure 3.18**) that this is the exact same profile as the delta of the bear spread from Chapter 2 because a short stock position hedged with a reverse-collar on a 1-to-1 basis is synthetically equivalent to a bear spread.

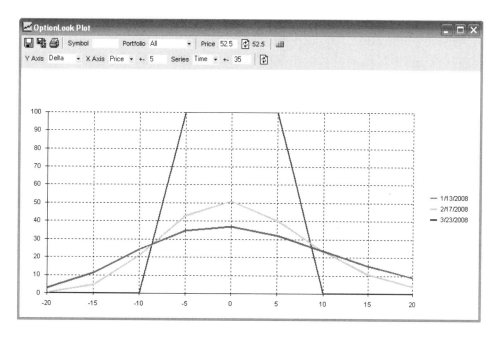

Figure 3.17 Delta of Collar-Hedged Stock vs. Underlying Price and Time to Expiration *Source: LiquidPoint, LLC*

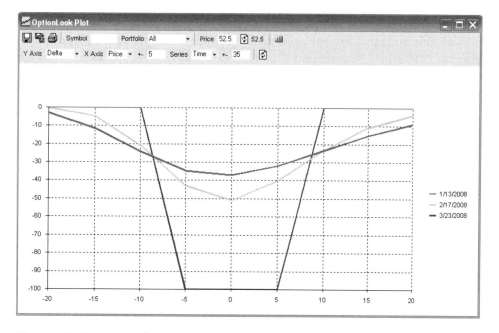

Figure 3.18 Delta of Reverse-Collar-Hedged Short Stock vs. Underlying Price and Time to Expiration *Source: LiquidPoint, LLC*

INVESTMENT OBJECTIVES

Collars and reverse-collars (*without* stock) are directional strategies, with the "long" option component positioned in the direction of the forecast move and the "short" option component positioned in the opposite direction. The usual reason traders choose a collar or reverse-collar, instead of another option strategy, to trade a directional forecast is that they are unsure of their timing.

If a trader is simply buying calls or puts, inaccurrate timing can be a very expensive proposition. An outright long call or long put position is subject to negative time decay, and if a trader is off on his or her timing forecast, each day that passes costs money. In addition, long calls and puts have a positive vega, and if the market slips into an unexpected holding pattern before the move, implied volatility may decline, lowering the value of purchased options. This scenario is the dreaded "double whammy" of poor timing.

Because the structure of the collar and reverse-collar is one long option and one short option, the timing issue is softened, so that time decay and implied volatility risks largely offset one another, allowing the trader to stay with the position longer while he waits for the forecast directional move to occur.

Market Outlook

• Sharp Directional Underlying Movement

The trader of a collar or reverse-collar should be forecasting a sharp directional move, beyond the strike of the long option of the position. The owner of a collar should be expecting the underlying price to move sharply *below* the strike of the long put component of the collar; the owner of a reverse-collar should be expecting the underlying price to move sharply *above* the strike of the long call component of the reverse-collar. As mentioned, the timing does not need to be precise with this type of position. **Figures 3.19** and **3.20** are good general examples of the type of movement the collar and reverse-collar trader should be expecting.

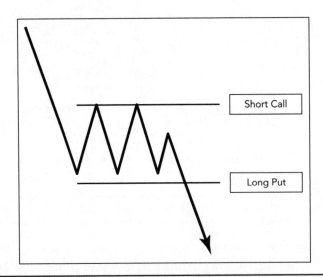

Figure 3.19 Market Forecast Suitable for the Collar

• Mind the Risk!

As with many option positions, the collar and reverse-collar positions are double-edged swords. They allow for the luxury of waiting for a sharp directional move without having to pay for time decay or risking

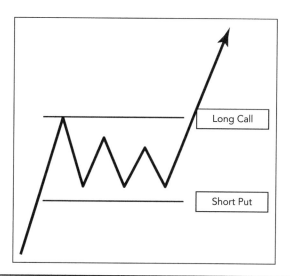

Figure 3.20 Market Forecast Suitable for the Reverse-Collar

a markdown in implied volatility levels, but this comes at a price: the severe risk of a naked short option position in the opposite direction of the forecast.

So, in addition to the forecast of a sharp directional move, the trader of the collar also should be prepared both financially and psychologically for the prospect of the underlying price moving in the opposite direction. Ultimately, this type of movement would give the trader the same position, but with momentum moving the wrong way.

The trader of a collar, with a bearish view of the underlying, should be prepared to become delta short if the underlying rises through the strike of the short call portion of his or her position, or have a stop-loss in place to close the short call. The trader of a reverse-collar, with a bullish view of the underlying, should be prepared to become delta long if the underlying drops below the strike of the short put portion of his or her position, or have a stop-loss in place to close the short put.

STRATEGY COMPONENT SELECTION

In addition to a large-magnitude bullish or bearish forecast, choosing the structure of a collar or reverse-collar requires an analysis of several market parameters:

- What is the current market forecast?
  - Bullish
  - Bearish
- What is the trigger price for the forecast move?
- Where is significant resistance (in the case of a collar)?
- Where is significant support (in the case of a reverse-collar)?

- What is the time horizon of the forecast move?
- What are current implied volatility conditions?
  - What is the base level of implied volatility?
  - Is there a significant implied volatility skew?
- What is the trader's risk appetite?
  - Large, able to accept open-ended risk
  - Moderate to small; must use a stop-loss

What Is One's Current Market Forecast?

This one is pretty simple. As we have stated, the collar is best suited to a forecast of a bearish move of large magnitude. A reverse-collar is best suited to a forecast of a bullish move of large magnitude. If one's forecast does not fall into one of these two categories, then a different strategy should be used.

What Is the Trigger Price of the Forecast Move?

For structuring purposes, it is important to have an idea of the trigger price—that is, the price that will be the "launch pad" of the forecast bullish or bearish move. This is important information because, ideally, the long put (in the case of a collar) or the long call (in the case of the reverse-collar) portion of the position should be located as close to the trigger price as possible to capture the majority of the forecast move.

Example

ABC is trapped in a range between 100.00 and 105.00. The trader believes that the next time it trades through 105.00 ABC is going to break out for a large upside move. In this case 105.00 is the trigger price. (In technical analysis lingo, this is sometimes referred to as the *pivot price*.)

Where Is the Significant Resistance (Collar)?

Again, for structuring purposes, it is important for the trader of a collar to have an idea of where significant overhead resistance lies. Ideally, this is where the short call portion of the position is located.

Example

The investor believes that GHF will collapse if it trades below 95.00. Currently GHF is trading at 100.00, and there is large overhead resistance at 105.00. The trader believes this is the ideal situation for a 95.00/105.00 collar. He decides to buy the 95.00 put at the trigger price and to sell the 105.00 call at resistance.

Where Is the Significant Support (Reverse-Collar)?

The trader of a reverse-collar will need to have an idea of where significant underlying support lies. Ideally, this is where the short put portion of the position should be located.

Example

The investor believes that ZYX will explode if it trades above 89.75. Currently ZYX is trading at 87.50, and there is significant support below the market at 85.00. The trader believes this is the ideal situation for an 85.00/90.00 reverse-collar. He decides to buy the 90.00 call at (approximately) the trigger price and sell the 85.00 put at support.

What Is the Time Horizon of the Forecast Move?

Even though the collar and reverse-collar are deliberately structured to allow for some sloppiness in timing, it is still important to have an idea—however it is arrived at—regarding when the underlying is going to make its move. The expiration chosen for construction of the collar or reverse-collar should comfortably cover this time horizon, with a couple extra weeks thrown in for good measure. There is nothing worse than being "right" about direction and not being "in" the marketplace.

Example

HIJ has been consolidating and the trader believes that if HIJ trades through 120.00 it will explode to the upside. Previous consolidation periods in HIJ have lasted between ten and fifteen business days (two and three weeks). Some of the available options expire in twenty-eight calendar days, and others expire in sixty calendar days. The trader believes that he needs the additional margin of error of the sixty-day option and constructs his reverse-collar using options of that expiry.

What Are the Current Implied Volatility Conditions?

Implied volatility structure sometimes can be the deciding factor when a trader is considering several different strategies to address a market view. When the possibilities include the collar or reverse-collar, the following implied volatility information should be a part of the decision-making process.

- **Base Level of Implied Volatility**

The base level of implied volatility is the general level of at-the-money implied volatility. Base level volatility should be evaluated in a historical context when approaching any trade, including a collar or reverse-collar. As mentioned, the structure of the collar or reverse-collar of one long option and one short option softens the exposure of the overall position to implied volatility. The positive vega of the long option and the negative vega of the short option act to cancel out the overall vega exposure of the position (when the underlying is between the strikes). This means that the collar and reverse-collar are good choices when one is looking to play a large-magnitude directional move and base levels of implied volatility are moderate to high.

However, if the base level of implied volatility happens to be low, it might be better to choose a long put over a collar or a long call over a reverse-collar, especially from a risk/reward standpoint. One would still have the right position for a large-magnitude move, but without the risk aspect of the collar or reverse-collar in the opposite direction.

• Implied Volatility Skew

Generally, in the case of equity and index options, the implied volatilities of the lower strike option rise as the strike prices fall, and vice versa. This often is referred to as the *implied volatility skew*. Trying to explain the implied volatility skew and the reason it exists could open a can of worms, and it probably deserves its own chapter, if not its own book.

It suffices to say, for our purposes, that different strikes of the same expiration often trade at different implied volatilities, depending on market conditions. In addition, implied volatilities of lower strike options tend to be higher than those of higher strike options.

When the implied volatilities are plotted against strike prices on a graph, they often exhibit a "smirk" or "smile." **Figure 3.21** is a good example of the implied volatility skew smirk.

If the market demonstrates a large implied volatility skew, sometimes a reverse-collar trade becomes more appetizing to the bullish trader because the implied volatility of the put option being sold could be much higher than the implied volatility of the call option being bought, giving the trader

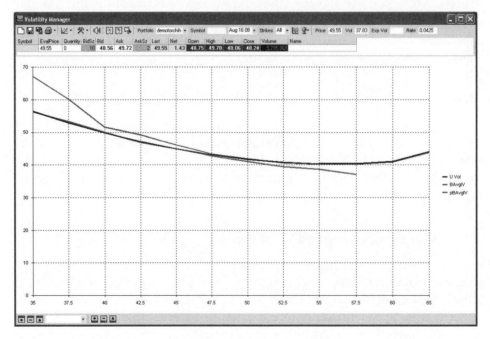

Figure 3.21 Implied Volatility Skew, January 2008

an additional "edge" to work with. Conversely, if the implied volatility skew is unusually flat, it can make a collar trade more appetizing to the bearish trader because the implied volatility of the call option being sold could be equal to or higher than that of the put option being bought, giving the trader a potential "skew" edge.

Example

The trader believes XYZ is about to make a substantial upside move, and is considering several bullish option strategies. The trader notices that, due to recent weakness, XYZ options have a steep implied volatility skew, meaning the out-of-the-money puts trade at much higher implied volatilities than the out-of-the-money calls. The trader decides he can address this implied volatility skew by using a reverse-collar for his bullish strategy.

What Is the Trader's Risk Appetite?

Risk breaks two ways. If the trader has plenty of capital to work with and is comfortable with the possibility that she might end up with a position if the underlying moves in the opposite direction—getting long delta with the market moving lower or getting short delta with the market moving higher—then there is no problem. The trader is simply getting long on weakness or short on strength instead of the other way around.

If the trader has a moderate-to-low risk appetite, though, an exit strategy will have to be put in place. In addition, stop-loss orders to close the open-ended risk of the short call component will need to be in place when trading collars, and stop-loss orders to close the semi-open-ended risk of the short put component will need to be in place when trading reverse-collars.

All traders should keep in mind that stop-loss orders do not provide any guarantees for how and when they will be executed, and they provide no coverage when the market is closed. If a trader loses sleep over the idea of a stock gapping up through his short call or down through his short put, then the collar and reverse-collar are not strategies that should be considered.

TRADE MANAGEMENT

There are several important issues to consider when contemplating using a collar or reverse-collar:

- What is the most efficient way to take any profits?
- How should one deal with adverse market movement?
- Where should the stop-loss orders be placed?
- What does one do if the underlying move fails to be triggered and expiry is approaching?

Collar and reverse-collar trade management must be broken into two categories: directional strategy and hedge. Both must be examined separately because the motivation for them is different.

Managing Speculative Directional Strategy

Managing collars and reverse-collars falls into the following categories:

- Managing the successful position (directional move in the forecast direction)

- Managing the unsuccessful position (directional move opposite the forecast direction)

- Managing the position that fails to trigger

Managing the Successful Position

When the trade goes along as hoped, it is important to actively manage the long put or long call component of the trade to squeeze the maximum profitability out of that portion of the position, while either closing out or deciding what to do about the residual and risky short option component of the trade that is now far out-of-the-money. This is usually accomplished by "rolling" the long option position along with the underlying by selling vertical spreads.

Rolling a long option position is an excellent way to manage a position that is "going your way." Rolling accomplishes three important things:

- It maintains the exposure in the direction of the breakout.

- It reduces risk and takes "money off the table."

- By accomplishing the above, it puts the trader in a strong psychological position and increases his "staying power."

Examples of Rolling

• Scenario 1

The trader, expecting a breakout to the downside after a period of consolidation, executes a 100/105 collar position. The market does indeed break down, and the trader aggressively manages the position by executing a series of rolling trades, accomplished by selling vertical put spreads, as shown in **Figures 3.22** and **3.23**.

In this scenario, the trader is rolling the long put portion of the collar down with the market. Every time the underlying appears to lose downward momentum, the trader sells a put vertical in order to reduce risk and take money off the table, all while maintaining exposure. The trader would continue to do this as long as he or she felt the down move would continue.

• Scenario 2

The trader, expecting a breakout to the upside after a period of consolidation, executes a 90/95 reverse-collar position. The market does indeed break out, and the trader aggressively manages the position by executing

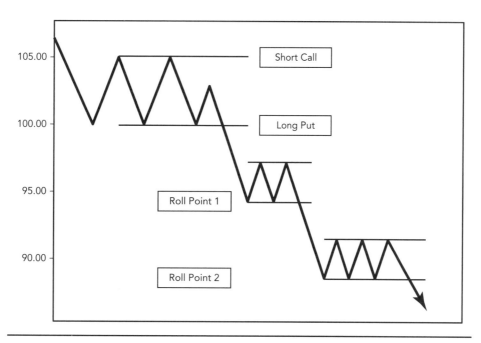

Figure 3.22 Collar Rolling Points in a Breakdown Situation

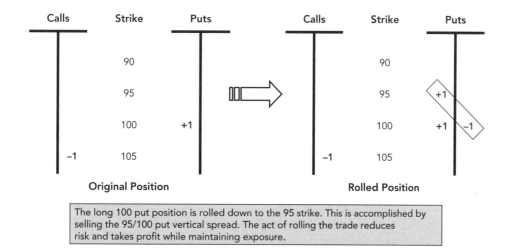

The long 100 put position is rolled down to the 95 strike. This is accomplished by selling the 95/100 put vertical spread. The act of rolling the trade reduces risk and takes profit while maintaining exposure.

Figure 3.23 Put Roll Diagrammed

a series of rolling trades, accomplished by selling vertical call spreads, as shown in **Figures 3.24** and **3.25**.

The long positions in scenarios 1 and 2 can be rolled as long as the trader feels the directional move is likely to continue. As soon as the trader feels the move is over, the position should be closed. It is also very important that the trader not forget the trailing short call of the successful collar or short put of the successful reverse-collar. Even though these options are out-of-the-money, it is never a good idea to leave short option positions open, no matter how far out-of-the-money they might be. Once the breakout has been confirmed in a particular direction and the short option side of a collar or reverse-collar loses most of its value, it should be closed. The trader should

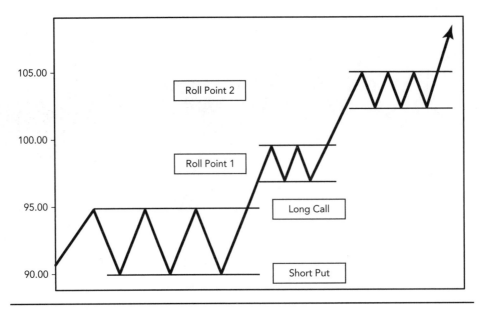

Figure 3.24 Reverse-Collar Rolling Points in a Breakout Situation

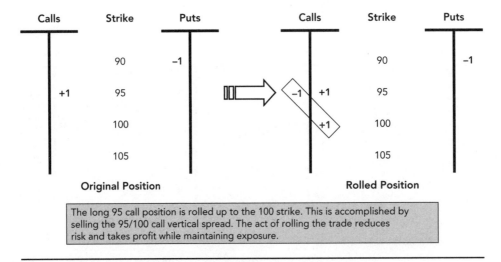

The long 95 call position is rolled up to the 100 strike. This is accomplished by selling the 95/100 call vertical spread. The act of rolling the trade reduces risk and takes profit while maintaining exposure.

Figure 3.25 Call Roll Diagrammed

be looking to profit from the opposing long position instead. Also note that additional execution costs associated with each spread used to roll the position will reduce profits.

Managing the Unsuccessful Position

When the trade is going against the trader, he will have to actively manage the short call or short put component of the trade while deciding what to do with the residual long put or long call component that is now far out-of-the-money.

Whenever one considers entering a trade, it always is important to have a risk-management strategy in place ahead of time. If, in fact, it becomes clear that one's forecast is incorrect, then it is time to get out the position, hopefully in an orderly fashion. This usually is accomplished through the use of stop-loss orders. As mentioned, stop-loss orders are buy or sell orders placed in the market that trigger if certain price conditions are met, at which point they are turned into market orders. Traders usually will use stop-loss orders to close losing positions if key price levels are violated, indicating an incorrect price forecast.

Example

The trader, expecting a breakout to the upside after a period of consolidation, executes a 90/95 reverse-collar position. Support is strong at the 90.00 level, and if this level is violated it will indicate that the trader's forecast is incorrect. The trader places a stop-loss order to buy back the 90 put with an 89.99 stop. Unfortunately, the market does break down and the stop-loss order is triggered, closing out the short put portion of the position at a loss, as shown in **Figure 3.26**.

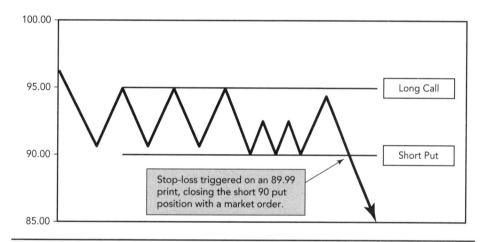

Figure 3.26 Stop-Loss Triggered

The important point to remember about managing risk with stop-loss orders is that they do not protect you when the market is closed. If there is a gap opening due to news or some other event, the market could gap significantly through the stop-loss level. Under these conditions, losses could be very large before the position can be closed.

With an unsuccessful position, once the short call of the collar or the short put of the reverse-collar is closed out, there will be an out-of-the-money call or put remaining. If there is any value left in the long option, the trader may want to close it out and salvage the remaining premium. If the option has little or no value, it can be held as a "lottery ticket," just in case the market decides to reverse course before expiration.

Managing the Position That Fails to Trigger

If a collar or reverse-collar strategy makes it all the way to expiration and does not trigger, the trader will have to decide whether he would like to extend the strategy further. This would be accomplished with calendar spreads: buying the calendar spread to roll the long option to a further expiry and selling the calendar spread to roll the short option to a further expiry.

Example

The trader is expecting a break to the downside after a period of consolidation and executes a 100/105 collar. Unfortunately, the market does not break down by expiration and the options are about to expire. The trader still feels confident that the market is going to break down and wishes to roll the position into the next expiration cycle. He rolls the position by buying the 100 put calendar spread and selling the 105 call calendar spread, as shown in **Figure 3.27**. There will be additional execution costs.

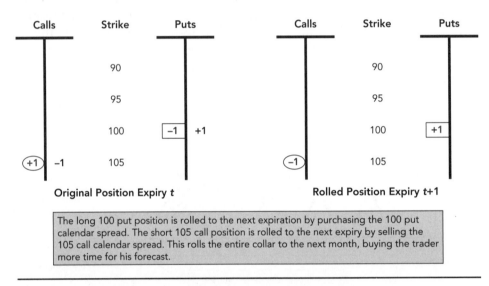

Figure 3.27 Rolling the Collar to a Further Expiration

Managing Hedging Strategy

Recall from "Strategy Overview," at the beginning of the chapter, that applying a collar as a hedge to a long underlying position converts the overall position to a synthetic bull spread with limited risk to the downside and limited upside potential. Remember also that applying a reverse-collar as a hedge to a short underlying position converts the overall position to a bear spread with limited risk to the upside and limited downside potential.

Generally, these hedging strategies are applied whenever a trader feels there is a threat to her position and would like to step into a limited-risk exposure until the threat passes. Such threats include strong support or resistance levels, government economic reports, earnings, or anything else that would make a trader nervous about her position. The trader will apply the collar or reverse-collar hedge when the threat level is high, and then unwind it when she feels comfortable again.

Example

The trader has been profitably long XYZ stock for some time. Now XYZ has traded up against a strong resistance level, and the trader feels there is a strong likelihood of a setback. He decides to hedge the position by wrapping a collar around it. If the stock corrects as he suspects, he will take profit on the collar when it retraces to a support level and once again has better upside potential, as shown in **Figure 3.28**.

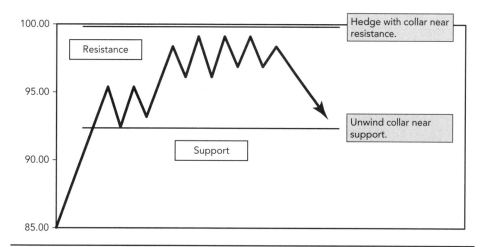

Figure 3.28 Hedging a Long Position with a Collar

CHAPTER 3 EXERCISE

1. The 110 put has a delta of –0.30, and the 120 call has a delta of +0.30. What is the delta of the 110/120 collar?

2. Combining a short underlying position with a reverse-collar creates a synthetic bear vertical spread. True or false?

3. Does the sensitivity of the delta of the collar increase or decrease as expiration approaches?

4. At-the-money options that are close to expiration have a greater gamma than at-the-money options with greater time left until expiration (assuming all other things being equal). True or false?

5. When the underlying price is near the long put, is the vega of the collar position positive or negative?

6. Is the theta of the reverse-collar positive or negative when the underlying is near the long call upper strike?

7. For a reverse-collar, the long put should be located as close to the trigger point as possible. True or false?

8. A "steep implied volatility skew" in ABC options means that the out-of-the-money (puts) (calls) trade at a much higher implied volatility than the out-of-the-money (puts) (calls).

9. Applying a collar to an existing long underlying position converts the overall position to what kind of spread?

10. The break-even point of a collar that is initiated for a debit is the lower strike minus the spread debit, and the break-even point of a collar that is initiated for a credit is the upper strike plus the spread credit. True or false?

Chapter 3 Exercise Answer Key

1. $-0.60 \; [(-0.30 \times 1) + (+30 \times -1)]$
2. True
3. Increases
4. True
5. Positive
6. Negative
7. False (The long call should be located close to trigger point; there is no long put.)
8. Puts, calls
9. Synthetic bull spread
10. True

CHAPTER 3 QUIZ

1. An investor has on a 100/110 collar. His trigger point was not reached by expiration. He decides to roll to the next expiration cycle. He can roll the position by (purchasing) (selling) the 100 put calendar spread and (purchasing) (selling) the 110 call calendar spread.

2. An investor has on the June 80/85 reverse-collar position. The market experiences a breakout. He can roll the position by (purchasing) (selling) the 85/90 vertical call spread.

3. ABC is trading at 170. He initiates the 150/190 collar for a debit. If ABC stays between 150 and 190 until expiration, will the position make or lose money?

4. Both the collar and reverse-collar are structured to minimize time decay as well as implied volatility risk. True or false?

5. Is determining the area of support of concern when initiating the collar or the reverse-collar spread?

6. Is determining the area of resistance of concern when initiating the collar or the reverse-collar spread?

7. The _____ should be located as close to the trigger price as possible when structuring the collar, while the _____ should be as close to the trigger price as possible for the reverse-collar.

8. ABC is trading at 95. He believes it is going to tank if it trades below 90. His technical indicators tell him there is a strong resistance at 100. Buying the 90/100 collar might be an appropriate strategy. True or false?

9. If the collar is initiated at a zero cost, what is the break-even point?

10. With a collar, what is the maximum upside profit potential on the long stock position?

Chapter 3 Quiz Answer Key

1. Purchasing, selling
2. Selling
3. Both the call and the put expire worthless. You would lose the amount of the debit, plus or minus any loss or profit made on the movement of the underlying stock.
4. True
5. Reverse-collar
6. Collar
7. Long put, long call
8. True
9. Purchase price of the underlying stock
10. Strike price of the call minus the purchase price of the underlying stock

4

Straddles and Strangles

CONCEPT REVIEW

Stop-loss order: A nonmarketable buy or a sell order placed in the market that is triggered if certain price conditions are met, at which point it is turned into a market order.

Consolidation: The movement of a stock's price within a well-defined pattern bounded by key support and resistance levels.

Breakout: A rise in the price of an underlying above a resistance level or a drop in the price below a support level.

STRATEGY OVERVIEW

Straddles and strangles fall into the category of "nondirectional" strategies. When one of these strategies is used, both a call and a put are either purchased or sold, simultaneously. This means that one is not necessarily forecasting a *direction* in the market, but rather a *magnitude*. These structures can be traded from the long side or the short side, depending on the type of movement expected in the underlying stock or index.

- *Long* straddles and strangles are used when a trader is forecasting a large magnitude move in either direction or an overall increase in implied volatility levels. The trader seeks to profit from an increase in the value of the position due to a rise in the intrinsic value of either the call or the put as they move in-the-money, or a rise in the extrinsic value of both the call and the put as implied volatility rises.

- *Short* straddles and strangles are used when a trader is forecasting little or no directional movement in the underlying stock or index and seeks to profit from a decrease in the overall value of the position due to time decay or falling implied volatility which will lead to a decline in extrinsic value of both the call and the put.

STRATEGY COMPOSITION

Long Straddles and Strangles

- **The Long Straddle**

The long straddle is a spread that consists of the simultaneous purchase of a call and a put of the same strike and same expiration cycle in a particular underlying stock or index. Usually, but not always, the trader uses an at-the-money strike when initiating a long straddle. This is because she usually wants to begin the trade close to delta neutral, since she does not know in which direction the underlying is going to move.

Figure 4.1 illustrates the structure of a long straddle at the 80 strike. For example, if the expiration cycle for the above structure were March, this position would be referred to as a "long March 80 straddle." At the point of initiation, the underlying usually would be in the 80 range (**Figure 4.2**).

Components: Long 1 March 80 call at $3.50
                     Long 1 March 80 put at $2.65

                     Long 1 March 80 straddle at $6.15

Calls	Strike	Puts
	75	
+1	80	+1
	85	

Figure 4.1 The Long Straddle

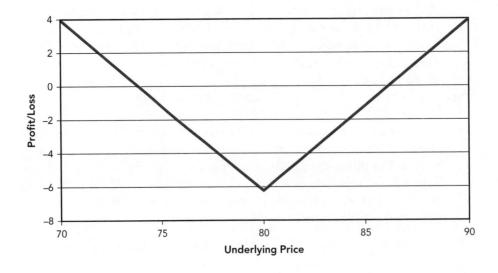

Figure 4.2 Long Straddle P&L Diagram

Maximum Profit: Unlimited to the upside; substantial to the downside
                   (to a stock price of zero)

Maximum Loss: Debit, or price paid to initiate strategy ($6.15)

Breakeven(s):   Put strike − debit (73.85); call strike + debit (86.15)

• The Long Strangle

The long strangle also is a spread that consists of the simultaneous purchase of a call and a put, but of different strikes. Usually, but not always, the trader uses out-of-the-money strikes that are approximately equidistant from the current underlying price when initiating a long strangle. Again, this is because the trader usually wants to begin the trade close to delta neutral.

Figure 4.3 illustrates the typical structure of a long strangle. For example, if the expiration cycle for the above structure were March, this position would be referred to as a "long March 720/740 strangle." At the point of initiation, the underlying usually would be in the 730 area (**Figure 4.4**).

Calls	Strike	Puts
	720	+1
	730	
+1	740	

Figure 4.3 The Long Strangle

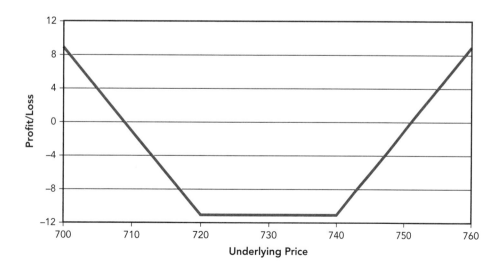

Figure 4.4 Long Strangle P&L Diagram

Components: Long 1 March 720 put at $5.50
                   Long 1 March 740 call at $6.00

                   Long 1 March 720/740 strangle at $11.50

Maximum Profit: Unlimited on the upside; substantial on the downside
                   (to a stock price of zero)

Maximum Loss: Debit, or price paid to initiate strategy ($11.50)

Breakeven(s):   Put strike − debit (709.50); call strike + debit (751.50)

Short Straddles and Strangles

• The Short Straddle

The short straddle is the opposite of the long straddle and consists of the simultaneous sale of a call and a put of the same strike and same expiration cycle in a particular underlying stock or index. As with the long straddle, usually, but not always, the at-the-money strike is used when a short straddle is initiated. This is because the trader usually wants to begin the trade close to delta neutral.

Figure 4.5 illustrates the structure of a short straddle at the 1240 strike. For example, if the expiration cycle for the above structure were March, this position would be referred to as a "short March 1240 straddle." At the point of initiation, the underlying usually would be in the 1240 area (**Figure 4.6**).

Calls	Strike	Puts
	1230	
−1	1240	−1
	1250	

Figure 4.5 The Short Straddle

Components: Short 1 March 1240 call at $14.75
                   Short 1 March 1240 put at $15.50

                   Short 1 March 1240 straddle at $30.25

Maximum Profit: Credit; amount received when initiating the strategy

Maximum Loss: Unlimited to the upside; substantial to the downside
                   (to a stock price of zero)

Breakeven(s):   Strike − credit (1,209.75); strike + credit (1,270.25)

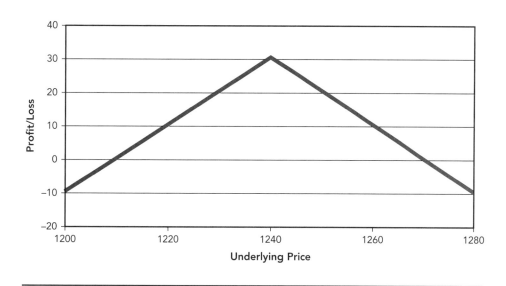

Figure 4.6 Short Straddle P&L Diagram

• The Short Strangle

The short strangle is the opposite of the long strangle and consists of the simultaneous sale of a call and a put, but of different strikes. As with the long strangle, usually, but not always, out-of-the-money strikes that are approximately equidistant from the current underlying price are used when initiating a short strangle. Again, this is because the trader usually wants to begin the trade close to delta neutral. **Figure 4.7** illustrates the structure of a short strangle.

Calls	Strike	Puts
	1250	−1
	1265	
−1	1280	

Figure 4.7 The Short Strangle

For example, if the expiration cycle for the above structure were March, this position would be referred to as a "short March 1250/1280 strangle." At the point of initiation, the underlying usually would be in the 1265 area (**Figure 4.8**).

Components: Short 1 March 1250 put at $16.50
                     Short 1 March 1280 call at $20.00

                     Short 1 Mar 1250/1280 strangle at $36.50

Maximum Profit: Credit; amount received when initiating the strategy

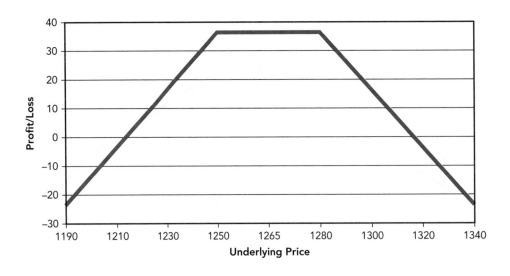

Figure 4.8 Short Strangle P&L Diagram

Maximum Loss: Unlimited to the upside; substantial to the downside
                     (to a strike price of zero)

Breakeven(s):   Put strike − credit (1,213.50); call strike + credit
                     (1,316.50)

THE GREEKS OF STRADDLES AND STRANGLES

Straddles and strangles are spreads that capitalize on movement (or lack thereof) in the underlying stock or index. In other words, *volatility* plays a key role in determining the success or failure of these strategies. As such, these strategies are geared to having a positive exposure (in the case of long straddles and strangles) or negative exposure (in the case of short straddles and strangles) to volatility, and are susceptible to the sensitivities that come with it.

With all else being equal, the Greeks of long straddles and strangles compared to short straddles and strangles usually are the exact opposite of one another.

The Long Straddle

The long straddle is composed of a long call and a long put, and it carries the sensitivities that all long option positions carry: positive gamma, positive vega, and negative theta (time decay). The delta of a long straddle is dependent on the location of the underlying versus the strike. Because of the way it is structured, the straddle will have a positive delta when the underlying is above the strike price, a negative delta when the underlying is below the strike price, and approximately a neutral delta when the underlying is at the strike price.

• Delta

The delta of a straddle is the sum of the position-adjusted deltas of its component options. For example the delta of the 100 straddle would be calculated as follows:

100 strike put delta = -0.50

100 strike call delta = 0.50

Long straddle delta = $(-0.50 \times 1) + (0.50 \times 1)$ or 0.00 (delta neutral)

In the above example, the 100 put has a negative delta but a positive (long) position, yielding a negative position-adjusted delta. The 100 call has a positive delta and a positive (long) position, yielding a positive position-adjusted delta. The position in the example above has a delta of zero, and so it is what is usually referred to as *delta neutral*.

The delta of a long straddle can range between $+100$ and -100 depending on the price of the underlying relative to the strike price involved, time left until expiration, implied volatility levels, and other factors. The delta will hover near zero when the underlying price is near the strike price. Because it is a position that capitalizes on movement, the delta becomes increasingly positive as the underlying stock or index moves above the strike, or increasingly negative as the underlying stock or index moves below the strike.

Figure 4.9 shows that the delta of a long straddle moves in favor of the trader as the underlying moves, becoming increasingly positive as the

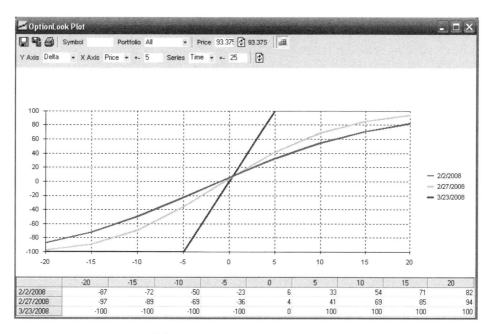

Figure 4.9 Long Straddle Delta vs. Underlying Price and Time to Expiration—Long XYZ March 93.375 Straddle
Source: LiquidPoint, LLC

underlying moves higher and negative as the underlying moves lower. The delta of the long straddle is approximately zero, or neutral, when the underlying price is at the strike price. Eventually, if the underlying moves far enough above or below the strike price, the delta will reach +100 or −100 when the long call or long put component goes deep in-the-money.

It also can be seen that the *rate* at which the delta of the long straddle changes is sensitive to the amount of time left until expiration. The sensitivity of the delta of the long straddle to changes in the underlying price increases as expiration approaches. Notice the difference in the delta generated at various times until expiration in Figure 4.9.

• Gamma

The gamma of a long straddle is the sum of the position-adjusted gammas of its component options. For example the gamma of the long 100 straddle would be calculated as follows:

100 strike put gamma = 0.05

100 strike call gamma = 0.05

Long straddle gamma = (0.05 × 1) + (0.05 × 1) or 0.10

A gamma of 0.10 means that the delta of the overall position will change by approximately 0.10 for every 1 point the underlying moves. Long options have positive gamma, and because the long straddle is composed of two long options, it also will have positive gamma. As was seen in Figure 4.9, a positive gamma means that the delta of the position will increase (become longer or less short) as the underlying moves up and will decrease (become shorter or less long) as the underlying moves down. Obviously, this is a very desirable characteristic in a position, but it carries a price, as we will see when we examine theta. Gamma is greatly dependent on moneyness and time to expiration. All things being equal, an at-the-money option near expiration will have a greater gamma than an at-the-money option with greater time left until expiration. However, short-dated options will "lose their gamma" more quickly than options with greater time until expiration. **Figure 4.10** shows the gamma of a long March 93.375.

Figure 4.10 demonstrates the dependency of the gamma of the long straddle on the location of the underlying and time until expiration. What is also demonstrated is that gamma itself is not linear. When expiration is near and the underlying price is close to the strike price of the long straddle, the position will have a large positive gamma. This dissipates quickly as the underlying moves away from the strike price. When there is greater time until expiration, the gamma curve is softer. The position still will have the greatest amount of gamma when the underlying is at the strike, but the rate of change in the gamma of the position as the underlying moves away from the strike is less drastic.

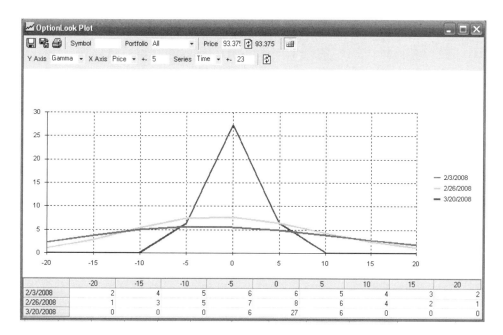

Figure 4.10 Long Straddle Gamma vs. Underlying Price and Time
to Expiration—Long XYZ March 93.375 Straddle
Source: LiquidPoint, LLC

• **Vega**

The vega of a long straddle is the sum of the position-adjusted vegas
of its component options. For example the vega of the long 100 straddle
would be calculated as follows:

$$100 \text{ strike put vega} = 0.18$$

$$100 \text{ strike call vega} = 0.15$$

$$\text{Long straddle} = (0.18 \times 1) + (0.15 \times 1) \text{ or } +0.33$$

This means that for every 1 percent change in implied volatility, the price
of the straddle would change by approximately 0.33, rising when implied
volatility rises and falling when implied volatility falls. Long options have
a positive vega, so the long straddle also will have a positive vega. Recall
from Chapter 1 that vega is very sensitive to time until expiration of the
options. Vega *increases* with time to expiration so that, all things being equal,
the vega of an option with a greater amount of time left until expiration will
be greater than that of an option with a lesser amount of time left until expiration. **Figure 4.11** shows the vega of the long XYZ March 93.375 straddle.

Figure 4.11 demonstrates the dependency of the vega of the straddle
on the location of the underlying price and time until expiration. This is
opposite the behavior of gamma. All things being equal, the vega of the
long straddle is greater when there is a larger amount of time left until
expiration.

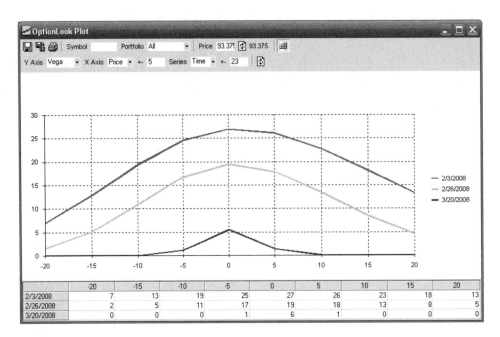

Figure 4.11 Long Straddle Vega vs. Underlying Price and Time
to Expiration—Long XYZ March 93.375 Straddle
Source: LiquidPoint, LLC

• Theta

The theta of a long straddle is the sum of the position-adjusted thetas
of its component options. For example, the theta of the long 100 straddle
would be calculated as follows:

100 strike put theta $= -0.02$

100 strike call theta $= -0.03$

Long straddle theta $= (-0.02 \times 1) + (-0.03 \times 1)$ or -0.05

This means that the value of the long straddle would decrease by
approximately 0.05 per calendar day. Because theta (time decay) is negative,
a long option position will have negative theta (negative time decay), so a
long straddle will have negative theta. Similar to gamma and vega, theta is
also dependent on moneyness, with at-the-money options having greater
theta than in- or out-of-the-money options of the same expiration. The
theta of an at-the-money option *increases* as time to expiration decreases
so that, all things being equal, the theta of an at-the-money option with a
lesser amount of time until expiration will be greater than the theta of an
at-the-money option with a greater amount of time until expiration. **Figure 4.12** shows the theta of the long XYZ March 93.375.

Figure 4.12 should look familiar. It is practically the mirror image of the
gamma graph of Figure 4.10. This is the "no free lunch" connection between
long gamma and negative theta. Having a position like a long straddle that
gets long when the market goes up or gets short when the market goes down
has a price tag, and it is the time decay that one experiences when holding

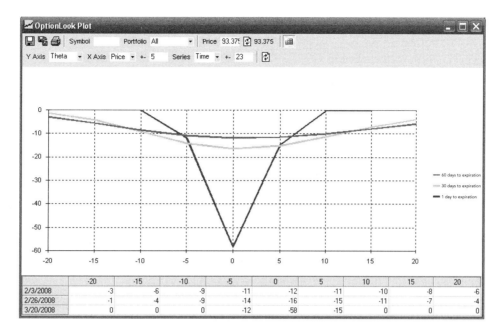

Figure 4.12 Long Straddle Theta vs. Underlying Price and Time to Expiration—Long XYZ March 93.375 Straddle
Source: LiquidPoint, LLC

such a position. As can be seen with the March 20, 2008 series in Figure 4.12, the theta of the long straddle, in absolute terms, reaches its peak when the underlying is at the strike price, and increases with the approach of expiration.

The Long Strangle

The long strangle, being a less aggressive version of the long straddle (long out-of-the-money options rather than at-the-money options), carries sensitivities that are similar to those of the long straddle.

• Delta

The delta of a long strangle is the sum of the position-adjusted deltas of its component options. For example, the delta of the long 100/110 strangle would be calculated as follows:

100 strike put delta = −0.25

110 strike call delta = +0.25

Long strangle delta = (−0.25 × 1) + (0.25 × 1) or 0.00 (delta neutral)

In the preceding example, the 100 put has a negative delta but a positive (long) position, yielding a negative position-adjusted delta. The 110 call has a positive delta and a positive (long) position, yielding a positive position-adjusted delta. The delta of a long strangle can range between +100 and −100 depending on the price of the underlying relative to the strike prices involved, time left until expiration, implied volatility levels, and other factors.

Because of the way it is structured, the delta of a long strangle sometimes can be difficult to quantify. When there is plenty of time left until expiration, the position generally will have a positive delta when the underlying is above the midpoint between the two strike prices, a negative delta when the underlying is below the midpoint between the two strike prices, and an approximately neutral delta when the underlying is at the midpoint between the strike prices. However, because the long strangle is composed of long out-of-the-money options, when near expiration the position will only have a positive delta when the underlying is above the strike of the long call, and a negative delta when the underlying is below the strike of the long put. When the position is between the two strikes, it will be approximately delta neutral. This effect can be seen in **Figure 4.13**.

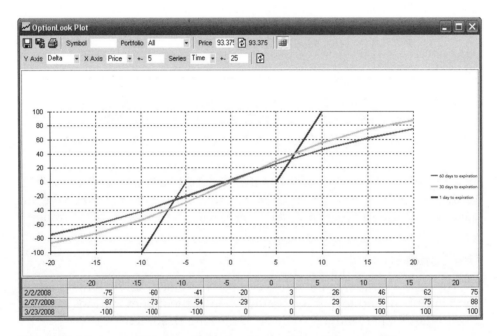

Figure 4.13 Long Strangle Delta vs. Underlying Price and Time to Expiration—Long XYZ March 86.625/100 Strangle
Source: LiquidPoint, LLC

It can be seen in Figure 4.13 that the delta of a long strangle, similar to that of the long straddle, moves in favor of the trader as the underlying moves, becoming increasingly positive as the underlying moves higher, and negative as the underlying moves lower.

The delta of the long strangle is approximately zero, or neutral, when the underlying price is exactly between the two strike prices. Eventually, if the underlying moves far enough above or below the strike price, the delta will reach +100 or −100 when the long call or long put component goes deep in-the-money. Note, however, the delta of the long strangle when expiration is close. It will be approximately neutral anywhere between the two strike prices.

Like the long straddle, the *rate* at which the delta of the long strangle changes is sensitive to the amount of time left until expiration. Again, notice in Figure 4.13 the difference in the delta generated at various times until expiration.

- **Gamma**

The gamma of a long strangle is the sum of the position-adjusted gammas of its component options. For example, the gamma of the long 100/110 strangle would be calculated as follows:

> 100 strike put gamma = 0.025
>
> 110 strike call gamma = 0.025
>
> Long strangle gamma = (0.025 × 1) + (0.025 × 1) or 0.05

A gamma of 0.05 means that the delta of the overall position would change by approximately 0.05 for every 1 point the underlying moved. Like the long straddle, the long strangle is composed of two long options, so it will have positive gamma. The delta of the position will increase (become longer or less short) as the underlying moves up and will decrease (become shorter or less long) as the underlying moves down. Unlike the long straddle, though, the long strangle has its long options located at different strikes, giving the graph of the gamma near expiration a double-peaked *M* aspect rather than the single-peak appearance associated with the gamma of a long straddle. **Figure 4.14** shows the gamma of a long strangle.

Figure 4.14 demonstrates the difference in the gamma between a long strangle near expiration and a long straddle near expiration. As expiration approaches, the gamma "accumulates" around the strikes of the long

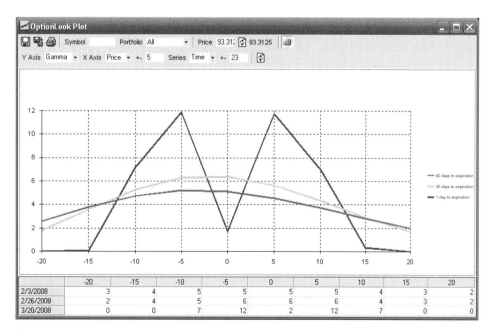

Figure 4.14 Long Strangle Gamma vs. Underlying Price and Time
to Expiration—Long XYZ March 86.625/100 Strangle
Source: LiquidPoint, LLC

options in two different locations. With a greater time left to expiration, the gamma of the long strangle and the long straddle have greater similarity. This is true of all of the Greeks.

• Vega

The vega of a long strangle is the sum of the position-adjusted vegas of its component options. For example, the vega of the long 100/110 strangle would be calculated as follows:

$$100 \text{ strike put vega} = 0.18$$

$$110 \text{ strike call vega} = 0.15$$

$$\text{Long strangle vega} = (0.18 \times 1) + (0.15 \times 1) \text{ or } +0.33$$

This means that for every 1 percent change in implied volatility, the price of the strangle would change by approximately 0.33, rising when implied volatility rises and falling when implied volatility falls. Long options have a positive vega, so the long strangle also will have a positive vega. **Figure 4.15** shows the vega of the long XYZ March 86.625/100 strangle.

Figure 4.15 shows the dependency of the vega of the long strangle on the location of the underlying price and time until expiration, with longer-dated options having greater sensitivity to implied volatility than their shorter-dated cousins. Note the difference in vega between the long strangle and the long straddle near expiration, with the double-peaked *M* aspect once again visible in the March 21, 2008, data series.

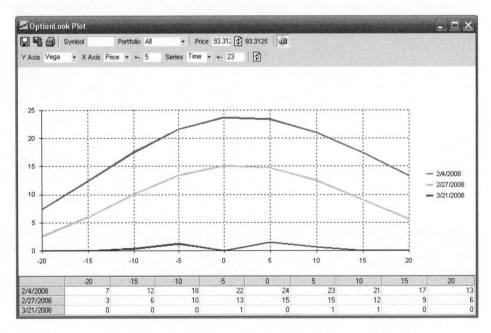

Figure 4.15 Long Strangle Vega vs. Underlying Price and Time
to Expiration—Long XYZ March 86.625/100 Strangle
Source: LiquidPoint, LLC

- **Theta**

The theta of a long strangle is the sum of the position-adjusted thetas of its component options. For example, the theta of the long 100/110 strangle would be calculated as follows:

100 strike put theta = -0.015

110 strike call theta = -0.015

Long strangle theta = $(-0.015 \times 1) + (-0.015 \times 1)$ or -0.03

This means that the value of the long strangle would decrease by approximately 0.03 per calendar day. As with the long straddle, the theta of the long strangle also is dependent on moneyness with at-the-money options having greater theta than in- or out-of-the-money options of the same expiration. **Figure 4.16** shows the theta of the long XYZ March 86.625/100 strangle.

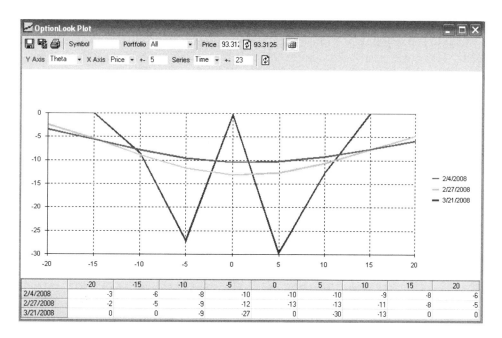

	-20	-15	-10	-5	0	5	10	15	20
2/4/2008	-3	-6	-8	-10	-10	-10	-9	-8	-6
2/27/2008	-2	-5	-9	-12	-13	-13	-11	-8	-5
3/21/2008	0	0	-9	-27	0	-30	-13	0	0

Figure 4.16 Long Strangle Theta vs. Underlying Price and Time to Expiration—Long XYZ March 86.625/100 Strangle
Source: LiquidPoint, LLC

As with the long straddle, the theta of the long strangle in Figure 4.16 is a mirror image of the gamma of the long strangle in Figure 4.14. Once again, note the difference in theta between the long strangle and the long straddle near expiration, with the double-valley *W* aspect visible in the March 21, 2008, data series.

The Short Straddle

Because the short straddle is composed of a short call and a short put, it carries the sensitivities that all short option positions carry: negative gamma, negative vega, and positive theta. The delta of a short straddle is dependent on the location of the underlying versus the strike. Because of the way it is structured, the straddle will have a negative delta when the underlying is above the strike price, a positive delta when the underlying is below the strike price, and an approximately neutral delta when the underlying is at the strike price.

• Delta

The delta of a short straddle is the sum of the position-adjusted deltas of its component options. For example, the delta of the 100 straddle would be calculated as follows:

100 strike put delta = −0.50

100 strike call delta = +0.50

Short straddle delta = (−0.50 × −1) + (0.50 × −1) or 0.00 (delta neutral)

In the above example, the 100 put has a negative delta and a negative (short) position, yielding a positive position-adjusted delta. The 100 call has a positive delta but a negative (short) position, yielding a negative position-adjusted delta. The position in the example above has a delta of zero, or is delta neutral.

The delta of a short straddle can range between +100 and −100 depending on the price of the underlying relative to the strike price involved, time left until expiration, implied volatility levels, and other factors. The delta will hover near zero when the underlying price is near the strike price. **Figure 4.17** shows the delta of a short XYZ March 93.375 straddle.

Figure 4.17 shows that the delta of a short straddle moves against the trader as the underlying moves, becoming increasingly negative as the underlying

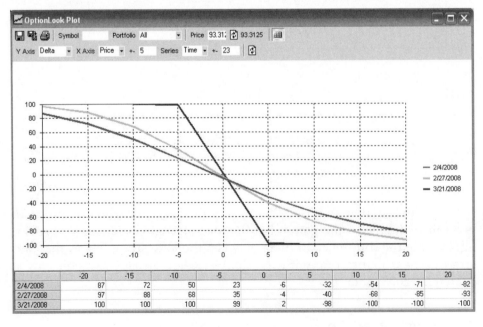

Figure 4.17   Short Straddle Delta vs. Underlying Price and Time
to Expiration—Short XYZ March 93.375 Straddle
Source: LiquidPoint, LLC

moves higher and positive as the underlying moves lower. The delta of the short straddle will be approximately zero, or neutral, when the underlying price is at the strike price. Eventually, if the underlying moves far enough above or below the strike price, the delta will reach −100 or +100 when the short call or short put component goes deep in-the-money.

As with the long straddle, the rate at which the delta of the short straddle changes is sensitive to the amount of time left until expiration. Notice in Figure 4.17 the difference in the delta generated at various times until expiration.

• Gamma

The gamma of a short straddle is the sum of the position-adjusted gammas of its component options. For example, the gamma of the short 100 straddle would be calculated as follows:

100 strike put gamma = 0.05

100 strike call gamma = 0.05

Short straddle gamma = (0.05 × −1) + (0.05 × −1) or −0.10

A gamma of −0.10 means that the delta of the overall position will change against the trader by approximately 0.10 for every 1 point the underlying moves. The delta of the position will decrease (become shorter or less long) as the underlying moves up, and increase (become longer or less short) as the underlying moves down. Obviously, this is a not a very desirable characteristic in a position, but there is a silver lining, as we can see when we examine theta. **Figure 4.18** illustrates the gamma of a short straddle.

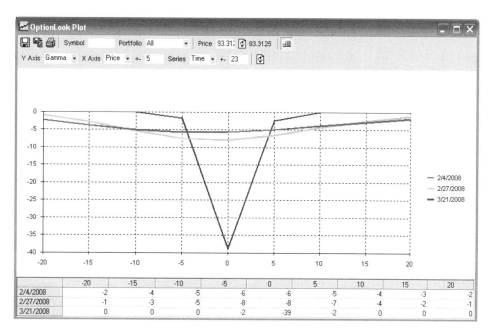

Figure 4.18 Short Straddle Gamma vs. Underlying Price and Time to Expiration—Short XYZ March 93.375 Straddle
Source: LiquidPoint, LLC

Figure 4.18 shows the dependency of the gamma of the short straddle on the location of the underlying and the time until expiration. The gamma of a short straddle is at its greatest when the underlying price is at the strike price. Short-dated at-the-money options have a higher gamma than at-the-money options with a greater amount of time to expiration.

• Vega

The vega of a short straddle is the sum of the position-adjusted vegas of its component options. For example, the vega of the short 100 straddle would be calculated as follows:

100 strike put vega = 0.18

100 strike call vega = 0.15

Short straddle vega = (0.18 × −1) + (0.15 × −1) or −0.33

This means that for every 1 percent change in implied volatility, the price of the straddle would change by approximately 0.33, rising by this amount when implied volatility rises and falling by this amount when implied volatility falls. So, the profitability of a short straddle position would increase by 0.33 per 1 percent fall in implied volatility or decrease by 0.33 per 1 percent increase in implied volatility. The vega increases with time to expiration so that, all things being equal, the vega of an option with a greater amount of time left until expiration will be larger than that of an option with a lesser amount of time left until expiration. **Figure 4.19** illustrates the vega of a short straddle.

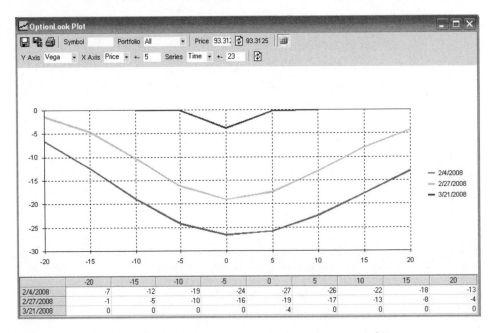

	-20	-15	-10	-5	0	5	10	15	20
2/4/2008	-7	-12	-19	-24	-27	-26	-22	-18	-13
2/27/2008	-1	-5	-10	-16	-19	-17	-13	-8	-4
3/21/2008	0	0	0	0	-4	0	0	0	0

Figure 4.19   Short Straddle Vega vs. Underlying Price and Time
to Expiration—Short XYZ March 93.375 Straddle
Source: LiquidPoint, LLC

Figure 4.19 shows how the vega of the short straddle depends on the location of the underlying price and time until expiration. All things being equal, the vega of the short straddle is greater when there is a larger amount of time left until expiration.

• **Theta**

The theta of a short straddle is the sum of the position-adjusted thetas of its component options. For example, the theta of the short 100 straddle would be calculated as follows:

100 strike put theta = −0.02

100 strike call theta = −0.03

Short straddle theta = (−0.02 × −1) + (−0.03 × −1) or +0.05

This means that the value of the straddle would decrease by approximately 0.05 per calendar day. Because theta (time decay) is negative, a short option position such as a short straddle will have positive theta (positive time decay), so the profitability of a short straddle position would increase by 0.05 per calendar day. The theta of an at-the-money option increases as the time to expiration decreases so that, all things being equal, the theta of an at-the-money option with a lesser amount of time until expiration will be greater than the theta of an at-the-money option with a greater amount of time until expiration. **Figure 4.20** illustrates the theta of a short straddle.

A position like the short straddle that responds negatively to underlying movement by becoming delta short when the market goes up or delta

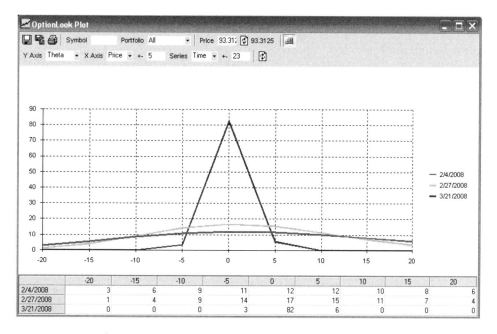

Figure 4.20 Short Straddle Theta vs. Underlying Price and Time to Expiration—Short XYZ March 93.375 Straddle
Source: LiquidPoint, LLC

long when the market goes down has the silver lining of a positive theta. In theory, if all things are equal, every day that passes makes the short straddle position more profitable. As shown by the March 21, 2008 series in Figure 4.20, the theta of the short straddle is always positive, and it reaches its peak when the underlying is at the strike price, increasing with the approach of expiration.

The Short Strangle

The short strangle is a less aggressive version of the short straddle, using short out-of-the-money options rather than at-the-money options. Its sensitivities are similar to those of the short straddle.

- ### Delta

The delta of a short strangle is the sum of the position-adjusted deltas of its component options. For example, the delta of the short 100/110 strangle would be calculated as follows:

100 strike put delta = −0.25

110 strike call delta = 0.25

Short strangle delta = (−0.25 × −1) + (0.25 × −1) or 0.00 (delta neutral)

In the above example, the 100 put has a negative delta and a negative (short) position, yielding a positive position-adjusted delta. The 100 call has a positive delta and a negative (short) position, yielding a negative position-adjusted delta. The position in the example above has a delta of zero; it is delta neutral.

With the short strangle, when there is plenty of time left until expiration, the position generally has a negative delta when the underlying is above the midpoint between the two strike prices, a positive delta when the underlying is below the midpoint between the two strike prices, and an approximately neutral delta when the underlying is at the midpoint between the strike prices. However, because the short strangle is composed of short out-of-the-money options, when near expiration, the position will only have a negative delta when the underlying is above the strike of the short call; it will have a positive delta when the underlying is below the strike of the short put. When between the two strikes, it will be approximately delta neutral. This effect can be seen in **Figure 4.21**.

Figure 4.21 shows that the delta of a short strangle moves against the trader as the underlying moves, becoming increasingly positive as the underlying moves lower and negative as the underlying moves higher. The delta of the short strangle is approximately zero, or neutral, when the underlying price is exactly between the two strike prices. Eventually, if the underlying moves far enough above or below the strike price, the delta will reach −100 or +100, when the short call or short put component

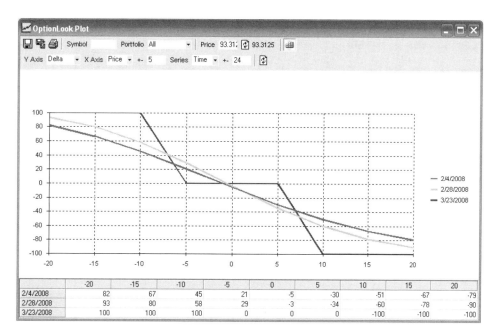

Figure 4.21 Short Strangle Delta vs. Underlying Price and Time
to Expiration—Short XYZ March 86.625/100 Strangle
Source: LiquidPoint, LLC

goes deep in-the-money. Note, however, the delta of the short strangle when expiration is close. It will be approximately neutral anywhere between the two strike prices.

• **Gamma**

The gamma of a short strangle is the sum of the position-adjusted gammas of its component options. For example, the gamma of the short 100/110 strangle would be calculated as follows:

100 strike put gamma = 0.025

110 strike call gamma = 0.025

Short strangle gamma = $(0.025 \times -1) + (0.025 \times -1)$ or -0.05

A gamma of -0.05 means that the delta of the overall position will change by approximately 0.05 for every 1 point the underlying moves. The short strangle has negative gamma, so the delta of the position will decrease (become shorter or less long) as the underlying moves up and will increase (become longer or less short) as the underlying moves down. Unlike the short straddle, the short strangle has its short options located at different strikes, giving the graph of the gamma near expiration the double-valley *W* aspect rather than the single valley associated with the gamma of a short straddle. **Figure 4.22** illustrates the gamma of a short strangle.

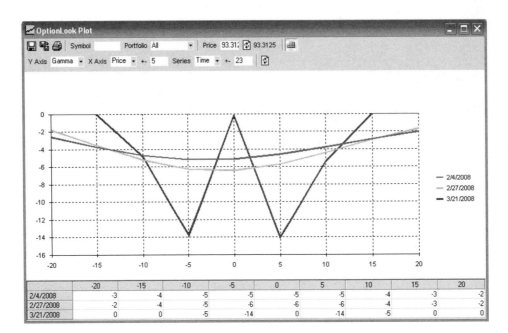

Figure 4.22 Short Strangle Gamma vs. Underlying Price and Time
to Expiration—Short XYZ March 86.625/100 Strangle
Source: LiquidPoint, LLC

Figure 4.22 shows the difference in the gamma between a short strangle near expiration and a short straddle near expiration. As expiration approaches, the gamma "accumulates" around the strikes of the short options in two different locations. With a greater time left to expiration, the gamma of the short strangle and gamma of the short straddle are more similar. Again, this is true of all of the Greeks.

• Vega

The vega of a short strangle is the sum of the position-adjusted vegas of its component options. For example, the vega of the short 100/110 strangle would be calculated as follows:

100 strike put vega = 0.10

110 strike call vega = 0.09

Short strangle vega = $(0.10 \times -1) + (0.09 \times -1)$ or -0.19

This means that for every 1 percent change in implied volatility, the price of the strangle will change by approximately 0.19, rising when implied volatility rises and falling when implied volatility falls. So the profitability of a short strangle position would increase by 0.19 for every 1 percent decrease in implied volatility and would decrease by 0.19 for every 1 percent increase in implied volatility. **Figure 4.23** illustrates the vega of a short strangle.

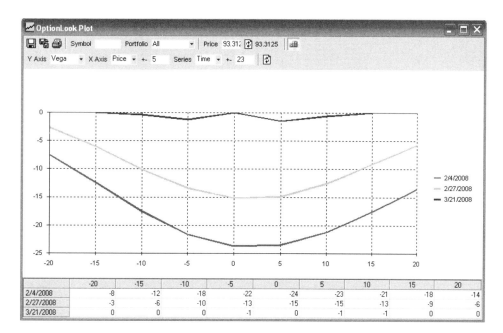

Figure 4.23 Short Strangle Vega vs. Underlying Price and Time to Expiration—Short XYZ March 86.625/100 Strangle
Source: LiquidPoint, LLC

Figure 4.23 illustrates the dependency of the vega of the short strangle on the location of the underlying price and the time until expiration, with shorter-dated options having less sensitivity to implied volatility than their longer-dated cousins.

• Theta

The theta of a short strangle is the sum of the position-adjusted thetas of its component options. For example, the theta of the short 100/110 strangle would be calculated as follows:

100 strike put theta = −0.015

110 strike call theta = −0.015

Short strangle theta = (−0.015 × −1) + (−0.015 × −1) or +0.03

This means that the value of the strangle would decrease by approximately 0.03 per calendar day, so the profitability of a short strangle position would increase by approximately 0.03 per calendar day. The theta of the short strangle is dependent on moneyness, with at-the-money options having greater theta than in- or out-of-the-money options of the same expiration. **Figure 4.24** illustrates the theta of a short strangle.

As with the short straddle, note that the theta of the short strangle increases as expiration approaches. Note also the difference in theta between the short strangle and the short straddle near expiration, with the double-peaked *M* aspect visible in the March 21, 2008, data series.

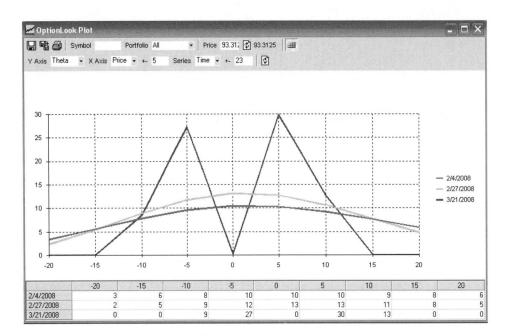

Figure 4.24 Short Strangle Theta vs. Underlying Price and Time
          to Expiration—Short XYZ March 86.625/100 Strangle
          Source: LiquidPoint, LLC

INVESTMENT OBJECTIVES

Straddles and strangles are nondirectional strategies designed to profit from the type of move forecast rather than the direction of a move. Long straddles and strangles are geared to profit from movement in the underlying position and/or increasing implied volatility. They also have limited risk and unlimited profit potential, but suffer from negative time decay. Short straddles and strangles are geared to profit from a lack of movement and/or declining implied volatility. They also have unlimited risk and limited profit potential, but have positive time decay. The investment objectives of these strategies are highlighted below.

Long straddles and strangles:

- Price appreciation due to a large gain in the intrinsic value of the long call or put

- Price appreciation due to an increase in implied volatility, raising the price of both the call and the put

Short straddles and strangles:

- Price depreciation due to the time decay of the short call and put

- Price depreciation due to the decrease in implied volatility, lowering the price of both the call and the put

STRATEGY COMPONENT SELECTION

Market Outlook: Long Straddles and Strangles

- **Large-Magnitude Movement in an Unknown Direction**

In this scenario, the trader of a long straddle or strangle should be looking for a large magnitude move (that is, a *breakout*) away from the strike price. This may be in response to an event such as an earnings report, a new product launch, a government report, a significant corporate event, or a macroeconomic event that will affect the market as a whole. It also could be technically driven. In fact, any situation that sets up an underlying stock or index for a large magnitude move in either direction is a candidate for a long straddle or strangle. The forecast move should be large enough that the position will pick up a significant increase in the intrinsic value of either the long call or long put, depending on which way the underlying stock or index moves. The owner of a long straddle or strangle should be expecting the underlying price to move sharply above or below the strike or strikes of the position. **Figure 4.25** is a good example of the type of movement the buyer of a long straddle or strangle should be expecting.

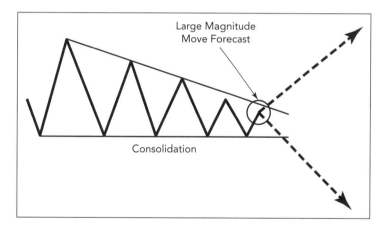

Figure 4.25 Breakout

- **Increase in Implied Volatility**

In this scenario, the trader of a long straddle or strangle should be looking for a general increase in the volatility of the underlying such that the implied volatility of the options increase. The trader is expecting to profit from a rise in the value of the straddle or strangle when the market participants mark up the level of implied volatility to reflect the increase in the volatility of the underlying. **Figure 4.26** illustrates this scenario.

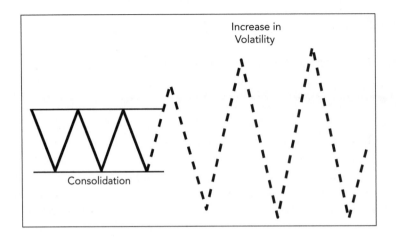

Figure 4.26 Volatility Increase

Market Outlook: Short Straddles and Strangles

• Low-Magnitude Directionless Movement

In this scenario, the trader of a short straddle or strangle should be looking for subdued low magnitude movement (that is, a *sideways* market) around the strike price. This scenario usually sets up after a period of volatile movement, when the market is in need of a "rest." It also could be seasonal, for example, during a holiday or post earnings, etc. Or it could be technically driven. The seller of a straddle or a strangle should be expecting the underlying price to move in a sideways fashion, and could profit from time decay and/or a decline in implied volatility. **Figure 4.27** illustrates a sideways market.

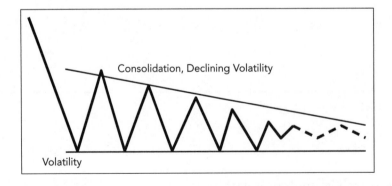

Figure 4.27 Sideways Market

• Risk: Long Straddles and Strangles

Because long straddles and strangles are composed of long calls and puts, risk is limited. This doesn't mean that they can be put on and then forgotten. Even though the risk is limited, long straddles and strangles still can produce painful losses if the trader's forecast is incorrect or his timing is off. Paying time decay on a long straddle or strangle position is like the death of a thousand cuts—each day's decay seems insignificant, but before you realize it, you are bleeding money. Movement of the underlying works in the trader's favor with a long straddle or strangle, but movement of the clock does not. Therefore, it is important to set both price and time constraints on these types of positions. It is important to quantify the price risk and the time risk you are willing to take before the trade is made and exit when the lesser of the two is reached.

- **Risk: Short Straddles and Strangles**

Because short straddles and strangles are composed of short calls and puts, risk is unlimited. This means they must be actively managed using stop-loss orders, as discussed in the previous chapter. The trader should be able to identify key price levels that, if breached, would indicate that her forecast of subdued movement is incorrect. If these levels are broken, the trade should be exited. It is also possible that the price of the straddle or strangle that the trader is short will rise without breaching key price levels, as might occur when volatility levels are generally rising. In this case, the trader should preset a stop-loss price on the structure itself, and exit the trade when this price is breached.

TRADE MANAGEMENT

Remember: It is crucial to have a risk management strategy in place before entering a trade!

If, in fact, it becomes clear that one's forecast is incorrect, then it is time to get out of the position—hopefully in an orderly fashion. This is usually accomplished through the use of stop-loss orders, which were discussed in Chapter 3. As a reminder, stop-loss orders are nonmarketable buy or sell orders placed in the market that trigger if and when certain price conditions are met, at which point they are turned into market orders. Traders usually use stop-loss orders to close losing positions if key price levels are violated, indicating an incorrect price forecast. There are several important issues to consider when trading straddles and strangles. Long straddles and strangles require different management from short straddles and strangles.

Long straddles and strangles:

- What is the most efficient way to take profits?

- How should poor timing be dealt with?

Short straddles and strangles:

- Where should stop-loss orders be placed?

- What should be done if the underlying isn't moving but implied volatility is rising?

Long Straddles and Strangles

• Breakout

When a long straddle or strangle becomes profitable, meaning that the large magnitude move the trader was forecasting occurs, it is important that he actively manages the long put or long call component of the trade that moves into the money and attempt to squeeze the maximum profitability out of that portion of the position. As with the collar and any other long-option-containing position, this is usually accomplished by "rolling" the long option position along with the underlying by selling vertical spreads. Rolling a long option position is an excellent way to manage a position that is going as planned. As discussed in the previous chapter, rolling accomplishes three important things:

- It maintains the investor's exposure in the direction of the breakout.

- It reduces risk and takes "money off the table."

- It puts the investor in a strong psychological position and increases his "staying power."

• Poor Timing

When trading a long straddle or strangle, it is important to not only have the correct market view (large magnitude breakout or rising implied volatility), but also to be fairly precise with timing. Because the long straddle or strangle has negative time decay, the clock is the enemy and every day that passes without the forecast movement is painful. Therefore, when an investor is trading straddles and strangles from the long side, it is important that she set a *time stop-loss* (a date in the future beyond which she will not carry the position) as well as a *price stop-loss* (a price below which she will not carry the position). When either one of these stop-loss levels is hit, the trader should exit the position.

Short Straddles and Strangles

• Breakout

Underlying movement is the enemy of the short straddle or strangle. If the forecast of subdued or low magnitude movement is incorrect, one will have to actively manage the short call or short put component of the position in order to help manage risk.

• Rising Implied Volatility

Sometimes when trading a short straddle or strangle, a trader might have the correct market view (subdued low-magnitude movement), but the implied volatility of the options rises anyway, causing the value of the straddle or strangle the trader is short to rise, creating losses. When implied volatility rises, it is because other market participants foresee increased volatility in the market place and begin pricing options accordingly. In the long run, they may not necessarily be correct; but this is their view at the time. Unfortunately, this situation creates near-term pain for one's trade, and it is difficult to know when this increase in implied volatility might begin to subside, if ever. Therefore, when a trader trades straddles and strangles from the short side, it is also important to set a stop-loss on the straddle or strangle price itself, at a price above which he will not carry the position. Even if the underlying stock or index is not moving, if this stop-loss level is hit, the position should be exited.

RISK AND REWARD, THERE IS NO FREE LUNCH!

Straddles and strangles can be very seductive trading vehicles. Traders with a weakness for the "long shot" can easily be blinded by the potential of long straddles and strangles—they give the appearance of making money in every direction and have unlimited profit potential. These traders tend to fall in love with their delta and gamma numbers and usually overlook the fact that they have to pay time decay and are exposed to declines in implied volatility. After some time passes and their forecasts are proven incorrect, they are left wondering where the money went. Traders looking for a "sure thing" can become addicted to short straddles and strangles. Short straddles and strangles profit from time decay, and what could be more certain than time passing? These traders tend to fall in love with their theta numbers and overlook the negative gamma or the unlimited risk aspects of their positions. They count their time decay income day after day only to see it all vanish when a large move takes place or implied volatility rises.

The bottom line is that there is no free lunch with straddles and strangles. For every upside there is a downside, and the risks have to be understood, factored into the forecast, and properly managed in a disciplined fashion if one is to be successful trading straddles and strangles (or using any other strategy).

CHAPTER 4 EXERCISE

1. If an investor purchases the following strangle, what are his break-even points?
   Long 1 XYZ May 130 put at $10.00
   Long 1 XYZ May 150 call at $12.00

2. Does a long straddle have a positive or a negative gamma?

3. Calculate the gamma of the long 100/115 strangle, if the call gamma = 0.02 and the put gamma = 0.02.

4. If a long strangle had a vega of 0.15, for every 1 percent change in the _____, the price of the strangle would change by 0.15.

5. The delta of the short straddle moves against the position as the underlying moves. True or false?

6. A long strangle has a positive vega. True or false?

7. Theta is the rate at which the _____ of the short straddle change is sensitive to the amount of time left until expiration.

8. Will the theta of the short strangle increase or decrease as expiration approaches?

9. Do short straddles and strangles have a negative or a positive time decay?

10. Does a long straddle have plus or minus vega, and does it have plus or minus theta?

Chapter 4 Exercise Answer Key

1. $108.00 ($130.00 − $22.00); $172.00 ($150.00 + $22.00)
2. Positive
3. 0.04 [(0.020 × 1) + (0.020 × 1)]
4. Implied volatility
5. True
6. True
7. Value
8. Increase
9. Positive
10. Plus; minus

CHAPTER 4 QUIZ

1. If you are expecting a "breakout" to take place, which two strategies might you employ?

2. If you were long the XYZ March 50 straddle and XYZ had dropped in price you might consider rolling down the put to 40, leaving you with the 40/50 _____.

3. If you initiate a short straddle with both options at-the-money, the options will each have a delta of approximately 50 and will offset each other just as with the long straddle. True or false?

4. What are the break-even points for the long straddle: strike (plus or minus) the premium on the downside, and strike (plus or minus) the premium on the upside?

5. The deltas will approach _____ as the at-the-money straddle nears expiration.

6. What is the maximum loss for the short straddle (include upside and downside)?

7. Short-dated at-the-money options have a (lower) (higher) gamma than at-the-money options with a greater amount of time to expiration.

8. A gamma of −0.10 means that the delta of the overall position would change *against* the trader by approximately _____ for every 1 point the underlying moves.

9. When trading straddles and strangles from the short side, it is important to set a _____ on the straddle or strangle price.

10. When an underlying is experiencing a subdued low-magnitude movement around the strike price, which two strategies might you consider employing?

Chapter 4 Quiz Answer Key

1. Long strangle and long straddle
2. Strangle
3. True
4. Minus; plus
5. Zero
6. On the upside, it is unlimited; on the downside, it is substantial down to zero in the underlying minus the credit you received when you initiated the position.
7. Higher
8. 0.10
9. Stop-loss order
10. Short straddle, short strangle

5

Butterflies
and Condors

CONCEPT REVIEW

Support level: Support is a price level or zone located below the current market price where buyers become more willing to buy and sellers are reluctant to sell.

Resistance level: Resistance is a price level or zone located above the current market price where sellers become more willing to sell and buyers are reluctant to buy.

Mean-reversion: The mean-reversion price or mean-reversion area is the price or area that the underlying stock or index seems to return to as it meanders in its trading range.

STRATEGY OVERVIEW

Butterflies and condors fit into the category of "directionless" strategies. In terms of market view they are similar to straddles and strangles in that the trader is not necessarily forecasting a particular direction in the market, but rather a magnitude of movement. Butterflies and condors can be traded from the long side or the short side, depending on the type of movement that is expected in the underlying stock or index:

- Long butterflies and condors (**Figures 5.1**, **5.2**, **5.3**, and **5.4**) are used when the trader is forecasting little or no directional movement or a "trading range" in the underlying stock or index and he or she seeks to profit from an increase in the overall value of the position due to time decay or falling implied volatility.

- Short butterflies and condors are used when the trader is forecasting a large magnitude move in either direction and he seeks to profit from a decrease in the value of the overall position.

STRATEGY COMPOSITION

Long Call Butterfly

Components: Long 1 March 130 call at $7.00
                   Short 2 March 135 calls at $5.00
                   Long 1 March 140 call at $4.00

                   Initiated for a debit of $1.00

Maximum Profit: $(K_3 - K_1) \div 2 -$ debit $(140 - 130/2 = \$1.00 = \$4.00)$

Maximum Loss: Debit, or price paid to initiate strategy ($1.00)

Breakeven(s): $K_1 +$ debit ($131.00); $K_3 -$ debit ($139.00)

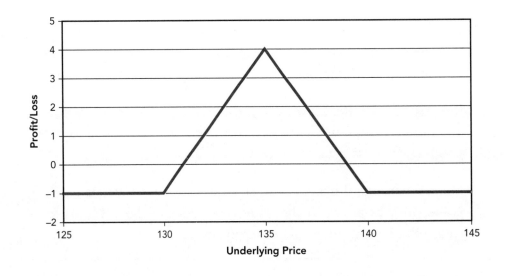

Figure 5.1 Long Call Butterfly P&L Diagram

Long Call Condor

Components: Long 1 March 55 call at $14.00
                   Short 1 March 60 call at $10.00
                   Short 1 March 65 call at $7.00
                   Long 1 March 70 call at $4.25

                   Initiated for a $1.25 debit

Maximum Profit: $K_3 - K_2 -$ debit or $K_2 - K_1 -$ debit ($3.75)

Maximum Loss: Debit, or price paid to initiate strategy ($1.25)

Breakeven(s): $K_1 +$ debit ($56.25); $K_4 -$ debit ($68.75)

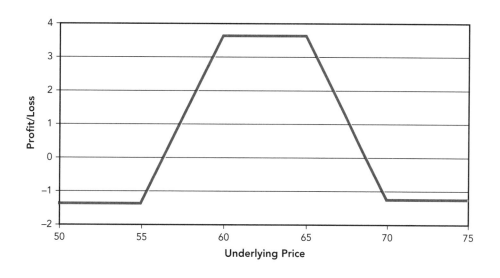

Figure 5.2 Long Call Condor P&L Diagram

Long Iron Butterfly

Components: Long 1 April 130 put at $3.00
                     Short 1 April 135 call at $5.50
                     Short 1 April 135 put at $5.00
                     Long 1 April 140 call at $3.50

                     Initiated for a $4.00 credit

Maximum Profit: Credit received ($4.00)

Maximum Loss: $K_2 - K_1$ − credit ($135.00 − $130.00 − $4.00 = $1.00)

Breakeven(s): K_2 − credit ($131.00); K_2 + credit ($139.00)

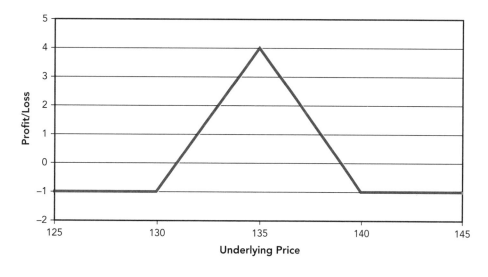

Figure 5.3 Long Iron Butterfly P&L Diagram

Long Iron Condor

Components:	Long 1 March 55 put at $1.50
	Short 1 March 60 put at $2.50
	Short 1 March 65 call at $5.25
	Long 1 March 70 call at $3.00
	Initiated for a $3.25 credit
Maximum Profit:	Limited to credit received
Maximum Loss:	$K_2 - K_1$ − credit ($60.00 − $55.00 − $3.25 = $1.75)
Breakeven(s):	K_2 − credit ($56.75); K_3 + credit ($68.25)

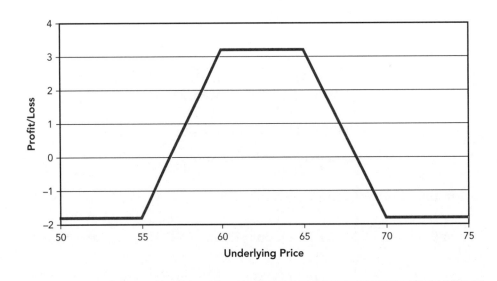

Figure 5.4 Long Iron Condor P&L Diagram

The similarities between butterflies and condors and straddles and strangles are no accident. Long butterflies contain an embedded synthetic short straddle wrapped by a synthetic long strangle. Long condors contain an embedded short strangle wrapped by a synthetic long strangle that is further out-of-the-money. This type of structure allows the properly positioned long butterfly or condor to potentially profit from time decay and/or falling implied volatility just as a short straddle or short strangle would. The big difference is that the long strangle "wrap" of both structures limits the risk in the position, making it a more attractive "direction-less" strategy for risk-averse traders.

Short butterflies contain an embedded synthetic long straddle wrapped by a synthetic short strangle. Short condors contain an embedded long strangle wrapped by a synthetic short strangle that is further out-of-the-money. This type of structure allows the properly positioned short butterfly or condor to potentially profit from sharp movement similar to a long straddle or long strangle would. The big difference is that the short strangle "wrap" of both structures limits the profit potential in the position (albeit with less exposure to time decay), making it a much less attractive "large move" strategy. For this reason we will focus on the long butterfly and long condor strategy in this book.

Long Butterflies and Condors

• The Long Butterfly

The long butterfly is a unique option strategy that can be used to address a directionless market. The classic long butterfly is constructed using three adjacent strikes, purchasing the lower strike option, selling two of the middle strike options, and purchasing the higher strike option. The long butterfly has several variations and can be constructed using calls, puts, or a mixture of both. **Figures 5.5**, **5.6**, and **5.7** illustrate the three basic forms of the long butterfly.

Calls	Strike	Puts
+1	100	
−2	105	
+1	110	

Figure 5.5 Long Call Butterfly

Calls	Strike	Puts
	100	+1
	105	−2
	110	+1

Figure 5.6 Long Put Butterfly

Calls	Strike	Puts
	100	+1
−1	105	−1
+1	110	

Figure 5.7 Long Iron Butterfly

Strike selection is very important when addressing the directionless market with a long butterfly. The middle strike should be located in the middle of the expected trading range. Placing the middle strike of the long butterfly at-the-money creates a position that does not have a directional bias and has a positive theta. Recall that at-the-money options have a higher theta than away-from-the-money options, so even though a long butterfly has an equal number of long and short options, locating the middle strike at-the-money gives the structure a positive theta.

• The Long Condor

A long condor is another limited-risk strategy that an investor can use to trade in a directionless market. Condors usually are lumped into the butterfly family because a condor is really just a variation of the butterfly. A long condor has the same general "+1/−2/+1" structure as the long butterfly; the difference is that the two short contracts that make up the "body" of the long condor are distributed over two strikes instead of one.

An investor could use a long condor when he expects a directionless market with a wider trading range, or a trading range that seems to move between strikes. The long condor also can be constructed using calls, puts, or a mixture of both. **Figures 5.8**, **5.9**, and **5.10** illustrate the three basic forms of the long condor.

Calls	Strike	Puts
+1	100	
−1	105	
−1	110	
+1	115	

Figure 5.8 Long Call Condor

Calls	Strike	Puts
	100	+1
	105	−1
	110	−1
	115	+1

Figure 5.9 Long Put Condor

Calls	Strike	Puts
	100	+1
	105	−1
−1	110	
+1	115	

Figure 5.10 Long Iron Condor

As with the long butterfly, the middle strikes should be located in the middle of the expected trading range. Placing the middle strikes of the long condor in the middle of the range creates a position that does not have a directional bias and has a positive theta. Stretching the "body" of the structure over two strikes rather than one gives the trader a larger range of potential profitability that can help cover a wider trading range. But this extra coverage is not free: A condor typically is more expensive than a butterfly. The extra premium spent buying a condor rather than a butterfly buys a larger range of potential profitability, but maximum profit is decreased and maximum loss is increased by the amount of the premium spent.

Time Decay

If a market is directionless, hovering around the same prices every day or floundering inside a trading range, the only thing really changing on a day-to-day basis is the passage of time. The driving force behind a long butterfly or condor strategy is time decay and/or declining implied volatility. The price of an option has two components: intrinsic value and extrinsic value. Intrinsic value is the amount by which an option is in-the-money. A call option is in-the-money if the price of the underlying is above the strike price. A put option is in-the-money if the price of the underlying is below the strike price. Any remaining value is extrinsic value. At-the-money options and out-of-the-money options are composed entirely of extrinsic value. The amount of extrinsic value in an option depends on many factors, including underlying price, interest rates, dividends, time until expiration, and implied volatility. The more uncertainty there is about the option's possible value at expiration (in the case, for example, of higher volatility and greater time to expiration), the greater the extrinsic value of the option. Conversely, the more certainty there is about an option's value at expiration (in the case, for example, of lower volatility and less time until expiration), the lower the extrinsic value of the option.

Theoretically, an option loses a portion of its extrinsic value every day, and over time, an option will lose all of its extrinsic value. This is referred to as *time decay*. Because of time decay, buyers of options theoretically lose money every day, while sellers of options theoretically gain money every day. Time decay is quantified by theta. If a long butterfly or condor is properly located around the trading range, the position will have positive time decay or a positive theta and will theoretically increase in value with each passing day. We will explore this further in the following section.

THE GREEKS OF LONG BUTTERFLIES AND CONDORS

As mentioned in "Strategy Overview," long butterflies and condors are directionless strategies that seek to profit from time decay and/or the decline of implied volatility as the market marks time by moving sideways. Because of the structure of long butterflies and condors—short options in the middle, or the "body," and long options on the perimeter, or the "wings"— the Greeks will be sensitive to the location of the underlying price versus the strike prices of the position. When the underlying price is near the short options of the body, the position will carry the characteristics of a short option position—short gamma, short vega, and positive theta—which are desirable characteristics if the underlying is moving in a trading range and hovering around the short strike(s). When the underlying price is near the long options of the wings, the position will carry the characteristics of a long option position—long gamma, long vega, and negative theta—which are undesirable characteristics if the underlying is moving in a trading range.

The Long Butterfly

- **Delta**

The delta of a long butterfly is dependent on the location of the underlying versus the strike. Because of the way it is structured, the long butterfly will have a positive delta when the underlying is below the middle strike price and a negative delta when the underlying is above the middle strike price; the delta will be approximately neutral when the underlying is at the middle strike price. On an extreme move up or down, the delta will eventually become neutral since the structure has limited risk.

The delta of a long butterfly is the sum of the position-adjusted deltas of its component options. For example, the delta of the long 500/510/520 call butterfly would be calculated as follows:

$$500 \text{ strike call delta} = 0.60$$

$$510 \text{ strike call delta} = 0.50$$

$$520 \text{ strike call delta} = 0.40$$

$$\text{Long call butterfly delta} = (0.60 \times 1) + (0.50 \times -2) + (0.40 \times 1) \text{ or } 0.00$$

The delta of the long 500/510/520 put butterfly would be calculated as follows:

$$500 \text{ strike put delta} = -0.40$$

$$510 \text{ strike put delta} = -0.50$$

$$520 \text{ strike put delta} = -0.60$$

$$\text{Long put butterfly delta} = (-0.40 \times 1) + (-0.50 \times -2) + (-0.60 \times 1) \text{ or } 0.00$$

The delta of the long 500/510/520 iron butterfly would be calculated as follows:

500 strike put delta = −0.40

510 strike put delta = −0.50

510 strike call delta = 0.50

520 strike call delta = 0.40

Long iron butterfly delta = (−0.40 × 1) + (−0.50 × −1) + (0.50 × −1) + (0.40 × 1) or 0.00

Note how the deltas of all three versions of the long butterfly are the same. This is because they are synthetically equivalent to one another. The Greeks of the call, put, and iron butterflies of the same strikes and expiration will always be identical.

Figure 5.11 shows that the delta of a long butterfly is positive when the underlying is below the middle strike, negative when the underlying is above the middle strike, and approximately neutral when it is at the middle strike. This makes sense because the point of maximum profitability of a long butterfly is at the middle strike. Also note the sensitivity of the delta of the long butterfly to the amount of time left until expiration. As expiration approaches, the delta of the long butterfly becomes much more sensitive to changes in the underlying price. Notice the differences in the delta generated at various times until expiration in Figure 5.11.

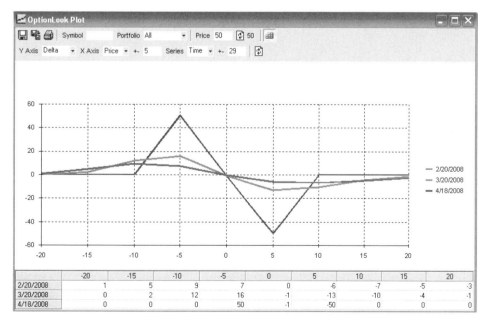

Figure 5.11 Long Butterfly Delta vs. Underlying Price and Time to Expiration—Long April 45/50/55 Butterfly
Source: LiquidPoint, LLC

- **Gamma**

The gamma of a long butterfly is the sum of the position-adjusted gammas of its component options. For example, the gamma of the long 500/510/520 call butterfly would be calculated as follows:

$$500 \text{ strike call gamma} = 0.05$$

$$510 \text{ strike call gamma} = 0.10$$

$$520 \text{ strike call gamma} = 0.06$$

$$\text{Long call butterfly gamma} = (0.05 \times 1) + (0.10 \times -2) + (0.06 \times 1) \text{ or } -0.09$$

A gamma of -0.09 means that the delta of the overall position would change against the trader by approximately 0.09 for every 1 point the underlying moved. In other words, if the underlying moved up by 1 point, the position would become 0.09 deltas shorter, and if the underlying moved down by 1 point, the position would become 0.09 deltas longer. Negative gamma positions always move against the trader. Obviously, this is not a very desirable characteristic in a position, but there is a silver lining as we will see when we examine theta. Gamma is greatly dependent on the moneyness and the time to expiration. All things being equal, an at-the-money option near expiration will have a greater gamma than an at-the-money option with greater time left until expiration.

Figure 5.12 shows the dependency of the gamma of the long butterfly on the location of the underlying and the time until expiration. When expiration

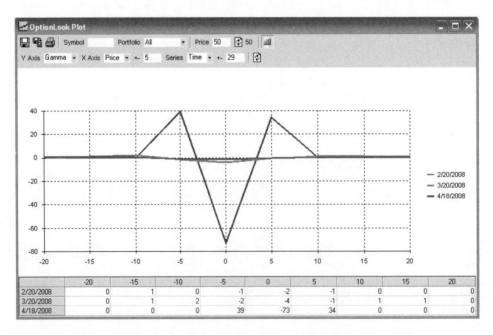

Figure 5.12 Long Butterfly Gamma vs. Underlying Price and Time to Expiration—Long April 45/50/55 Butterfly
Source: LiquidPoint, LLC

is near and the underlying price is close to the short options at the body, or middle, strike price of the long butterfly, the position will have a large negative gamma. This reverses quickly as the underlying moves away from the middle strike price into the area of the long wings of the outer strikes. When there is greater time until expiration, the gamma curve is much softer.

• Vega

The vega of a long butterfly is the sum of the position-adjusted vegas of its component options. For example, the vega of the long 500/510/520 call butterfly would be calculated as follows:

$$500 \text{ strike call vega} = 0.15$$

$$510 \text{ strike call vega} = 0.20$$

$$520 \text{ strike call vega} = 0.17$$

$$\text{Long call butterfly vega} = (0.15 \times 1) + (0.20 \times -2) \\ + (0.17 \times 1) \text{ or } -0.08$$

This means that for every 1 percent change in implied volatility, the price of the long butterfly would change by approximately 0.08. Because an at-the-money long butterfly is short vega, the value of the butterfly will fall when implied volatility rises and rise when implied volatility falls. **Figure 5.13** illustrates the vega of a long butterfly.

Because of the +1/−2/+1 structure of the long butterfly, the position will be short vega when the underlying price is near the short middle strike

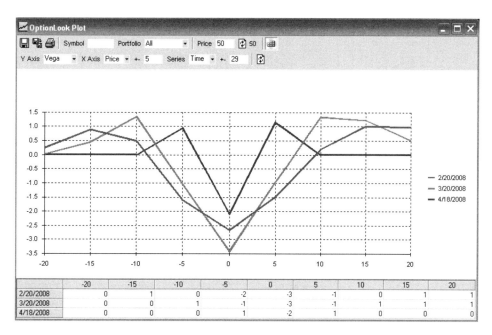

Figure 5.13 Long Butterfly Vega vs. Underlying Price and Time to Expiration—Long April 45/50/55 Butterfly
Source: LiquidPoint, LLC

and will reverse to being long vega when the underlying price is near the long wing strikes. Recall from Chapter 1 that vega increases with time to expiration so that, all things being equal, the vega of an option with a greater amount of time left until expiration will be larger than that of an option with a lesser amount of time left until expiration. Figure 5.13 clearly shows the dependency of the vega of the butterfly on the location of the underlying price and the time until expiration.

- **Theta**

The theta of a long butterfly is the sum of the position-adjusted thetas of its component options. For example, the theta of the long 500/510/520 call butterfly would be calculated as follows:

$$500 \text{ strike call theta} = -0.02$$

$$510 \text{ strike call theta} = -0.06$$

$$520 \text{ strike call theta} = -0.03$$

$$\text{Long call butterfly theta} = (-0.02 \times 1) + (-0.06 \times -2) \\ + (-0.03 \times 1) \text{ or } 0.07$$

This means that the value of an at-the-money long butterfly would increase by approximately 0.07 per calendar day. Because an at-the-money long butterfly has positive theta, the value of the at-the-money butterfly will rise as time passes and option values decay. **Figure 5.14** illustrates the theta of a long butterfly.

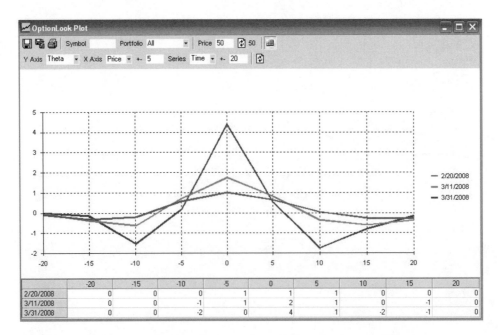

Figure 5.14   Long Butterfly Theta vs. Underlying Price and Time
to Expiration—Long April 45/50/55 Butterfly
Source: LiquidPoint, LLC

The long butterfly position will have positive theta when the underlying price is near the short middle strike and will reverse to having negative theta when the underlying price is near the long wing strikes. Recall that the theta of an at-the-money option increases as time to expiration decreases so that, all things being equal, the theta of an at-the-money option with a lesser amount of time until expiration will be greater than the theta of an at-the-money option with a greater amount of time until expiration. This is apparent in Figure 5.14.

The Long Condor

Owing to similarities in their structure—long two outside strike options, short two inside strike options—the Greeks of the long condor are similar to those of the long butterfly. However, because the two short options are located at two adjacent strikes rather than the same strike, there are obvious differences.

- **Delta**

The delta of a long condor is the sum of the position-adjusted deltas of its component options. For example, the delta of the long 500/510/520/530 call condor would be calculated as follows:

$$500 \text{ strike call delta} = 0.60$$

$$510 \text{ strike call delta} = 0.50$$

$$520 \text{ strike call delta} = 0.40$$

$$530 \text{ strike call delta} = 0.25$$

$$\text{Long call condor delta} = (0.60 \times 1) + (0.50 \times -1) + (0.40 \times -1) + (0.25 \times 1) \text{ or } -0.05$$

The delta of the long 500/510/520/530 put condor would be calculated as follows:

$$500 \text{ strike put delta} = -0.40$$

$$510 \text{ strike put delta} = -0.50$$

$$520 \text{ strike put delta} = -0.60$$

$$530 \text{ strike put delta} = -0.75$$

$$\text{Long put condor delta} = (-0.40 \times 1) + (-0.50 \times -1) + (-0.60 \times -1) + (-0.75 \times 1) \text{ or } -0.05$$

The delta of the long 500/510/520/530 iron condor would be calculated as follows:

$$500 \text{ strike put delta} = -0.40$$

$$510 \text{ strike put delta} = -0.50$$

$$520 \text{ strike call delta} = 0.40$$

530 strike call delta = 0.25

$$\text{Long iron condor delta} = (-0.40 \times 1) + (-0.50 \times -1)$$
$$+ (0.40 \times -1) + (0.25 \times 1) \text{ or } -0.05$$

Note how the deltas of all three versions of the long condor are the same. This is because they are synthetically equivalent to one another. The Greeks of the call, put, and iron condors of the same strikes and expiration will always be identical as seen in **Figure 5.15**.

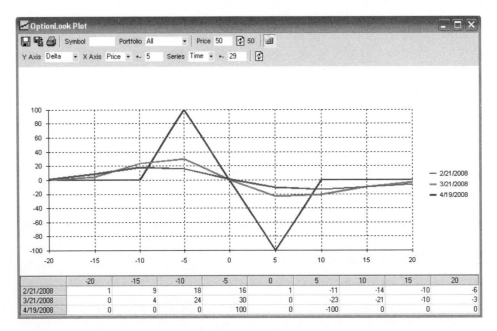

	-20	-15	-10	-5	0	5	10	15	20
2/21/2008	1	9	18	16	1	-11	-14	-10	-6
3/21/2008	0	4	24	30	0	-23	-21	-10	-3
4/19/2008	0	0	0	100	0	-100	0	0	0

Figure 5.15 Long Condor Delta vs. Underlying Price and Time
to Expiration—Long April 42.50/47.50/52.50/57.50 Condor
Source: LiquidPoint, LLC

Similar to the long butterfly, the delta of the long condor is positive when the underlying is below the midpoint between the two inside strikes, negative when the underlying is above the midpoint between the two inside strikes, and approximately neutral when the underlying is at the midpoint between the two inside strikes. This makes sense because the point of maximum profitability of a long condor is anywhere between the middle strikes. Once again, note the sensitivity of the delta of the long condor to the amount of time left until expiration. As expiration approaches, the delta of the long butterfly becomes much more sensitive to changes in the underlying price.

• **Gamma**

The gamma of a long condor is the sum of the position-adjusted gammas of its component options. For example, the gamma of the long

500/510/520/530 call condor is calculated as follows:

500 strike call gamma = 0.05

510 strike call gamma = 0.10

520 strike call gamma = 0.06

530 strike call gamma = 0.02

Long call condor gamma = $(0.05 \times 1) + (0.10 \times -1)$
$+ (0.06 \times -1) + (0.02 \times 1)$ or -0.09

A gamma of -0.09 means that the delta of the overall position would change against the trader by approximately 0.09 for every 1 point the underlying moved. In other words, if the underlying moved up by 1 point, the position would become 0.09 deltas shorter, and if the underlying moved down by 1 point, the position would become 0.09 deltas longer. Negative gamma positions always move against the trader. Gamma is greatly dependent on the moneyness and the time to expiration. All things being equal, an at-the-money option near expiration will have a greater gamma than an at-the-money option with greater time left until expiration.

Figure 5.16 clearly shows the dependency of the gamma of the long condor on the location of the underlying and the time until expiration. When expiration is near and the underlying price is near the strikes of the short options of the long condor body, the position will have a large negative gamma. This reverses quickly as the underlying moves away from the middle strike price into the area of the long wings of the outer strikes. Once again when there is greater time until expiration, the gamma curve softens.

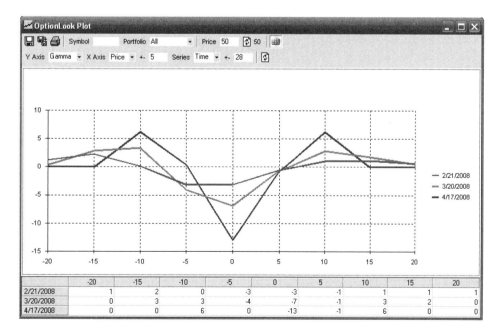

Figure 5.16 Long Condor Gamma vs. Underlying Price and Time
to Expiration—Long April 42.50/47.50/52.50/57.50 Condor
Source: LiquidPoint, LLC

• **Vega**

The vega of a long condor is the sum of the position-adjusted vegas of its component options. For example, the vega of the long 500/510/520/530 call condor is calculated as follows:

500 strike call vega = 0.15

510 strike call vega = 0.20

520 strike call vega = 0.17

530 strike call vega = 0.14

Long call condor vega = $(0.15 \times 1) + (0.20 \times -1) + (0.17 \times -1) + (0.14 \times 1)$ or -0.08

This means that for every 1 percent change in implied volatility, the price of the long condor would change by approximately $0.08. Because an at-the-money long condor is short vega, the value of the condor will fall when implied volatility rises and rise when implied volatility falls. **Figure 5.17** illustrates the vega of a long condor.

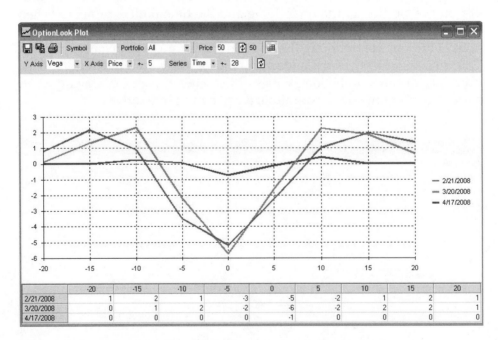

Figure 5.17 Long Condor Vega vs. Underlying Price and Time to Expiration—Long April 42.50/47.50/52.50/57.50 Condor
Source: LiquidPoint, LLC

Because of the $+1/-1/-1/+1$ structure of the long condor, the position will be short vega when the underlying price is near the short middle strikes and will reverse to being long vega when the underlying price is near the long wing strikes. Figure 5.17 shows the dependency of the vega of the long condor on location of the underlying price and time until expiration.

• **Theta**

The theta of a long condor is the sum of the position-adjusted thetas of its component options. For example, the theta of the long 500/510/520/530 call condor would be calculated as follows:

500 strike call theta $= -0.02$

510 strike call theta $= -0.06$

520 strike call theta $= -0.03$

530 strike call theta $= -0.01$

Long call condor theta $= (-0.02 \times 1) + (-0.06 \times -1)$
$+ (-0.03 \times -1) + (-0.01 \times 1)$ or 0.06

This means that the value of an at-the-money long condor would increase by approximately 0.06 per calendar day. Because an at-the-money long condor has positive theta, the value of the at-the-money condor will rise as time passes and option values decay. **Figure 5.18** illustrates the theta of a long condor.

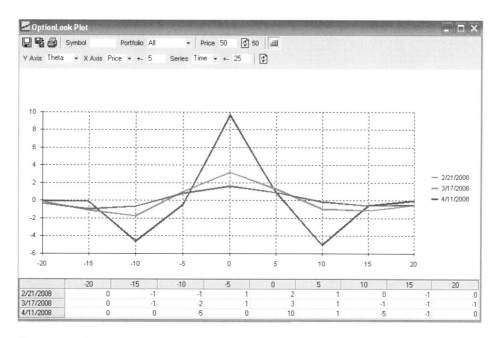

Figure 5.18 Long Condor Theta vs. Underlying Price and Time to Expiration—Long April 42.50/47.50/52.50/57.50 Condor
Source: LiquidPoint, LLC

Like the long butterfly, the long condor will have positive theta when the underlying price is near the short middle strikes and will reverse to having negative theta when the underlying price is near the long wing strikes. Recall that the theta of an at-the-money option *increases* as time to expiration decreases so that, all things being equal, the theta of an at-the-money option with a lesser amount of time until expiration will be greater than the theta of an at-the-money option with a greater amount of time until expiration. This means that the theta of an at-the-money long condor will increase over time. This is apparent in Figure 5.18.

INVESTMENT OBJECTIVES

Long butterflies and condors are strategies most often used to attempt to profit from the underlying stock or index moving in a sideways, or directionless, fashion. As the underlying price meanders back and forth, making no progress in either direction, time passes and the value of a properly located long butterfly or condor theoretically will increase in value. The key, therefore, is to locate directionless situations. This is sometimes easier said than done, and there is no right or wrong way to go about identifying directionless situations.

Identifying the Directionless Market

Directionless markets usually are identified by observing price action. Technical analysis tools can be especially helpful in identifying a directionless stock or index. Bar charts, candlestick charts, point-and-figure charts, and other types of graphic representation of price action over time are helpful in finding directionless stocks or indices. The trader can employ technical indicators, particularly "strength of trend" indicators to identify situations where trend strength is low and a directionless market is likely to persist. "Eyeballing" a price chart may be sufficient, but there are a few basic concepts that should be understood.

Support and Resistance

Support and resistance levels represent price levels or zones where supply (selling pressure) or demand (buying pressure) materializes and halts rising or falling prices. Support and resistance levels can form within uptrends, downtrends, or directionless markets.

- **Support**

Support is a price level or zone located below the current market price where buyers become more willing to buy and sellers become more reluctant to sell. The buyers overwhelm the sellers in or near these zones, forcing the price back up and preventing the price from falling below the support level. Support levels or zones are determined by connecting reaction lows, or "valleys," of price action with a line. Obviously it takes at least two reaction lows near the same price to form a support level, and the more reaction lows that occur in this area, the "stronger" the support level is seen to be. **Figure 5.19** illustrates support levels.

- **Resistance**

Resistance is a price level or zone located above the current market price where sellers become more willing to sell and buyers are reluctant to buy. Sellers overwhelm buyers in or near these zones, forcing the price back down and preventing the price from rising above resistance. Resistance

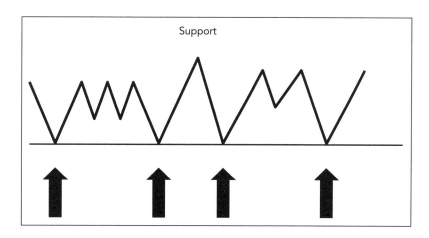

Figure 5.19 Support

levels or zones are determined by connecting reaction highs, or "peaks," of price action with a line. It takes at least two reaction highs near the same price to form a resistance level, and the more reaction highs that occur in this area, the "stronger" the resistance level is seen to be. **Figure 5.20** illustrates resistance levels.

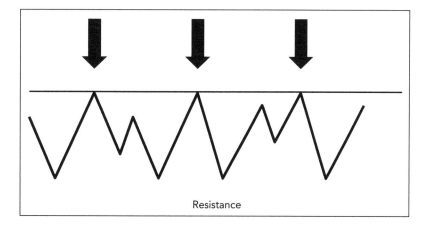

Figure 5.20 Resistance

The Trading Range Market

When the forces of supply and demand equalize, a stalemate occurs and the market moves sideways between support and resistance levels until one side can build up enough strength to finally overwhelm the other. Visualize two opposing armies entrenched directly across the battlefield from each other, neither having enough strength to break through the lines of the other. Attacks by both sides on each other's lines are easily repulsed, and neither side moves. The stalemate persists until one side finally builds up enough strength to break through the lines of the other. This is analogous to the classic directionless market, as shown in **Figure 5.21**.

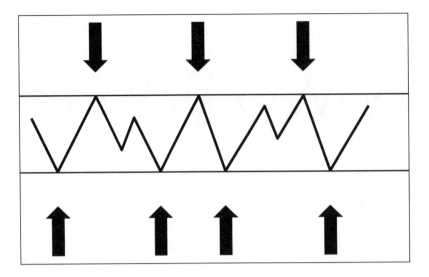

Figure 5.21 Trading Range

Important Factors

Regardless of which methods or tools the investor uses to identify the directionless market, a trader must identify some important factors when analyzing a stock or index if considering a directionless market option strategy. Most important are the price levels involved. Support and resistance levels need to be identified, along with the point or area to which price tends to revert as it meanders up and down. These levels are of key importance for selecting strikes when the investor constructs the strategy. It is also important that the stock or index being analyzed appears likely to remain in the directionless mode for a period of time that matches the time horizon of the investor.

STRATEGY SELECTION

Regardless of how one arrives at a view of a directionless market (technical, fundamental, or other type of analysis), the following information is necessary when selecting the strikes and expiration cycle for a long butterfly or condor strategy:

- Support and resistance levels
- Mean-reversion price or area
- Projected time in the trading range

Support and Resistance Levels

Support and resistance levels (see the preceding section, "Investment Objectives") are needed to define the boundaries of the trading range. This information is important for selecting the structure of one's long butterfly or condor. It is also important for risk management, as will be seen in the next section, "Trade Management."

Mean-Reversion Price or Area

The mean-reversion price, or mean-reversion area, is the price or area that the underlying stock or index seems to return to as it meanders in its trading range. This information is needed for structuring a long butterfly or condor. **Figure 5.22** is an example of a mean-reversion area.

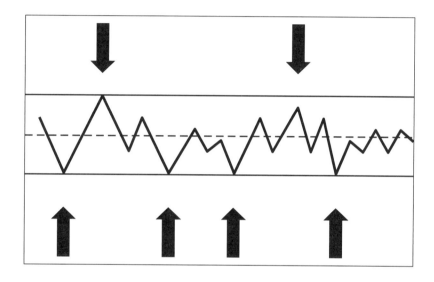

Figure 5.22 Mean-Reversion Area of a Trading Range

Projected Time in the Trading Range

Like any trend, the directionless trend must end. It is important for the trader to have a forecast of how long the directionless phase will last, to select the expiration cycle of his long butterfly or condor.

Strike Selection

Support and resistance levels and the mean-reversion price (or area) are needed for strike selection. It is important to cover the trading range with the range of profitability (see "Strategy Composition") of the long butterfly or condor. If the underlying is moving sideways through a narrow range and seems to revert to a particular price, and there is a strike price available at that particular price, then one would want to construct a long butterfly position with the body (the short middle strike) at that price. It is also important to locate the wings (the long outer strikes) near the support and resistance levels to limit risk in case of a breakout in the trading range. In **Figure 5.23**, the underlying is moving sideways in a range between 97.50 (support) and 102.50 (resistance) with 100.00 seeming to be the mean-reversion point. In this case a long 97.50/100/102.50 butterfly seems to make sense.

If the underlying is moving through a wider trading range and it seems to return to a mean-reversion area or zone rather than a particular price, or if strike prices do not match up well against important price levels, the strategy may have to be "stretched" into a long condor (or even a pterodactyl) to "fit" the range. In **Figure 5.24**, the underlying is moving sideways in a range

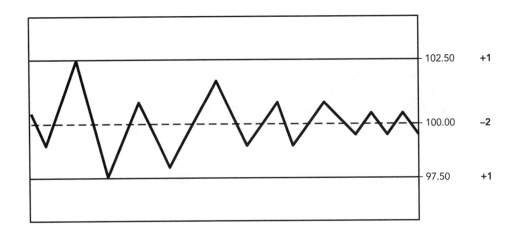

Figure 5.23 Long Butterfly Strike Selections

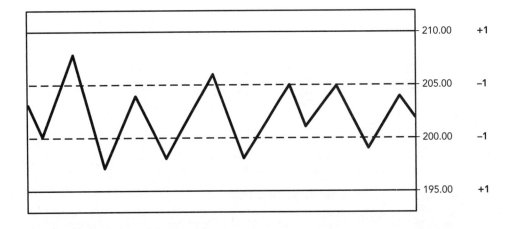

Figure 5.24 Long Condor Strike Selections

between 195.00 (support) and 210.00 (resistance) with the 200.00–205.00 zone seeming to be the mean-reversion area. In this case, a long butterfly does not have a large enough range of profitability to cover this area. A long 195/200/205/210 condor would be a better selection.

Expiry Selection

To select the expiration month, the trader must forecast the projected time the underlying will be in the trading range. If the trader is estimating that the trading range will persist for thirty days, then he or she would need to use options that expire before that time. If he is forecasting a trading range that will persist for some time, which expiration should he choose? Long butterflies and condors made up of shorter-dated options will bear fruit more quickly than their longer-dated cousins (assuming the trader is correct about the trading range), but they are also more risky because they cost more. If, for example, one's forecast is for the trading range to persist for ninety days, it might be better to use a blend of the expirations occurring in that time period.

TRADE MANAGEMENT

One of the reasons long butterflies and condors are popular strategies for taking a short volatility position to reflect the directionless market view is that they are limited-risk positions. Recall from "Strategy Overview" that a long butterfly is synthetically a short straddle with a long strangle wrap and that a long condor is synthetically a short strangle with a long strangle wrap that is further out-of-the-money. It is the synthetic long strangle wraps that make these positions limited-risk positions. If the underlying moves outside of the long wing strike, the long option "kicks in" to limit risk. With a long butterfly or condor, one can take a short volatility position and not worry about waking up splattered against the wall by a market-moving event.

The fact that long butterflies and condor positions have limited risk makes things a little easier from the risk management standpoint, but the position must still be managed. Points to consider:

- What is the most efficient way to take potential profits?
- What if the trading range begins to widen?
- What if the trading range narrows?
- How should one manage risk and/or take losses?

Taking Profits

Discipline, discipline, discipline . . . One of the biggest concerns in managing positions with positive time decay is knowing when to leave the party. Because a properly located long butterfly or condor (one where the underlying is hovering near the short strike(s) of the body) will theoretically increase in value every day, the temptation to try to get "one more day, just one more day" of time decay is always there. Inevitably, in trying to capture 0.10 worth of time decay by holding the position "just one more day," the trader loses $3.00 worth of accumulated profits when the underlying breaks out of the range and goes on a directional tear. Here are some important tips:

- **Take Partial Profits**

If an investor is fortunate enough to have a profitable long butterfly or condor position, he can consider taking partial profits occasionally by scaling out of the trade. For example, if a position consists of ten long butterflies, the investor should not be afraid to take profits on two here and two there. He can slowly scale out of the position as it goes in his favor. This action results in profits and limits the remaining risk.

- **Watch Market Action**

Remember the reason the investor got into this trade in the first place: He had a market forecast of sideways behavior and/or declining implied volatility. If the underlying stock or index in which he has the position starts to behave as though this trend may end, he should get out!

- **Use Your Head**

As a corollary to the above, don't be foolish and take a long butterfly or condor into a situation that might lead to a breakout or a pickup in volatility—earnings, government reports, and so on—unless it is part of the game plan.

- **Use Synthetics to Exit**

Again, long butterflies and condors have synthetic components—a long butterfly is synthetically a short straddle with a long strangle wrap, and a long condor is synthetically a short strangle with a long strangle wrap that is further out-of-the-money. Use this knowledge to exit the trade in a clever fashion.

For example, an investor has been long a butterfly and has been fortunate that his forecast of sideways movement about his short strike was correct. Now he would like to take profits because he feels that the climate may be changing and volatility might pick up. He decides that a clever choice is to cover the synthetic short straddle at the inside strikes by buying back the actual straddle, leaving him with a long, low-cost synthetic long strangle at the outside strikes. **Figures 5.25**, **5.26**, and **5.27** illustrate this procedure:

Calls	Strike	Puts
+1	100	
−2	105	
+1	110	

Figure 5.25 Existing Long Call Butterfly Position

Calls	Strike	Puts
+1	100	
+1 −2	105	+1
+1	110	

Figure 5.26 Purchase of the Straddle at the Short Strike

Calls	Strike	Puts
+1	100	
−1	105	+1
+1	110	

Figure 5.27 Resulting Synthetic Long Strangle

The result in Figure 5.27 is a synthetic long 100/110 strangle. A short call/long put at the 105 strike combined with a long call at the 100 strike is synthetically equivalent to a long 100 put; that combined with an existing long 110 call yields a synthetic long 100/110 strangle.

Modifying to Fit the Trading Range

What if the forecast of a directionless market was correct but the investor happened to choose the wrong strikes or the trading range happens to be wider or narrower than his initial forecast? In these cases it is possible to modify an existing long butterfly or condor position by adding or subtracting additional butterflies to widen or narrow the position to fit the new range. For example, although a trader correctly forecasted a directionless market, he structured his long butterfly position so that the short strike was 105.00, but the underlying seemed to be trading between 105.00 and 110.00, rather than reverting to 105.00 as the trader had forecasted. He decided to purchase an additional butterfly to "roll" his long butterfly into a long condor, giving him additional range coverage. **Figures 5.28, 5.29,** and **5.30** illustrate this procedure.

Calls	Strike	Puts
+1	100	
−2	105	
+1	110	

Figure 5.28 Existing Long Call Butterfly Position

Calls	Strike	Puts
+1	100	
+1 −2	105	
+1 −2	110	
+1	115	

Figure 5.29 Purchase of the Additional Butterfly at Higher Strikes

Calls	Strike	Puts
+1	100	
−1	105	
−1	110	
+1	115	

Figure 5.30 Resulting Long Condor

The result in Figure 5.30 is a long 100/105/110/115 condor. If the trading range had moved lower than the projected trading range, the trader would have needed to purchase an additional butterfly at the lower strikes. Even though the above example uses calls, the same procedure can be used with put or iron butterflies, since they are all synthetically equivalent.

As another example, let's say that the forecast of a directionless market was correct and the trader's purchase of the 100/105/110/115 put condor has paid off. Now the underlying seems to be "homing in" on the 105 strike. The trader decides to use this as an opportunity to take some money off the table by selling the embedded 105/110/115 put butterfly out of his condor and leaving him long the 100/105/110 put butterfly. **Figures 5.31**, **5.32**, and **5.33** illustrate this procedure.

Calls	Strike	Puts
	100	+1
	105	−1
	110	−1
	115	+1

Figure 5.31 Existing Long Put Condor Position

Calls	Strike	Puts	
	100	+1	
	105	−1	−1
	110	+2	−1
	115	+1	−1

Figure 5.32 Sale of the Put Butterfly at Higher Strikes

Calls	Strike	Puts
	100	+1
	105	−2
	110	+1
	115	

Figure 5.33 Resulting Long Put Butterfly

The result in Figure 5.33 is a long 100/105/110 put butterfly. The act of selling a higher strike put butterfly out of the condor takes money off the table and rolls the position into a long butterfly at the lower three strikes. If the underlying had homed in on the 110 strike rather than the 105 strike, the trader would have had to sell the 100/105/110 put butterfly to roll the position up instead. Even though the preceding example uses puts, the same procedure can be used with call or iron condors, since they are all synthetically equivalent.

Managing Risk and Taking Losses

As soon as the price action proves the forecast for a directionless market to be incorrect by breaking through a key support or resistance level, one needs to exit the trade. This is why support and resistance levels—or some method for choosing boundaries for a long butterfly or condor trade—are so important. They are needed for structuring purposes, but also for risk management purposes. Support or resistance levels or boundaries need to be the "lines in the sand." If the underlying moves outside these levels, the forecast is incorrect and one needs to exit the trade, as shown in **Figure 5.34**.

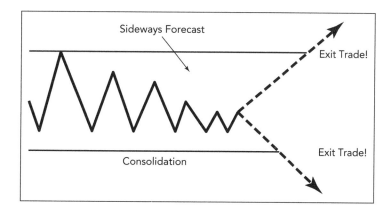

Figure 5.34 Breakout from the Trading Range

CHAPTER 5 EXERCISE

1. A long butterfly contains an embedded synthetic short straddle wrapped by a synthetic long _____.

2. Placing the middle strike of the long butterfly at the underlying's current price creates a position that has a (positive) (negative) theta.

3. A long condor can be used when one expects a sideways market with a wider range. True or false?

4. The long butterfly will have a (positive) (negative) delta when the underlying is trading below the middle strike, and a (positive) (negative) delta when the underlying is above the strike.

5. The Greeks of the call, put, and iron butterflies, having the same strikes and times to expiration, should always be equal. True or false?

6. In the case of the long butterfly, does a gamma of –0.07 mean that the overall delta of the position would change for or against the trader for every 1 point the underlying moves?

7. Does an at-the-money long butterfly have a negative or a positive theta?

8. The delta of the long condor is approximately neutral at the midpoint between the two middle strikes. True or false?

9. When it is near expiration, and the underlying is near the strikes of the short options, will the position have a large positive or negative gamma?

10. Is a long at-the-money condor long or short vega? Therefore, will the value of the condor rise or fall when implied volatility rises?

Chapter 5 Exercise Answer Key

1. Strangle
2. Positive
3. True
4. Positive, negative
5. True
6. Against
7. Positive
8. True
9. Negative
10. Short, fall

CHAPTER 5 QUIZ

1. Calculate the theta of the following long call condor:

   410 strike call theta = −0.03
   420 strike call theta = −0.07
   430 strike call theta = −0.04
   440 strike call theta = −0.02

2. Will the theta of the at-the-money long condor increase or decrease over time?

3. If a trader is long a butterfly and decides to cover the synthetic short straddle at the inside strikes, what position is he left with?

4. An investor has on a long butterfly position, and he decides he needs additional range coverage. He can purchase an additional _____ in order to roll his long butterfly, turning it into a _____.

5. An investor has on the 105/110/115/120 put condor. The underlying seems to be staying around the 110 strike. He could decide to take some profits here by selling the 110/115/120 put butterfly, leaving him with the _____.

6. In reference to the case in question 5, if the underlying had been hovering around 115, the investor would have had to sell the 105/110/115 put to roll the butterfly up. True or false?

7. If an investor is incorrect in his forecast, and the underlying breaks through a key support or resistance level, what should he do?

8. If a trader has on the long 60/65/70 iron butterfly position, what should he do to convert this position to a bear spread?

9. A trader has on the 50/55 bull put spread. After the market rallies and a new resistance level is identified, he predicts a sideways market. He could convert the position into an iron butterfly by selling the _____.

10. If a trader buys the 50/55/60 put butterfly after he already has on the long 45/50/55 put butterfly, what is the resulting position?

Chapter 5 Quiz Answer Key

1. $(-0.03 \times 1) + (-0.07 \times -1) + (-0.04 \times -1) + (-0.02) = 0.06$
2. Increase
3. Synthetic long strangle at the outer strikes
4. Butterfly, long condor
5. 105/110/115 put butterfly
6. True
7. Exit the trade—stay disciplined.
8. Close out the 60/65 bull put spread.
9. 55/60 bear call spread
10. Long the 45/50/55/60 put condor

6

Calendar
Spreads

CONCEPT REVIEW

Term structure: Implied volatility levels generally differ for different expiration cycles.

Jelly roll: A long jelly roll is composed of a long call time spread and a short put time spread; a short jelly roll is the combination of a short call time spread and a long put time spread.

STRATEGY OVERVIEW

Calendar spreads employ options of the same class but with different expiration cycles to capture specific market scenarios. Calendar spreads break down into two general categories: *horizontal* calendar spreads (often called *time spreads*) and *diagonal* calendar spreads. Horizontal calendar spreads are composed of options of the same class and strike price but with different expirations; diagonal calendar spreads are composed of options of the same class, but with different strike prices and different expirations. Calendar spreads are wonderfully complex and can be used to capture a number of different market scenarios depending on how they are constructed. We will introduce only horizontal calendar spreads in this chapter. Horizontal calendar spreads (time spreads):

- Can be composed of calls or puts
- Can be long or short
- Can have a bullish or bearish bias
- Can have a sideways bias
- Can have a movement bias (large move in either direction) (**Figures 6.1** and **6.2**)

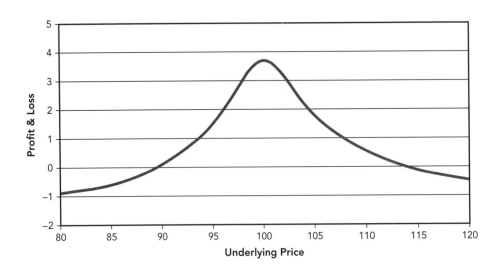

Figure 6.1 Long 100 Call Calendar/Time

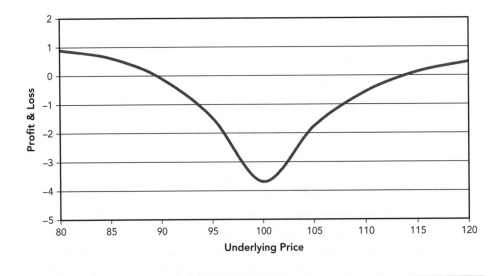

Figure 6.2 Short 100 Call Calendar/Time

A horizontal calendar spread involves the simultaneous purchase and sale of options of the same class (calls or puts) and strike prices, but with different expiration cycles. Depending on which strike and expiration is purchased and which strike and expiration is sold, the time spread can have a bullish, bearish, neutral, or movement bias (large move in either direction).

Naming Conventions

Time spread terminology can be confusing because these spreads can be composed of calls or puts of a variety of expiration cycles. To keep it straight, keep the concept of buying and selling time in mind. If one buys a call or put of a longer-dated expiration than the call or put that is sold, one is buying time and is long the time spread; if one buys a call or put of a shorter-dated expiration than the call or put that is sold, one is selling time and is short the time spread.

STRATEGY COMPOSITION

Long Calendar

Long Call Calendar:	Purchase deferred call; sell near term call, same strike price.
Long Put Calendar:	Purchase deferred put; sell near term put, same strike price.
Maximum Profit:	Cannot be determined
Maximum Loss:	Limited to premium paid for the spread
Example:	Purchase deferred 100 call at $6.10; sell near term 100 call at $3.80.
Maximum Profit:	Cannot be determined
Maximum Loss:	Premium paid is $2.30

Short Calendar

Short Call Calendar:	Sell deferred call, purchase near term call, same strike price.
Short Put Calendar:	Sell deferred put, purchase near term put, same strike price.
Maximum Profit:	Premium received
Maximum Loss:	Difference in price of the two options at expiration of the short-dated option. The amount of this risk cannot be quantified at the outset of the trade.
Example:	Sell deferred 100 call at $6.10, purchase near term 100 call at $3.80.
Maximum Profit:	Premium received: $2.30
Maximum Loss:	Cannot be determined

- **Long Time Spreads**

A long time spread is composed of a long option of a particular class, strike, and expiration and a short option of the same class and strike but of an expiration of a shorter duration. **Figure 6.3** illustrates the structure of a long call time spread.

Expiration 1			Expiration 2		
Calls	Strike	Puts	Calls	Strike	Puts
−1	100		+1	100	

Figure 6.3 Long Call Time Spread

Figure 6.4 illustrates the structure of a long put time spread.

Expiration 1			Expiration 2		
Calls	Strike	Puts	Calls	Strike	Puts
	100	−1		100	+1

Figure 6.4 Long Put Time Spread

- **Short Time Spreads**

A short time spread is composed of a long option of a particular class, strike; and expiration and a short option of the same class and strike but of an expiration of a longer duration. **Figure 6.5** illustrates the structure of a short call time spread.

Expiration 1			Expiration 2		
Calls	Strike	Puts	Calls	Strike	Puts
+1	100		−1	100	

Figure 6.5: Short Call Time Spread

Figure 6.6 illustrates the structure of a short put time spread.

Expiration 1			Expiration 2		
Calls	Strike	Puts	Calls	Strike	Puts
	100	+1		100	−1

Figure 6.6 Short Put Time Spread

Time Spread Strategy

Because time spreads consist of an equal number of calls or puts purchased and sold—that is, the ratio is always one long call to each short call or one long put to each short put—the structures have limited risk and limited return. Long-dated options generally are more expensive than shorter-dated options of the same class and strike (the exception usually being deep-in-the-money put options). Therefore, buying a time spread results in a debit and selling a time spread usually results in a credit. The risk to the buyer is limited to the initial debit; the risk to the seller is limited to the difference in the price of the two options at the expiration of the short-dated option. The amount of this risk cannot be quantified at the outset of the trade.

The buyer of the time spread wants the value of the spread to expand in price; the seller of the time spread wants the value of the spread to contract in price. As was seen is "Strategy Composition," the point of maximum value of a time spread is when the underlying price is at the strike, of the short-dated option on expiration. This is the price/time target of the time spread buyer. The value of the time spread contracts as the underlying price moves away from the strike price. This is the price target of the time spread seller—as far away from the strike as possible. The strategies available to buyers and sellers of time spreads break down into the following:

- Long time spreads
  - Bullish
  - Bearish
  - Neutral
- Short time spreads
  - Large move away from the strike, in either direction

Because the long time spread reaches its point of maximum profitability at the strike, at expiration it can structured to be bullish, bearish, or neutral, depending on where the strike price of the time spread is located in relation to the current underlying price. If the strike of a long time spread is above the current underlying price, it has a bullish bias; if it is below the current underlying price, it has a bearish bias; and if it is equal to the current underlying price, it is neutral.

The seller of a time spread wants the underlying price to move away from the strike in any direction, which generally causes the value of the spread to contract. So, technically, a short time spread also can be bullish or bearish. Keeping in mind that the seller of a time spread wants the underlying price to move as far away from the strike as possible, a short time spread with a strike above the current underlying price is bearish; the seller would like the underlying price to continue to move down, away from the strike. A short time spread with a strike below the current underlying price is bullish; the seller would like the underlying price to continue to move up, away from the strike.

THE GREEKS OF THE TIME SPREAD

Now would be a great time to refer back to Chapter 1 to review the Greeks, and especially the way the delta, gamma, vega, and theta of an option change over time. Time spreads, being composed of long and short option positions in different expiration months, have unique sensitivities that basically amount to the differences in option sensitivity to changes in market conditions over time. These differences can be exploited to capture certain market scenarios; however, they can be difficult to visualize, even with the help of graphics. Getting familiar with how the Greeks of an option "age" over time will help in understanding the workings of the time spread.

Long Time Spreads

• **Delta**

The delta of a long time spread is the difference between the deltas of the long-dated option and the short-dated option. For example, the delta of the long XYZ $(t + n, t)$ 100 call time spread would be calculated as follows:

$$(t) = \text{closest month}$$

$$(t + n) = \text{farther-out month}$$

$$\text{long XYZ } (t + n) \text{ 100 call delta} = 0.55$$

$$\text{short XYZ } t \text{ 100 call delta} = 0.50$$

$$\text{long XYZ } (t + n, t) \text{ 100 call time spread delta} = 0.55 - 0.50 \text{ or } 0.05$$

Remember that puts have a negative delta, so the delta of the long XYZ $(t + n, t)$ 100 put time spread would be calculated as follows:

$$\text{long XYZ } (t + n) \text{ 100 put delta} = -0.45$$

$$\text{short XYZ } t \text{ 100 put delta} = -0.50$$

$$\text{long XYZ } (t + n, t) \text{ 100 put time spread delta} = -0.45 - (-0.50) \text{ or } 0.05$$

Recall that the point of maximum profitability of a long time spread is when the underlying price is at the strike, at expiration. Therefore, it makes sense that the delta of a long time spread is positive when the underlying price is below the strike price and negative when the underlying price is above the strike price. This is evident in **Figures 6.7** and **6.8**.

What also can be seen in Figures 6.7 and 6.8 is that the delta of the long call time spread becomes increasingly sensitive as expiration approaches. Recall that the delta of a short-dated option is much more sensitive to

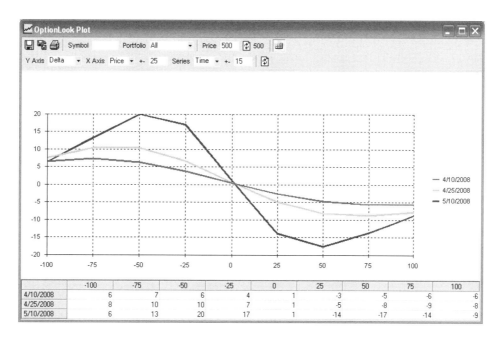

	-100	-75	-50	-25	0	25	50	75	100
4/10/2008	6	7	6	4	1	-3	-5	-6	-6
4/25/2008	8	10	10	7	1	-5	-8	-9	-8
5/10/2008	6	13	20	17	1	-14	-17	-14	-9

Figure 6.7 Call Time Spread Delta vs. Time to Expiration—Long XYZ
June/May 500 Call Time Spread, Underlying Price = 500
Source: LiquidPoint, LLC

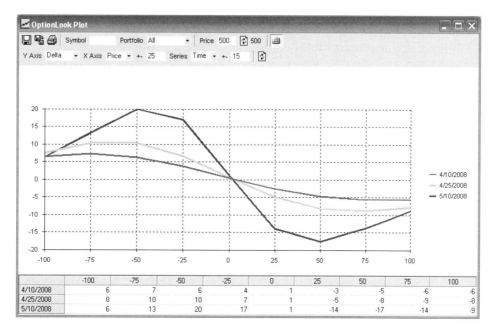

	-100	-75	-50	-25	0	25	50	75	100
4/10/2008	6	7	6	4	1	-3	-5	-6	-6
4/25/2008	8	10	10	7	1	-5	-8	-9	-8
5/10/2008	6	13	20	17	1	-14	-17	-14	-9

Figure 6.8 Put Time Spread Delta vs. Time to Expiration—Long XYZ
June/May 500 Put Time Spread, Underlying Price = 500
Source: LiquidPoint, LLC

"moneyness" (the location of the underlying price relative to the strike price) than that of a long-dated option. In other words, short-dated at-the-money options have a greater gamma than longer-dated at-the-money options. Therefore, the long time spread will have negative gamma when the underlying price is near the strike price. This means that as the underlying price moves away from the strike price, the delta of the short-dated option will change faster than the delta of the long-dated option, generating a long delta when the underlying price drops below the strike price and a short delta when the underlying price rises above the strike price. In the May 10, 2008, series shown in Figures 6.7 and 6.8, the rate of change of the delta near the strike price is much greater than that of the other series.

Long Call Time Spread vs. Long Put Time Spread

You may have noticed a remarkable similarity between Figure 6.7, the delta of a long call time spread, and Figure 6.8, the delta of a long put time spread. In fact, they are identical. The long call time spread of a particular strike and set of expirations is synthetically equivalent to the long put time spread of the same strike and set of expirations. Much like call and put vertical spreads, call and put time spreads are linked by a neutral interest-rate-driven structure called the *jelly roll*. We will discuss this later in the chapter, but it suffices to say that the delta, gamma, theta, and vega of call and put time spreads (which have the same underlyings, same strikes, same set of expirations) are identical. Going forward, we will be exploring the Greeks of the generic "long time spread."

- **Gamma**

The gamma (the rate of change of the delta) of a long time spread is the sum of the position-adjusted gammas of its component options. Recall from Chapter 1 that a long option position will have a positive gamma while a short option position will have a negative gamma. So, in the case of the long time spread, the long-dated option will generate positive gamma while the short-dated option will generate negative gamma. For example, the gamma of the long XYZ $(t + n, t)$ 100 time spread would be calculated as follows:

$$\text{long XYZ } (t + n) \text{ 100 gamma} = 0.05$$

$$\text{short XYZ } t \text{ 100 gamma} = 0.10$$

$$\text{long XYZ } (t + n, t) \text{ 100 time spread gamma} = 0.05 - 0.10 \text{ or } -0.05$$

The gamma of a long time spread is negative when the underlying price is at or around the strike price because the short-dated option has a larger gamma than the long-dated option. However, the gamma curve of the short-dated option has greater convexity than that of the long-dated option, so if the underlying price moves far enough away from the strike price, the gamma of the long time spread will flip back to positive as illustrated in **Figure 6.9**.

As can be seen in the May 10, 2008, data series in the following figure, the gamma of the long time spread is negative when the underlying price

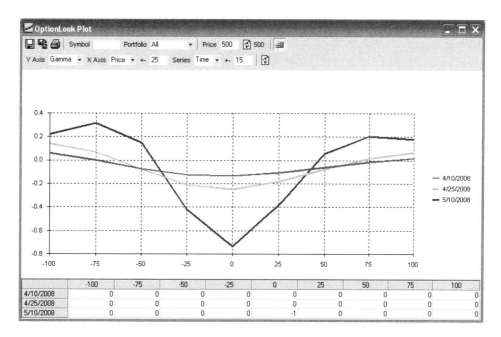

Figure 6.9 Long Time Spread Gamma vs. Time to Expiration—Long XYZ
June/May 500 Time Spread, Underlying Price = 500
Source: LiquidPoint, LLC

is near the strike price. When the expiration of the short-dated option is near and the gamma of the short-dated option is very high (the May 500 time spread in this case), the gamma of the time spread can be very negative. As always, this is less pronounced when there is greater time until the expiration of the first option, as can be seen with the April 20, 2008, and the April 25, 2008, data series in Figure 6.9.

- **Vega**

The vega (the sensitivity to changes in implied volatility) of a long time spread is the sum of the position-adjusted vegas of its component options. Recall from Chapter 1 that a long option position will have a positive vega while a short option position will have a negative vega, and that a long-dated option will have a larger vega than a shorter-dated option of the same strike. The vega of the long XYZ $(t + n, t)$ 100 time spread would be calculated as follows:

$$\text{long XYZ } (t + n) \text{ 100 vega} = 0.15$$

$$\text{short XYZ } t \text{ 100 vega} = 0.08$$

$$\text{long XYZ } (t + n, t) \text{ 100 time spread vega} = 0.15 - 0.08 \text{ or } 0.07$$

As can be seen in **Figure 6.10**, the vega of the long time spread is positive, with the magnitude dependent on the time differential between the expiration of the two component options and the time until expiration of the short-dated option. The vega of an option diminishes as the expiration approaches, so the vega of the long time spread generally will rise as the expiration of the short-dated option approaches.

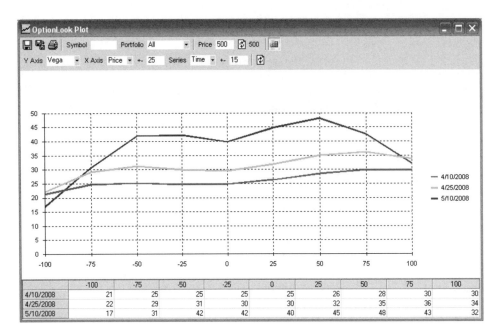

Figure 6.10 Long Time Spread Vega vs. Time to Expiration—Long XYZ
June/May 500 Time Spread, Underlying Price = 500
Source: LiquidPoint, LLC

• Theta

The theta (the sensitivity to the passage of time) of a long time spread is the sum of the position-adjusted thetas of its component options. Recall from Chapter 1 that a long option position will have a negative theta while a short option position will have a positive theta and that a short-dated at-the-money option will have a larger theta than a longer-dated at-the-money option of the same strike. The theta of the long XYZ $(t + n, t)$ 100 time spread would be calculated as follows:

$$\text{long XYZ } (t + n) \text{ 100 theta} = -0.06$$

$$\text{short XYZ } t \text{ 100 theta} = -0.13$$

$$\text{long XYZ } (t + n, t) \text{ 100 time spread theta} = -0.06 - (-0.13) \text{ or } 0.07$$

This means that the value of the time spread would theoretically expand by approximately 0.07 per day, all else being equal. Of course, the theta of the long time spread also is dependent on the location of the underlying relative to strike prices, time left until expiration, implied volatility levels, and other factors. **Figure 6.11** illustrates the theta of the long time spread.

As can be seen in the following figures, and like the other Greeks, the theta of the long time spread is greatly dependent on the location of the underlying and the time until expiration. Notice that the theta of the position is positive when the underlying price is near the strike price, but if the underlying price moves far enough away from the strike price in either direction, the theta of the long time spread can become negative. Like the gamma, the theta of an at-the-money option increases rapidly as expiration approaches and the theta of a long time spread will generally increase as expiration approaches.

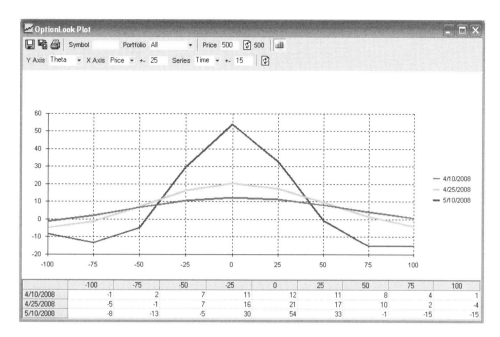

Figure 6.11 Long Time Spread Theta vs. Time to Expiration—Long XYZ June/May 500 Time Spread, Underlying Price = 500
Source: LiquidPoint, LLC

Short Time Spreads

Given that the Greeks of the short time spread are the exact opposite of those of the long time spread, the following examples may seem repetitive, but the Greeks of time spreads can be difficult, so more review is better than less review in this case.

- **Delta**

The delta of a short time spread is the difference between the deltas of the short-dated option and the long-dated option. For example, the delta of the short XYZ $(t, t + n)$ 100 call time spread would be calculated as follows:

$$\text{long XYZ } t \text{ 100 call delta} = 0.50$$

$$\text{short XYZ } (t + n) \text{ 100 call delta} = 0.55$$

$$\text{short XYZ } (t, t + n) \text{ 100 call time spread delta} = 0.50 - 0.55 \text{ or } -0.05$$

Puts have a negative delta, so the calculation of the delta of the short XYZ $(t, t + n)$ 100 put time spread would be calculated as follows:

$$\text{long XYZ } t \text{ 100 put delta} = -0.50$$

$$\text{short XYZ } (t + n) \text{ 100 put delta} = -0.45$$

$$\text{short XYZ } (t, t + n) \text{ 100 put time spread delta} = -0.50 - (-0.45) \text{ or } -0.05$$

Recall that the point of maximum loss of a short time spread is when the underlying price is at the strike, at expiration. Therefore, it makes sense that the delta of a short time spread is negative when the underlying price is below the strike price and positive when the underlying price is above the strike price. With a short time spread, one would like the underlying price to move away from the strike price as quickly as possible. One does not want the underlying price to return to the strike price. **Figures 6.12** and **6.13** illustrate this.

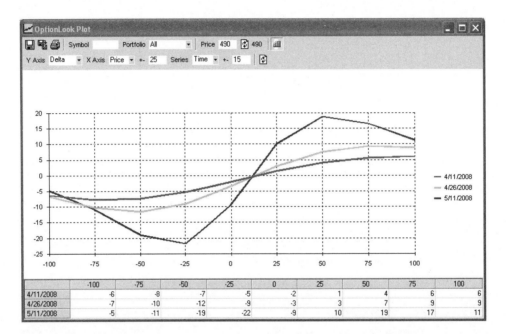

Figure 6.12 Short Call Time Spread Delta vs. Time to Expiration—Short XYZ June/May 500 Call Time Spread, Underlying Price = 490
Source: LiquidPoint, LLC

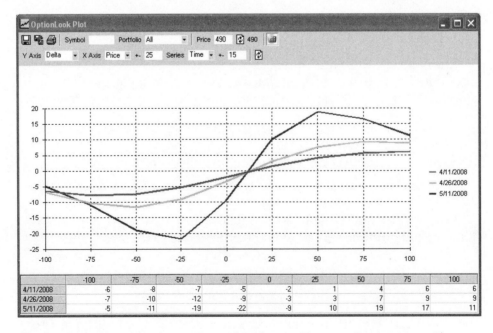

Figure 6.13 Short Put Time Spread Delta vs. Time to Expiration—Short XYZ June/May 500 Put Time Spread, Underlying Price = 490
Source: LiquidPoint, LLC

Notice in Figures 6.12 and 6.13 that the deltas of the short call time spread and the short put time spread (same strikes, same set of expirations) are identical. This is because the call and the put time spreads are synthetically equivalent, and again, we will discuss the relationship of call time spreads and put time spreads later in the chapter. Notice also that the delta of the short call time spread becomes increasingly sensitive as expiration approaches. Recall that the delta of a short-dated option is much more sensitive to moneyness than that of a long-dated option. In other words, short-dated at-the-money options have a greater gamma than longer-dated at-the-money options, and therefore the short time spread will have a positive gamma when the underlying price is near the strike price.

This means that as the underlying price moves away from the strike price, the delta of the short-dated option will change faster than the delta of the long-dated option, generating a long delta when the underlying price rises above the strike price and a short delta when the underlying price drops below the strike price. In the May 11, 2008, series shown in Figures 6.12 and 6.13, the rate of change of the delta near the strike price is much greater than it is with the other series.

- **Gamma**

The gamma (the rate of change of the delta) of a short time spread is the sum of the position-adjusted gammas of its component options. Recall from Chapter 1 that a long option position will have a positive gamma while a short option position will have a negative gamma. So, in the case of the short time spread, the long-dated option will generate a negative gamma while the short-dated option will generate a positive gamma. For example, the gamma of the short XYZ $(t, t + n)$ 100 time spread would be calculated as follows:

$$\text{long XYZ } t \text{ 100 gamma} = 0.10$$

$$\text{short XYZ } (t + n) \text{ 100 gamma} = 0.05$$

$$\text{long XYZ } (t, t + n) \text{ 100 time spread gamma} = 0.10 - 0.05 \text{ or } +0.05$$

The gamma of a short time spread is positive when the underlying price is at or around the strike price because the short-dated option has a larger gamma than the long-dated option. However, the gamma curve of the short-dated option has greater convexity than that of the long-dated option, so if the underlying price moves far enough away from the strike price, the gamma of the short time spread will flip back to negative as illustrated in **Figure 6.14**.

As can be seen from the May 11, 2008, data series in Figure 6.14, the gamma of the short time spread is positive when the underlying price is near the strike price. When the expiration of the short-dated option is near and the gamma of the short-dated option is very high (the May 500 time spread in this case), the gamma of the short time spread can be very positive. As always, this is less pronounced when there is greater time until the expiration of the first option, as can be seen with the April 11, 2008, and the April 26, 2008, data series.

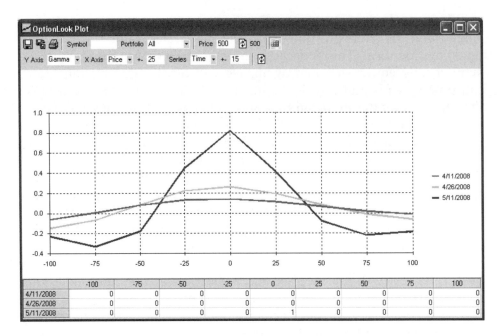

Figure 6.14 Short Time Spread Gamma vs. Time to Expiration—Short XYZ June/May 500 Time Spread, Underlying Price = 500
Source: LiquidPoint, LLC

- **Vega**

The vega (the sensitivity to changes in implied volatility) of a short time spread is the sum of the position-adjusted vegas of its component options. Recall from Chapter 1 that a long option position will have a positive vega while a short option position will have a negative vega and that a long-dated option will have a larger vega than a shorter-dated option of the same strike. The vega of the short XYZ $(t, t + n)$ 100 time spread would be calculated as follows:

$$\text{long XYZ } t \text{ 100 vega} = 0.08$$

$$\text{short XYZ } (t + n) \text{ 100 vega} = 0.15$$

$$\text{short XYZ } (t, t + n) \text{ 100 time spread vega} = 0.08 - 0.15 \text{ or } -0.07$$

Figure 6.15 illustrates the vega of the short time spread.

As can be seen in the preceding figure, the vega of the short time spread is negative, with the magnitude dependent on the time differential between the expiration of the two component options and the time until expiration of the short-dated option. The vega of an option diminishes as the expiration approaches, so the vega of the short time spread will generally fall as the expiration of the short-dated option approaches.

- **Theta**

The theta (the sensitivity to the passage of time) of a short time spread is the sum of the position-adjusted thetas of its component options. Recall

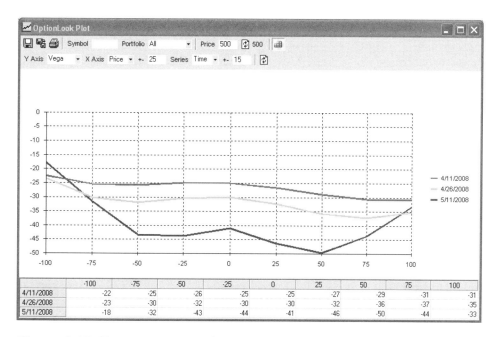

	-100	-75	-50	-25	0	25	50	75	100
4/11/2008	-22	-25	-26	-25	-25	-27	-29	-31	-31
4/26/2008	-23	-30	-32	-30	-30	-32	-36	-37	-35
5/11/2008	-18	-32	-43	-44	-41	-46	-50	-44	-33

Figure 6.15 Short Time Spread Vega vs. Time to Expiration—Short XYZ June/May 500 Time Spread, Underlying Price = 500
Source: LiquidPoint, LLC

from Chapter 1 that a long option position will have a negative theta while a short option position will have a positive theta and that a short-dated at-the-money option will have a larger theta than a longer-dated at-the-money option of the same strike. The theta of a short time spread with the underlying price at or near the strike is negative. The theta of the short XYZ $(t, t + n)$ 100 time spread would be calculated as follows:

$$\text{long XYZ } t \text{ 100 theta} = -0.13$$

$$\text{short XYZ } (t + n) \text{ 100 theta} = -0.06$$

$$\text{short XYZ } (t, t + n) \text{ 100 time spread theta} = -0.13 - (-0.06) \text{ or } -0.07$$

This means that the value of the time spread would theoretically expand by approximately 0.07 per day, all else being equal (a loss to a trader short the time spread). The theta of the short time spread is also dependent on the location of the underlying relative to strike prices, time left until expiration, implied volatility levels, and other factors. **Figure 6.16** illustrates the theta of the short time spread.

In the following figure, the theta of the short time spread is highly negative when the underlying price is near the strike price, but if the underlying price moves far enough away from the strike price in either direction, the theta of the long time spread can become positive. The theta of the short-dated at-the-money option increases rapidly as expiration approaches, and therefore the time decay of the short time spread will generally increase as the expiration approaches.

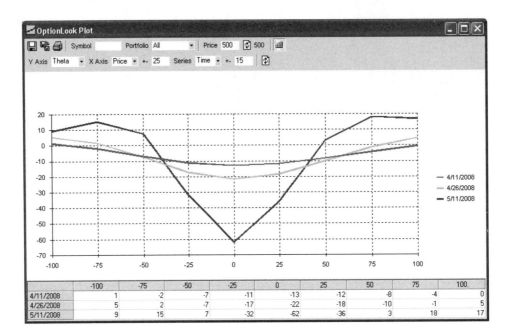

Figure 6.16 Short Time Spread Theta vs. Time to Expiration—Short XYZ
June/May 500 Time Spread, Underlying Price = 500
Source: LiquidPoint, LLC

INVESTMENT OBJECTIVES

As mentioned in "Strategy Overview," time spreads can be used in a variety of situations. Depending on the location of the strike price versus the current underlying price, and whether the time spread is long or short, time spreads can be used as directional strategies or they can be used as directionless strategies. They can be used for high-velocity, high-magnitude directional movement, or for slow sideways movement. They can also be used to target extreme differences in implied volatility between two expiration months. Because of the unique sensitivities of an intermonth long/ short option combination, long and short time spreads (**Figure 6.17**) can be deployed to fit very specific market forecasts. Price, implied and timing factors all can be built into a single strategy. To recap:

Spread Type	Delta		Gamma	Vega	Theta
Long Time Spread	Up	−	Negative	Positive	Positive
	Dn	+			
Short Time Spread	Up	+	Positive	Negative	Negative
	Dn	−			

Figure 6.17 Summary of the Greeks for the Long and the Short Time
Spreads

- • Long Time Spreads
- • Negative gamma, positive vega, positive theta
  - — Sideways trade; rising implied volatility
  - — Directional move toward a target price

- • Short Time Spreads
- • Positive gamma, negative vega, negative theta
  - — Sharp movement away from the strike; falling implied volatility

- • Either Time Spread
- • Address large implied volatility differentials.

Sideways Trade

The long time spread can be used to address the underlying that is moving in a sideways or directionless fashion. Because the long time spread has a positive theta (a positive time decay), the value of an at-the-money long time spread should rise as the underlying price hovers near the strike price of the spread. Should the underlying price break out in either direction, risk is limited to the initial cost of the spread. Because the long time spread is also long vega, it can be a good choice for a forecast of sideways movement in the market or a particular underlying where implied volatility levels are already low.

Directional Moves Toward a Target Price

Long time spreads can be used as a directional strategy. If one's forecast is for the market to move to a certain price point in a certain time frame, an effective strategy can be a long time spread structured at the strike nearest the target price, with the short-dated option expiring at the time the trader expects the underlying to "arrive" at that price. A long time spread with a strike above the current underlying price is bullish because it is desirable for the underlying price to move up to that particular strike. A long time spread with a strike below the current underlying price is bearish because it is desirable for the underlying price to move down to that particular strike. Again, because the long time spread is long vega, it can be a good choice for a directional strategy when implied volatility levels are low.

Sharp Move Away from the Strike

The short time spread can be used to be a directionless "breakout" strategy. Sharp movement away from the strike causes the value of the time spread to decline. The short time spread is long gamma, meaning that movement in any direction away from the strike price will cause a change in the delta of the overall spread that is favorable to the trader. If the underlying price moves up away from the strike, the position will become long delta; if the underlying price moves down away from the strike, the position will become short delta (refer again to Figures 6.12 and 6.13). This behavior is similar to a long straddle or long strangle, but unlike the long straddle and strangle, the short time spread is short vega, so if the forecast also includes declining implied volatility after the breakout (this sometimes occurs after government reports are issued), or if overall implied volatility levels are already high, the short time spread might be a better choice than a long straddle or strangle for trading a breakout forecast.

Implied Volatility Differentials

Implied volatility is the options market's consensus about a particular underlying stock's expected volatility through the expiration date of the options. Implied volatility levels change constantly in response to the buyers and sellers of options entering and exiting the market in response to events and nonevents. Because there are different expectations associated with different expiration cycles and with the estimated volatility likely to occur during a particular time period, implied volatility levels generally differ for different expiration cycles. This is referred to as the *term structure* of implied volatility. The implied volatility of short-dated options will conform to short-term events, spiking when underlying price movement is volatile, collapsing when it is not, whereas the longer-dated options will trade more in line with the historical long-term volatility. This means that the term structure of implied volatility can show a great deal of variance, and this sometimes leads to opportunity for the time spreader. **Figure 6.18** is an example of the term structure of implied volatility after a recent low volatility period.

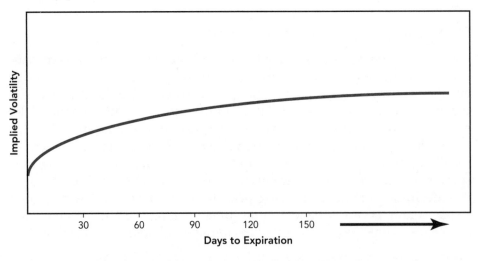

Figure 6.18 Term Structure of Implied Volatility—Recent Low Volatility

Figure 6.18 charts implied volatility levels over expiration dates. In this case, implied volatility is lower in the near-term expiration months than in the longer-term expiration months, which is indicative of an underlying that has been going through a "slow period" where short-term volatility has underperformed the mean long-term volatility. **Figure 6.19** is an

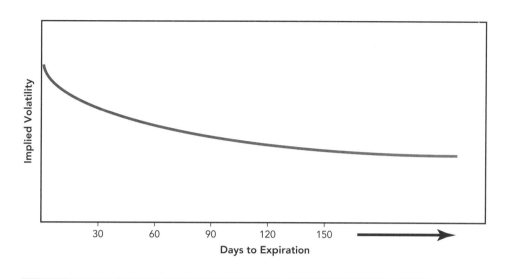

Figure 6.19 Term Structure of Implied Volatility—Recent High Volatility

example of what the term structure of implied volatility might look like if the underlying has gone through a recent period of high volatility.

The fluctuations in the term structure of implied volatility, as shown in Figures 6.18 and 6.19, can be incorporated into time spread strategies. The term structure of implied volatility of a stock that has gone through a recent slow period, such as the one in Figure 6.18, would favor a short time spread strategy, because one would be purchasing the short-dated option at a lower implied volatility than the long-dated option that is being sold. The term structure of a stock that has gone through a recent volatile period, such as the one shown in Figure 6.19, would favor a long time spread strategy, since one would be purchasing the long-dated option at an implied volatility that is lower than that of the short-dated option that is being sold. Although term structure is important and can add to (or subtract from) the quality of one's time spread strategy, it is not necessarily enough to warrant a trade in and of itself. It is important that one's forecast for price movement (or nonmovement as the case may be) also justifies the selected time spread strategy.

STRATEGY COMPONENT SELECTION

So how should one structure his or her time spread strategy? There are many variables involved:

- What is one's current market forecast?
  - Bullish
  - Bearish
  - Neutral
  - Breakout

- What is the magnitude of the forecast move?

  — Choose a target price.

- What is the time horizon of the forecast move?

  — Determine when you expect the target price to be reached.

- What is the term structure of implied volatility?

What Is One's Current Market Forecast?

Bullish, bearish, neutral, or breakout. There may be a time spread position to address each one of these forecasts. A bullish forecast might call for a long time spread at a strike price above the current underlying price, while a bearish forecast might call for a long time spread at a strike price below the current underlying price. A neutral forecast might call for a long time spread at a strike that corresponds to the current market price, and a forecast of breakout in either direction might call for a short time spread at a strike that corresponds to the current market price.

What Are the Magnitude and Time Horizon of the Forecast Move?

For structuring purposes, it is important for the investor to have an idea of a target price—where she thinks the underlying is likely to go if her bullish or bearish forecast is correct—and the time horizon over which she thinks the move will take place. Both factors are important because, as we saw in "Strategy Composition," the point of maximum profitability of a long time spread is at the strike price, at the expiration of the short-dated option. Ideally, the investor would like the underlying price to move to this strike price at or near expiration to capture the maximum amount of profit.

Example

The trader believes ABC is set to move from the 100.00 level to the 90.00 level over the next thirty days. What strikes should he or she incorporate into a bearish long time spread strategy to target an optimal potential return on this move?

- **Answer**

Her strategy could be long a time spread at the 90.00 strike, with a short-dated option at the expiration closest to the trader's forecast thirty-day time horizon.

What Is the Term Structure of Implied Volatility?

Obviously, this will play a large part in time spread strategy selection. If the current term structure of implied volatility is in alignment with one's price/time forecast for the underlying it can be the deciding factor for choosing a time spread over another strategy. If the current term structure of implied volatility is in opposition to one's forecast, it can force one into a strategy other than a time spread.

Example 1

The investor believes that GHF is about to move from 100.00 to 110.00 and would like to capture this move with a limited-risk options strategy. After careful examination of the term structure of implied volatility, he notices that the implied volatilities of short-dated options are very depressed relative to long-dated options. This eliminates a bullish long time spread from consideration.

Example 2

The investor believes HIJ is going to move up from 120.00 to 130.00 in the next thirty days, and would like to capture this move with a limited-risk options strategy. After careful examination of the term structure of implied volatility, she notices that the implied volatility of the options expiring in thirty days are very elevated compared to the implied volatility of the options expiring in ninety days. Based on this, she decides to implement a long time spread, buying the ninety-day option and selling the thirty-day option at the 130.00 strike.

At the Point of Execution: Call Time Spread or Put Time Spread?

• Pricing Anomalies

As we mentioned earlier in our examination of the Greeks of time spreads, long call and put time spreads and short call and put time spreads (having the same underlyings, strike prices, and expirations) are synthetically equivalent to one another. They have identical sensitivities and risk-reward characteristics; the only difference is price. Call time spreads usually are more expensive than the put time spreads of the same strikes and expirations. As usual, this difference comes down to cash flows and carrying costs.

Option prices are based on the theoretical forward price of the underlying instrument corresponding to their particular expiration date. The forward price of a stock is equivalent to the spot price plus financing costs (minus discounted dividends, if any). This means that, in general, the forward price of a stock rises over time, and therefore the forward price used to calculate option values will be (absent large dividends) progressively higher with each expiration month. When the strike price is factored into the equation, the result is a cost of carry differential from one expiration month to the next, and this interest rate differential is captured in a structure commonly known as the *jelly roll*.

• The Jelly Roll

A jelly roll is composed of a long time spread and a short time spread, one composed of puts, the other of calls, having the same strikes and same expiration. **Figures 6.20** and **6.21** illustrate the structure of a jelly roll spread.

Calls	Strike	Puts
−1	100	+1

Calls	Strike	Puts
+1	100	−1

Figure 6.20 Long Jelly Roll

Calls	Strike	Puts
+1	100	−1

Calls	Strike	Puts
−1	100	+1

Figure 6.21 Short Jelly Roll

Combining a long call time spread and a short put time spread (which have the same strikes, same expiration) creates a long jelly roll spread; combining a short call time spread and a long put time spread (which have the same strikes, same expiration) creates a short jelly roll spread.

- **Jelly Roll Value**

The jelly roll is a neutral structure with an interest-rate component. It has no delta, no gamma, no theta, and no vega—it can't because it is composed of offsetting positions in two synthetically equivalent spreads: long time spread + short time spread = neutral. It does, however, have an interest-rate component, and it is this component that explains the difference in pricing between call and put time spreads. Absent any early exercise situations, the value of a jelly roll should always equal the cost of carry differential of the expirations, adjusted by the strike price:

$$\text{Jelly roll value}[1] = K \times (d_2 - d_1) \times (r \div 360)$$

Where:
  K = Strike price
  d_2 = Days to expiry of the long-dated options

d_1 = Days to expiry of the short-dated options
r = Annualized interest rate

For example, what is the fair value of the sixty-day/ninety-day 100 strike jelly roll at 6 percent interest?

$$\text{Jelly roll value} = K \times (d_2 - d_1) \times (r \div 360)$$
$$= 100 \times (90 - 60) \times (0.06 \div 360) = 0.50$$

This value is embedded into the price differential of the call time spread and the put time spread; that is, the call time spread is worth $0.50 more than the put time spread. Another way to look at the relationship is as follows:

Call time spread (CTS) − Put time spread (PTS) = Jelly roll value (JR)

or

$$CTS - PTS = JR$$

This means that the value of the call time spread should always exceed the value of the put time spread by the value of the jelly roll. Buying the put time spread for less than the call time spread does not save money unless one is buying it for less than CTS − JR. Selling the call time spread for more than the put time spread does not make a great sale, unless one is selling it for more than PTS + JR.

• Practical Uses

When it comes time to "pull the trigger" on a call or put time spread, whether at the point of entry or exit, we can evaluate which structure is a better trade by incorporating the jelly roll formula into the evaluation process. Remember: CTS − PTS = JR. If the equation does not balance, there may be a relative advantage available.

Example

An investor decides market conditions in XYZ call for a long time spread. He decides to buy a sixty-day option and sell a twenty-eight-day option at the 50 strike. Interest rates are 5 percent.
You receive the following quotes:

Call time spread: $1.25 − $1.35

Put time spread: $1.15 − $1.20

Which time spread offer represents the best value?

• Answer

$$\text{Jelly roll value} = K \times (d_2 - d_1) \times (r \div 360)$$
$$= 50 \times (60 - 28) \times (0.05 \div 360) = +0.22$$

You can then evaluate the offers:

CTS − PTS = JR

1.35 − 1.20 = 0.15; less than the ~0.22 value of the jelly roll

Therefore, the call time spread is theoretically underpriced and represents a better potential value when buying a time spread.

Here are some easier and faster shortcuts:

Long time spread rules:

- If the call time spread ask minus the put time spread ask is greater than the value of the jelly roll, the put time spread appears cheap.

- If the call time spread ask minus the put time spread ask is less than the value of the jelly roll, the call time spread appears cheap.

Short time spread rules:

- If the call time spread bid minus the put time spread bid is greater than the value of the jelly roll, the call time spread appears rich.

- If the call time spread bid minus the put time spread bid is less than the value of the jelly roll, the put time spread appears rich.

Important note: These rules could also be used when exiting a trade.

TRADE MANAGEMENT

Time spreads can be fairly tame when it comes to risk, with the risk limited to the purchase price when long and the risk "sort of limited" but unquantifiable when short (more in a moment)—as long as they are closed out before the expiration of the short-dated option. The risk of early exercise of a short deep-in-the-money leg of a time spread also exists. We will examine some of these scenarios in this section. As always, one's game plan should be laid out in advance of making the trade. Important questions to consider:

- What is the most efficient way to take profits? Losses?

- What should be done if the underlying reaches the investor's target ahead of schedule?

- What should the investor do if a breakout fails to materialize?

- What should the investor do if he is completely wrong on direction?

- What should the investor do at expiration?

These are all questions that need to be considered *before* the trade. Once again, our overarching risk management protocol: *If you are wrong, get out!*

This means that if any of the assumptions that went into your market forecast turn out to be wrong you should get out of the position.

Taking Profits and Losses

There are two points at which to exit a trade: when one's market forecast has been met or when one's market forecast has changed. In the case of the former, one should always have profit and loss targets going into a trade; if they are met, one should assess the situation and decide whether to lock in profits. We are very big fans of scaling into and out of positions. Scaling out is a very powerful and positive way to extract any profits from a position because it builds a level of comfort—taking money off the table and limiting risk while staying with one's forecast. In the case of the latter, when the market forecast changes, it means the original assumptions used for selecting a certain strategy are no longer valid. The trade should be liquidated, or at the very least, modified.

In the case of liquidation, there are two ways to exit a time spread. One is to liquidate the original position and (recalling the preceding section, "Strategy Component Selection") the other is to liquidate via the synthetically equivalent position. It should be remembered, however, that exiting a time spread position with a synthetically equivalent position will result in a jelly roll position that will need to be managed and may eventually have assignment risk. Also, additional trades will incur additional commission charges. For these reasons, this type of position might be more trouble than it is worth for many traders.

• How to Exit

The decision whether to liquidate using the original position versus the synthetic equivalent (without commission considerations) depends on two factors: price and liquidity. Price is simple enough if one remembers to apply the pricing rules from the previous section and to use the most advantageously priced time spread to liquidate the position. The other factor is liquidity, and liquidity issues usually have to do with the moneyness of the individual options that compose the time spread. As options move in-the-money, they acquire a larger delta, and this makes hedging them riskier for market makers. Accordingly, market makers will widen the bid-ask spread of in-the-money options to compensate for this risk. Conversely, out-of-the-money options have a lower delta, making hedging them less risky for market makers. This usually results in out-of-the-money options having a narrower bid-ask spread than their in-the-money counterparts. The net effect on time spreads is that a time spread consisting of in-the-money options will usually have a wider bid-ask spread than a time spread consisting of out-of-the-money options, because an in-the-money call time spread has a synthetically equivalent out-of-the-money put time spread and an in-the-money put time spread has a synthetically equivalent out-of-the-money call time spread. This moneyness effect can make using synthetically equivalent positions to exit a trade very effective.

Example 6.1 Liquidation of a Long Call Time Spread

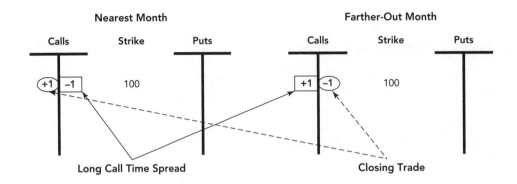

In the preceding case, the original position is simply liquidated by the execution of the reverse position; in Example 6.1, a short call time spread liquidates an existing long call time spread. Sometimes liquidity or pricing issues can arise in liquidating the original spread. In that event, the synthetically equivalent spread may be used to close the position (Example 6.2).

Example 6.2 Liquidation of a Long Call Time Spread via a Synthetically Equivalent Put Time Spread

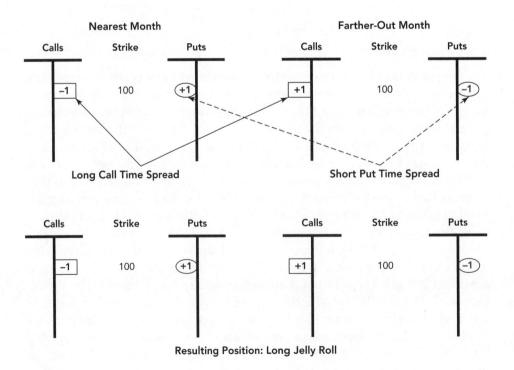

Early Arrival—Underlying Price Arrives at Target Price Ahead of Schedule

It can be maddening to the long time spreader to get the direction right and the timing wrong, correctly forecasting a directional move but making very little profit on a long time spread because time decay has not yet had a chance to work on the short-dated option. This sets up a dilemma: Should the trader hang on and hope that the underlying price will "hang around" the strike price for awhile and capture some time decay? Should he simply exit? Or is there an adjustment that can be made?

First of all, he must examine the market and see if his forecast needs to be adjusted. Was he wrong or was his timing just a bit off? It is very difficult for traders to be totally honest with themselves in these situations because they tend to rationalize in favor of their positions. If the trader truly believes that the underlying is going to now move sideways at the current level, then by all means, he should hold the position. However, if the nature of the movement has changed and the underlying is now moving at a higher velocity than initially forecast, then it is best to exit because the position is wrong.

There is another possibility: The time spread could be "rolled" to a new target strike. The trader must feel very strongly about his forecast of movement by the underlying to the new target before doing this: It is involved and will generate a lot of commissions because he will have to execute two vertical spreads in two separate expiration months. See Example 6.3.

Example 6.3 "Rolling Up" a Long Call Time Spread

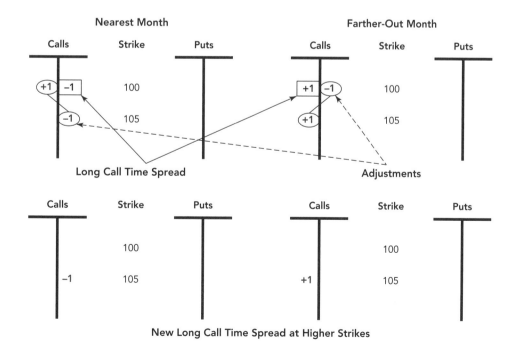

New Long Call Time Spread at Higher Strikes

Late Arrival—Underlying Price Does Not Move When Expected

Let's say an investor had forecast a breakout within a certain time period and decided to trade a short time spread to target the anticipated move. His breakout failed to materialize and he is now eating the time decay generated by his short, at-the-money time spread. What should he do? He was wrong. He should get out!

• Incorrect Direction

An investor had forecast a move lower and executed a long put time spread at the strike near his target zone. Now the underlying price has moved higher through resistance. What should he do? He was wrong. He needs to get out!

• Expiration

Expiration is the trickiest time for time spread management—long or short. The position must be closed out or rolled; otherwise, a pure directional position will be the result, and it is possible that is could involve a position in the underlying. Let's examine the outcome of both long and short time spreads taken through the expiration process (Example 6.4a).

Note that a short calendar spread involves potentially unlimited (for calls) or substantial (for puts) risk after the expiration of the near-term long option. Additionally, a short calendar spread may be treated as an uncovered position for margin purposes.

Example 6.4a Long Call Time Spread—Underlying Price Above the Strike Price

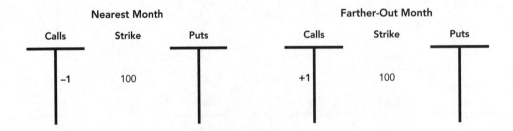

With the underlying price above the strike price at expiration, the short call in the expiration month will be exercised, leaving the trader with a short stock position against a long call in the deferred month. See Example 6.4b.

Example 6.4b Long Call Time Spread—Underlying Price Above
the Strike Price

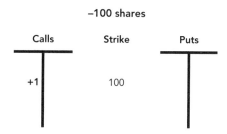

The position in Example 6.4b is known as a synthetic long put.

Example 6.5a Long Call Time Spread—Underlying Price Below
the Strike Price

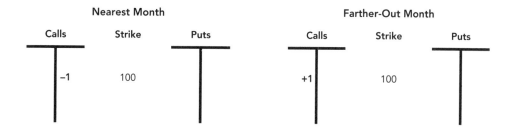

With the underlying price below the strike price at expiration, the short call in the expiration month will expire worthless, leaving the trader with a long call in the deferred month. See Example 6.5b.

Example 6.5b Long Call Time Spread—Underlying Price Below the
Strike Price

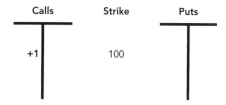

Example 6.6 Long Put Time Spread—Underlying Price Above the Strike Price

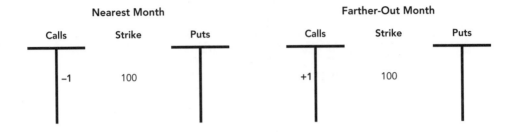

With the underlying price above the strike price at expiration (Example 6.6), the short put in the expiration month will expire worthless, leaving the trader with a long put in the deferred month.

Example 6.7a Long Put Time Spread—Underlying Price Below the
           Strike Price

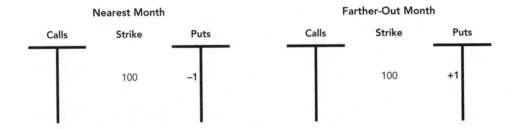

With the underlying price below the strike price at expiration, the short put in the expiration month will be exercised, leaving the trader with a long stock position against a long put in the deferred month (Example 6.7b).

Example 6.7b Long Put Time Spread—Underlying Price Below the
           Strike Price

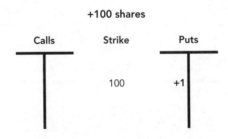

This position is known as a synthetic long call.

What is the best way to deal with expiration? Unless the original plans included the possibility of ending up with a naked directional position, synthetic or otherwise, it is best to exit on or before expiration day.

CHAPTER 6 EXERCISE

1. Which are examples of long put time spreads?

    A long or a short 1 June 105 put
    A long or a short 1 August 105 put

2. As the seller of a time spread, one would want the underlying price to move as far away as possible from the strike price. True or false?

3. Is it a long or a short time spread that can be either bullish, bearish, or neutral?

4. Calculate the delta of the following put time spread:

    XYZ (August 2008) 110 put delta = −0.35
    XYZ (June 2008) 110 put delta = −0.45

5. Is it a long or a short time spread that will have negative gamma when the underlying is near the strike price?

6. Will a short dated at-the-money option have a greater or a lesser theta than a longer dated at-the-money option of the same strike?

7. Should the value of an at-the-money long time spread rise or fall as the underlying price hovers near the strike price of the spread?

8. Long time spreads have (limited) (unlimited) risk and (limited) (unlimited) reward potential.

9. What do long time spreads have: positive or negative gamma; positive or negative vega; and positive or negative theta?

10. If you buy the ATM time spread and the underlying moves significantly in either direction, the spread will decrease, or narrow in value (assume no change in volatility). True or false?

Chapter 6 Exercise Answer Key

1. Short, long
2. True
3. Long
4. XYZ August/June 110 put time spread delta = −0.35 − (−0.45) = 0.10
5. Long
6. Greater
7. Rise
8. Limited, limited

9. Negative gamma, positive vega, positive theta.
10. True. The at-the-money time spread is the most expensive.

CHAPTER 6 QUIZ

1. Calculate the vega of the following short call time spread:

   XYZ (June) 110 call vega = 0.05
   XYZ (July) 110 call vega = 0.10

2. If implied volatility levels are low, and the forecast is for a sideways market in an underlying, a long time spread might be a strategy to employ to take advantage of this situation. True or false?

3. Which is bullish, a long or a short time spread with a strike above the current price?

4. Would the term structure of implied volatility of a stock that has gone through a recent slow period favor a long or a short time spread strategy?

5. If the term structure of implied volatility shows a sharp upward slope, would this indicate that short-dated implied volatilities are much lower or higher than longer-dated implied volatilities?

6. Assume that the market has been moving sideways for some time and that implied volatility levels are low. A trader decides to purchase the calendar spread with the strike price at exactly the price of the underlying. Determine the following:

   Delta: positive, neutral, or negative
   Gamma: positive, neutral, or negative
   Theta: positive, neutral, or negative
   Vega: positive, neutral, or negative

7. An investor anticipates that XYZ is going to rally from 130.00 to 140.00 in thirty days. He notices that implied volatility levels of all the options expiring in thirty days are high compared to the volatility of all options expiring in sixty days. To capture this move with a limited-risk strategy, would he buy or sell the sixty-day option and buy or sell the thirty-day option at the 140.00 strike?

8. An investor holds a long June/July call time spread. At expiration, if the underlying is above the strike price, the short June call will be exercised. What position is he left with?

9. To create a long jelly roll spread, do you need to combine a long or a short call time spread with a long or a short put time spread?

10. If the call time spread ask price minus the put time spread ask price is less than the value of the jelly roll, is the call time spread expensive or cheap?

Chapter 6 Quiz Answer Key

1. 110 call vega $= 0.05 - (0.10) = -0.05$
2. True
3. Long
4. Long
5. Lower
6. Neutral, negative, positive, positive
7. Buy sixty-day, sell thirty-day
8. Synthetic long put
9. Long call time spread, short put time spread
10. Cheap

CHAPTER NOTE

1. Assuming no early exercise considerations

7

Ratio Spreads

CONCEPT REVIEW

Volatility skew: A graphic representation of implied volatility levels associated with different strike prices, the curves' shape is often referred to as a "smile" or "smirk."

Congestion: An area where a security trades below resistance and above support levels.

STRATEGY OVERVIEW

Ratio spreads strategies can be used when one forecasts a complex market scenario, involving market direction, implied volatility levels, and timing. They may be especially effective for contratrend trading.

The term *ratio spread* is used when referring to any structure that involves the purchase of an option that is underwritten by the sale of a greater number of further out-of-the-money options of the same class and expiration cycle. For example, buying one March 100 call and selling two March 110 calls is a call ratio spread; buying one June 90 put and selling three June 75 puts is a put ratio spread.

The *ratio* of the ratio spread is determined by the number of further out-of-the-money options sold per nearer-the-money option purchased. Common ratios used by ratio spreaders are 1 to 2 (two sold for every one purchased), 2 to 3 (three sold for every two purchased), and 1 to 4 (four sold for every one purchased). However, any ratio may be used. Depending on the ratio used, the strikes involved, the time to expiration, and implied volatility levels, the spread could be executed for a debit, even money, or a credit.

Because ratio spreads are net short of options (there are always more short options in the position than long options), they generally will have a short volatility bias, meaning they will be short vega and will benefit from declining volatility. For the same reason, they generally will have a positive theta, meaning that the position will benefit from the passage of time. For these reasons ratio spreads can be most effective when one is expecting a low-magnitude directional move coupled with either declining implied volatility or the passage of time:

- *Call ratio spreads* could be used when forecasting a low-magnitude upward directional move that will be accompanied by declining volatility or that will take a great deal of time to materialize. Usually this takes the form of a contratrend recovery or "bounce" scenario in which the market has been declining with rising implied volatility and the trader is forecasting a bounce or mild correction, during which the underlying will trade higher for a time while implied volatility declines.

- *Put ratio spreads* could be used when one is forecasting a low-magnitude downward directional move that will be accompanied by declining volatility or that will take a great deal of time to materialize. Usually this takes the form of a contratrend sell-off or "correction" scenario in which the market has been rising and the trader is forecasting a sell-off or mild correction, during which the underlying will trade lower for a time while implied volatility declines.

Risk

Because they generally are used as contratrend trading vehicles, ratio spreads usually are constructed so that they have minimal cost or even a credit. Then, if the prevailing trend resumes, the position in that direction has little or no risk. It needs to be emphasized, however, that a ratio spread is net short of options and therefore has open-ended risk in the direction of the short options. Therefore, one's market forecast should assume only a remote possibility of the market moving through the short strike of the position with any velocity. The risk-averse trader should probably avoid the ratio spread entirely and instead use a limited-risk spread with similar characteristics, such as a vertical spread or a long butterfly.

STRATEGY COMPOSITION

Call Ratio Spreads

As mentioned in the previous section, the call ratio spread (**Figure 7.1**) consists of a long call at a particular strike, usually, but not necessarily, at-the-money or slightly out-of-the-money, underwritten by the sale of more than one further out-of-the-money call of the same expiration cycle.

Components: Long 1 Jan. 105 call at $3.40
Short 2 Jan. 110 calls at $2.00
= Jan. 105/110 call ratio spread at $0.60 (credit)

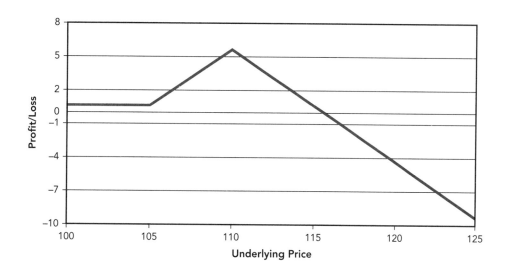

Figure 7.1 Call Ratio Spread P&L Diagram

Maximum Profit: $(K_2 - K_1)$ + credit or − debit (to initiate spread)
($110.00 − $105.00 + $0.60 = $5.60)

Maximum Loss: Unlimited on the upside; on the downside, limited to the amount of the debit (if initiated for a debit)

Breakeven(s):   On the downside: K_1 + debit (if done for a debit)
On the upside: [(number of short calls × short call breakeven) − (number of long calls × long call breakeven)]/(number of short calls − number of long calls) [(2 × $112.00) − (1 × $108.40)]/(2 − 1) = $115.60

Figures 7.2 and **7.3** illustrate the structure of some basic call ratio spreads.

Calls	Strike	Puts
+1	100	
−2	105	

Figure 7.2 1-to-2 Call Ratio Spread

Calls	Strike	Puts
+1	100	
−3	105	

Figure 7.3 1-to-3 Call Ratio Spread

Previously discussed spreads are evident in the structure of the call ratio spread. One can view a call ratio spread as a bull call spread with one or more extra short calls at the upper strike (see **Figure 7.4**) or in the case of a 1-to-2 call ratio spread, a long call butterfly with an extra short call at the upper strike (see **Figure 7.5**).

Calls		Strike	Puts
+1		100	
−1	−1	105	

Figure 7.4 Bull Call Spread with an Extra Short Call

Calls		Strike	Puts
+1		100	
−2		105	
+1	−1	110	

Figure 7.5 Long Call Butterfly with an Extra Short Call

The bull call spread and the long call butterfly are limited-risk positions that address mild upward movement and declining implied volatility and the passage of time, as do call ratio spreads. The addition of the extra short option at the upper strike of both of those structures reduces risk to the downside and converts the spread to a call ratio spread—a more aggressive strategy geared for taking advantage of declining implied volatility and time decay.

Put Ratio Spreads

The put ratio spread (**Figure 7.6**) consists of a long put at a particular strike, usually, but not necessarily, at-the-money or slightly out-of-the-money, underwritten by the sale of more than one further out-of-the-money puts of the same expiration cycle.

Components: Long 1 Aug. 860 put at $2.00
Short 2 Aug. 855 puts at $1.75
= Aug. 855/860 put ratio spread at $1.50 (credit)

Maximum Profit: $(K_2 − K_1)$ + credit, or − debit ($6.50)

Maximum Loss: On the downside, substantial to zero
On the upside, a debit if incurred for a debit.

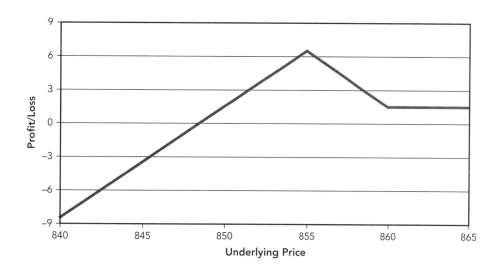

Figure 7.6 P&L Diagram

Breakeven(s):   On the upside: K_2 − debit (if done for a debit)
On the downside: [(number of short puts × short put breakeven) − (number of long puts × long puts breakeven)]/(number of short puts − number of long puts) [(2 × \$853.25) − (1 × \$858)] / (2 − 1) = \$848.50

Figures 7.7 and **7.8** illustrate the structure of some basic put ratio spreads.

Calls	Strike	Puts
	100	−2
	105	+1

Figure 7.7 1-to-2 Put Ratio Spread

Calls	Strike	Puts
	100	−3
	105	+1

Figure 7.8 1-to-3 Put Ratio Spread

As with the call ratio spread, it is obvious that some other previously discussed spread structures are represented in the put ratio spread. A put ratio spread can be viewed as a bear put spread with an extra short put(s) at the lower strike (see **Figure 7.9**) or a long put butterfly with an extra short put at the lower strike (see **Figure 7.10**).

Calls	Strike	Puts
	100	−1 −1
	105	+1

Figure 7.9 Bear Put Spread with an Extra Short Put

Calls	Strike	Puts
	100	+1 −1
	105	−2
	110	+1

Figure 7.10 Long Put Butterfly with an Extra Short Put

The bear put spread and the long put butterfly are limited-risk positions that address mild downward movement and declining implied volatility and the passage of time, as do put ratio spreads. The addition of the extra short option at the lower strike of both of those structures limits risk to the upside and converts the spread to a put ratio spread— a more aggressive and unlimited-risk spread geared for taking advantage of declining implied volatility and time decay.

THE GREEKS OF RATIO SPREADS

Ratio spreads are complex positions. They are composed of a long option at a particular strike that has the sensitivities of a long option and a greater number of short options at a different strike that have the sensitivities of short options. The combined position is sensitive to changes in underlying price, implied volatility, and the time until expiration. We will examine the Greeks of basic 1-to-2 call and put ratio spreads. Visualizing the ratio spread as an out-of-the-money long butterfly without the extra long option on the furthest out-of-the-money "wing" can help one to better understand the behavior of the position.

The 1-to-2 Call Ratio Spread

- **Delta**

The delta of a call ratio spread is dependent on the location of the underlying versus the strike, time to expiration, and implied volatility. Depending on the interplay of those three factors, the delta can be long, neutral, or short at any particular underlying price. The delta of a complex position can be difficult to visualize without looking at graphs, but a good method for visualizing how the delta of a complex position responds to changing market conditions is to think of the delta of an option as the odds that the option will finish in-the-money. Continuing with the horse racing analogy, the favorites (the in-the-money and at-the-money options) would have higher deltas (odds) than the long shot (the out-of-the-money options). As the race continued toward the finish line (expiration approaches), the deltas (odds) of the in-the-money options would continue to rise toward 100 while the deltas of the out-of-the-money options would fall toward zero.

The delta of a call ratio spread is the sum of the position-adjusted deltas of its component options. For example, the delta of the 100/105 1-to-2 call ratio spread would be calculated as follows:

100 strike call delta = 0.50

105 strike call delta = 0.20

1-to-2 call ratio spread delta = (0.50 × 1) + (0.20 × −2) or 0.10

The delta of the same spread with greater time until expiration or higher implied volatility might look something like this:

100 strike call delta = 0.50

105 strike call delta = 0.30

1-to-2 call ratio spread delta = (0.50 × 1) + (0.30 × −2) or −0.10

The delta of the same spread with less time until expiration or lower implied volatility might look something like this:

100 strike call delta = 0.50

105 strike call delta = 0.10

1-to-2 call ratio spread delta = (0.50 × 1) + (0.10 × −2) or 0.30

Figure 7.11 illustrates the relationship of the delta of a call ratio spread to time until expiration.

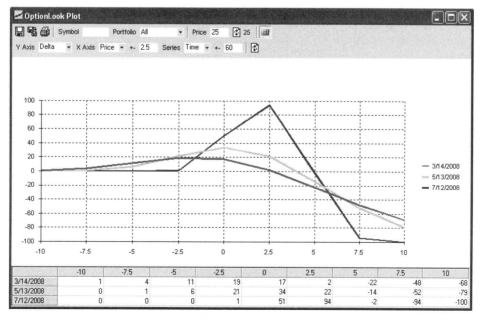

Figure 7.11 1-to-2 Call Ratio Spread Delta vs. Underlying Price and Time
to Expiration: July 25/30 1-to-2 Call Ratio Spread
Source: LiquidPoint, LLC

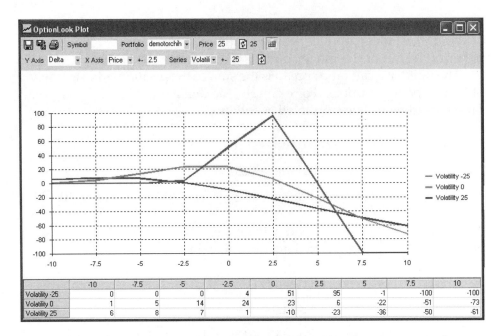

Figure 7.12 1-to-2 Call Ratio Spread Delta vs. Underlying Price and
Implied Volatility: July 25/30 1-to-2 Call Ratio Spread
Source: LiquidPoint, LLC

Figure 7.11 shows that the delta of the call ratio spread becomes increasingly positive with modest upward movement over time. As time passes, the delta of the short out-of-the money options decrease faster than that of the long at- or near-the-money option. This causes the delta of the spread to "grow" to positive over time, as long as the underlying does not rally too sharply. Obviously, if the underlying rises far enough, the delta of the position will flip to negative. The same effect can be observed with declining implied volatility in **Figure 7.12**. Notice the similarity in this graph and the preceding one and recall that the effect of declining volatility on option positions mimics the passage of time.

• Gamma

The gamma of a call ratio spread is the sum of the position-adjusted gammas of its component options. For example, the gamma of the 100/105 1-to-2 call ratio spread is calculated as follows:

100 strike call gamma = 0.10

105 strike call gamma = 0.04

1-to-2 call ratio spread gamma = $(0.10 \times 1) + (0.04 \times -2)$ or 0.02

The gamma of the call ratio spread is highly sensitive to the location of the underlying relative to the strikes. As with any spread made up of both long and short options, the position will take on the gamma characteristics of the underlying option position at the nearest strikes. A ratio spread includes

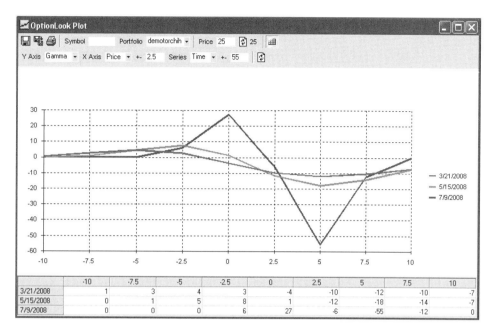

Figure 7.13 Call Ratio Spread Gamma vs. Underlying Price and Time to Expiration: July 25/30 1-to-2 Call Ratio Spread
Source: LiquidPoint, LLC

more short options than long options, so gamma quickly becomes negative as the underlying price rises, or as implied volatility rises. **Figure 7.13** illustrates the relationship of the gamma of a call ratio spread to the underlying price and the time to expiration.

The preceding figure shows how the gamma of the call ratio spread depends on the location of the underlying and the time until expiration. When expiration is near and the underlying price is closest to the long option at the lower strike, the spread will have a positive gamma; when the underlying price is closer to the short options at the upper strike, the spread will have a large negative gamma. When there is greater time until expiration, the gamma curve is much softer. The effect of the passage of time on the gamma of the call ratio spread is again mimicked by falling implied volatility, as illustrated by **Figure 7.14**.

Note the similarities between Figures 7.13 and 7.14 and recall that the effects of declining volatility on the sensitivity of an option position mimics the passage of time.

• **Vega**

The vega of a call ratio spread is the sum of the position-adjusted vegas of its component options. For example, the vega of the 100/105 1-to-2 call ratio spread is calculated as follows:

100 strike call vega = 0.15

105 strike call vega = 0.10

1-to-2 call ratio spread vega = $(0.15 \times 1) + (0.10 \times -2)$ or -0.05

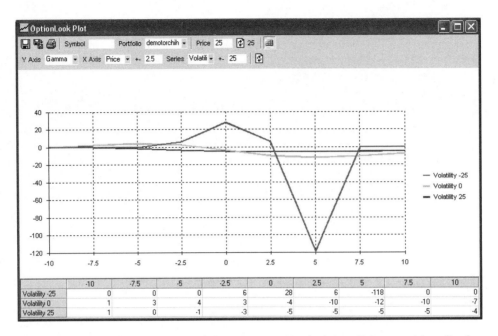

Figure 7.14 Call Ratio Spread Gamma vs. Underlying Price and Implied
Volatility: July 25/30 1-to-2 Call Ratio Spread
Source: LiquidPoint, LLC

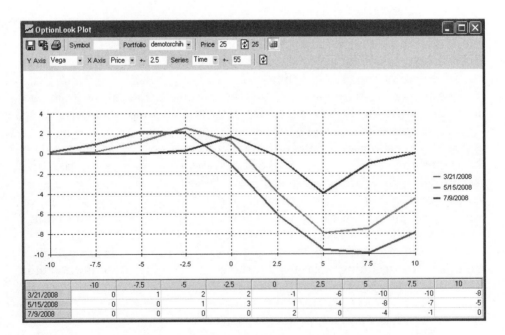

Figure 7.15 Call Ratio Spread Vega vs. Underlying Price and Time
to Expiration: July 25/30 1-to-2 Call Ratio Spread
Source: LiquidPoint, LLC

This means that for every 1 percent change in implied volatility, the
price of the call ratio spread would change by approximately 0.05. Because
the call ratio spread is generally short vega, the value of the spread will
fall when implied volatility rises and rise when implied volatility falls.
Figure 7.15 illustrates the vega of the call ratio spread.

The vega of the spread is positive when the underlying price is near the strike of the long option, and then becomes negative when the underlying price moves toward the strike of the short options. Recall from Chapter 1 that vega increases with the time to expiration so that, all things being equal, the vega of an option with a greater amount of time left until expiration will be larger than that of an option with a lesser amount of time left until expiration. With regard to the call ratio spread, this means that the overall amount of positive or negative vega generated by the position will decline as expiration approaches.

• Theta

The theta of the call ratio spread is the sum of the position-adjusted thetas of its component options. For example, the theta of the 100/105 1-to-2 call ratio spread would be calculated as follows:

$$100 \text{ strike call theta} = -0.06$$

$$105 \text{ strike call theta} = -0.04$$

$$1\text{-to-2 call ratio spread theta} = (-0.06 \times 1) + (-0.04 \times -2) \text{ or } +0.02$$

This means that the value of the call ratio spread would increase by approximately 0.02 per calendar day (all else being equal). Because a call ratio spread generally has *positive* theta, the value of the spread will rise as time passes and option values decay. **Figure 7.16** illustrates the theta of a call ratio spread.

Figure 7.16 illustrates how the sensitivity of the position depends on the location of the underlying price and the time until expiration. When the

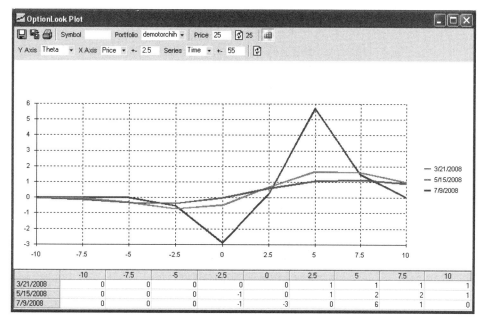

Figure 7.16 Call Ratio Spread Theta vs. Underlying Price and Time
to Expiration: July 25/30 1-to-2 Call Ratio Spread
Source: LiquidPoint, LLC

underlying price is near the strike of the long option, the call ratio spread will have negative theta, and when the underlying price is nearer the strike of the short options, the call ratio spread will have positive theta. Recall that the theta of an at-the-money option increases as time to expiration decreases and the theta of an out-of-the-money option decreases as time to expiration decreases, so the swings of negative to positive theta that occur as the underlying price shifts location between the long and short strikes become more dramatic.

The 1-to-2 Put Ratio Spread

• Delta

As with the call ratio spread, the delta of a put ratio spread is dependent on the location of the underlying relative to the strike, time to expiration, and implied volatility. The delta can be short, neutral, or long at any particular underlying price depending on those market factors. The delta of a put ratio spread is the sum of the position-adjusted deltas of its component options. For example, the delta of the 100/105 1-to-2 put ratio spread would be calculated as follows:

105 strike put delta = −0.60

100 strike put delta = −0.20

1-to-2 put ratio spread delta = (−0.60 × 1) + (−0.20 × −2) or −0.20

The delta of the same spread with greater time until expiration or higher implied volatility might look something like this:

105 strike put delta = −0.50

100 strike put delta = −0.30

1-to-2 put ratio spread delta = (−0.50 × 1) + (−0.30 × −2) or +0.10

The delta of the same spread with less time until expiration or lower implied volatility might look something like this:

105 strike put delta = −0.50

100 strike put delta = −0.10

1-to-2 put ratio spread delta = (−0.50 × 1) + (−0.10 × −2) or −0.30

Figure 7.17 illustrates the relationship of the delta of a put ratio spread to time until expiration.

The delta of the put ratio spread becomes increasingly negative with modest downward movement over time. As time passes, the delta of the short out-of-the money options decreases (in absolute terms) faster that the long at- or near-the-money option. This causes the delta of the spread to become increasingly negative over time, as long as the underlying

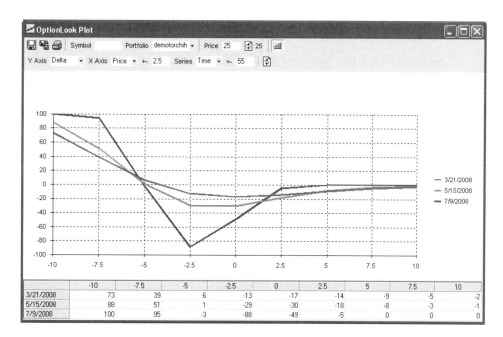

Figure 7.17 Put Ratio Spread Delta vs. Underlying Price and Time
to Expiration: July 25/30 1-to-2 Put Ratio Spread
Source: LiquidPoint, LLC

does not sell off too sharply. If the underlying falls far enough, the delta
of the position will flip to positive. The same effect can be observed with
declining implied volatility in **Figure 7.18**. Again, observe that the effect
of declining volatility on option positions mimics the passage of time.

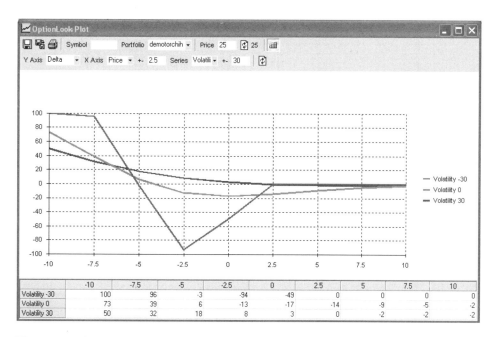

Figure 7.18 Put Ratio Spread Delta vs. Underlying Price and Implied
Volatility: July 25/30 1-to-2 Put Ratio Spread
Source: LiquidPoint, LLC

• **Gamma**

The gamma of a put ratio spread is the sum of the position-adjusted gammas of its component options. For example, the gamma of the 100/105 1-to-2 put ratio spread is calculated as follows:

$$105 \text{ strike put gamma} = 0.10$$

$$100 \text{ strike put gamma} = 0.04$$

$$1\text{-to-2 put ratio spread gamma} = (0.10 \times 1) + (0.04 \times -2) \text{ or } 0.02$$

As with the call ratio spread, the put ratio spread is highly sensitive to the location of the underlying relative to the strikes, and the position will take on the gamma characteristics of the underlying option position at the strikes nearest the underlying price. Gamma quickly becomes negative as the underlying price falls, or as implied volatility rises. **Figure 7.19** illustrates the relationship of the gamma of a put ratio spread to the underlying price and the time to expiration.

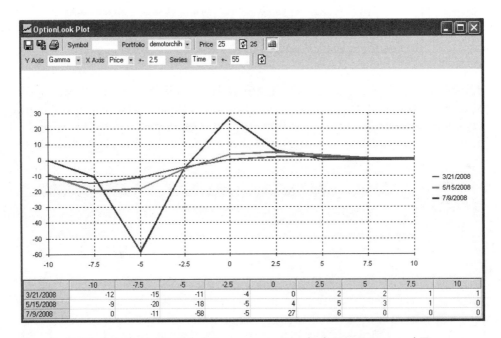

Figure 7.19 Put Ratio Spread Gamma vs. Underlying Price and Time
            to Expiration: July 25/30 1-to-2 Put Ratio Spread
            Source: LiquidPoint, LLC

When the underlying price is near the long option at the upper strike, the put ratio spread will have a positive gamma, shifting to negative as the underlying price moves lower toward the short options at the lower strike. Because at-the-money gamma rises and in- or out-of-the-money gamma falls as expiration approaches, the gamma of the put ratio spread will have a bigger swing as it moves from positive to negative. When there is greater time until expiration, the gamma curve is much softer. The effect of the passage of time on the gamma of

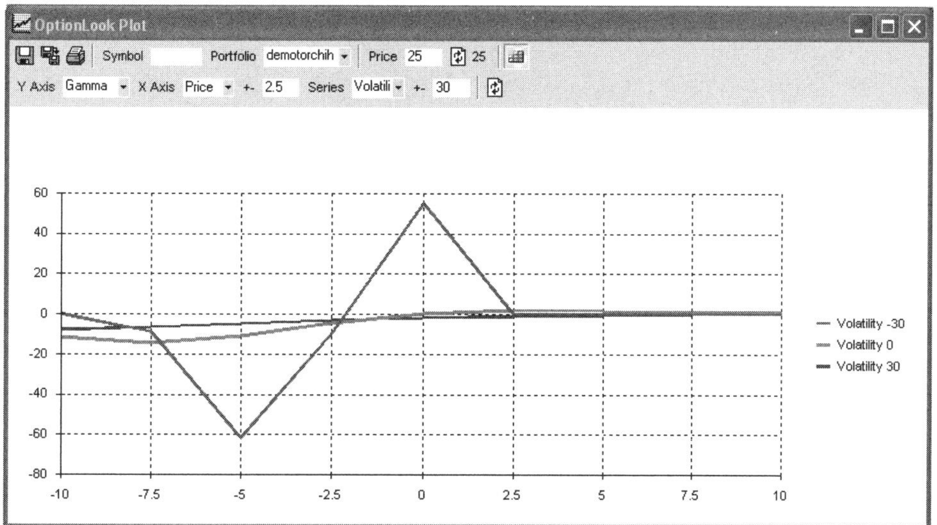

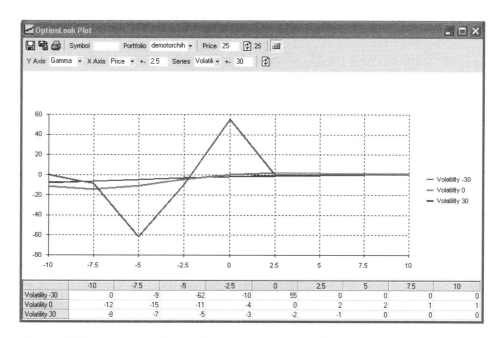

	-10	-7.5	-5	-2.5	0	2.5	5	7.5	10
Volatility -30	0	-9	-62	-10	55	0	0	0	0
Volatility 0	-12	-15	-11	-4	0	2	2	1	1
Volatility 30	-8	-7	-5	-3	-2	-1	0	0	0

Figure 7.20 Put Ratio Spread Gamma vs. Underlying Price and Implied Volatility: July 25/30 1-to-2 Put Ratio Spread
Source: LiquidPoint, LLC

the put ratio spread is again mimicked by falling implied volatility, as illustrated by **Figure 7.20**.

• Vega

The vega of a put ratio spread is the sum of the position-adjusted vegas of its component options. For example, the vega of the 100/105 1-to-2 put ratio spread is calculated as follows:

$$105 \text{ strike put vega} = 0.15$$

$$100 \text{ strike put vega} = 0.10$$

$$\text{1-to-2 put ratio spread vega} = (0.15 \times 1) + (0.10 \times -2) \text{ or } -0.05$$

This means that for every 1 percent change in implied volatility, the price of the put ratio spread would change by approximately 0.05. Because the put ratio spread is generally short vega, the value of the spread will fall when implied volatility rises, and rise when implied volatility falls. **Figure 7.21** illustrates the vega of the put ratio spread.

The vega of the spread is positive when the underlying price is near the strike of the long option, and then becomes negative when the underlying price moves toward the strike of the short options. Recall from Chapter 1 that vega increases with time to expiration so that, all things being equal, the vega of an option with a greater amount of time left until expiration will be larger than that of an option with a lesser amount of time left until expiration. With regard to the call ratio spread, this means that the overall amount of positive or negative vega generated by the position will decline as expiration approaches.

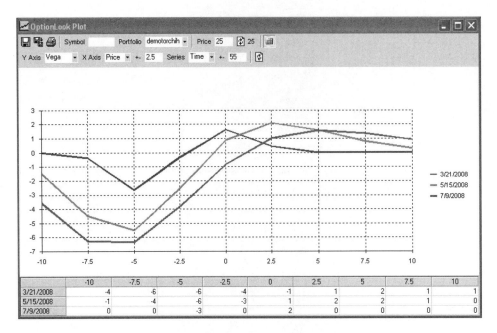

Figure 7.21 Put Ratio Spread Vega vs. Underlying Price and Time to Expiration: July 25/30 1-to-2 Put Ratio Spread
Source: LiquidPoint, LLC

- **Theta**

The theta of the put ratio spread is the sum of the position-adjusted thetas of its component options. For example, the theta of the 100/105 1-to-2 put ratio spread would be calculated as follows:

$$105 \text{ strike put theta} = -0.06$$

$$100 \text{ strike put theta} = -0.04$$

$$1\text{-to-2 put ratio spread theta} = (-0.06 \times 1) + (-0.04 \times -2)$$
$$\text{or } +0.02$$

This means that the value of the put ratio spread would increase by approximately 0.02 per calendar day (all else being equal). Because a put ratio spread generally has *positive* theta, the value of the spread will rise as time passes and option values decay. **Figure 7.22** illustrates the theta of a put ratio spread.

The put ratio spread generally will have positive theta when the underlying price is nearest the strike of the short options. When the underlying price is near the strike of the long option, the spread may have a negative theta. Recall that the theta of an at-the-money option increases as time to expiration decreases and the theta of an out-of-the-money option decreases as time to expiration decreases, so as expiration approaches, the theta of the put ratio spread will have bigger swings as it moves from positive to negative. When there is greater time until expiration, the theta curve is much softer.

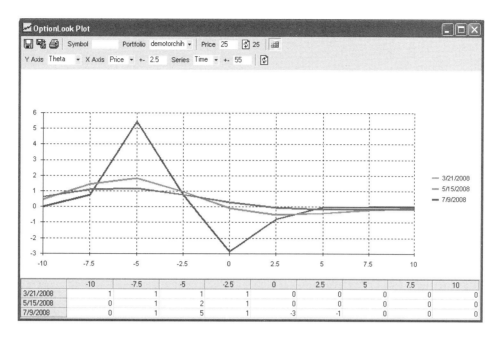

Figure 7.22 Put Ratio Spread Theta vs. Underlying Price and Time
to Expiration: July 25/30 1-to-2 Put Ratio Spread
Source: LiquidPoint, LLC

INVESTMENT OBJECTIVES

Because of their asymmetrical risk-reward properties—limited risk in one direction and unlimited risk in another—and their short vega/positive theta characteristics, ratio spreads can be especially suited to situations that favor limited movement in the direction of the short strike with declining volatility and the passage of time. Both declining volatility and the time decay work to expand the value of a ratio spread. In addition, the passage of time and/or declining implied volatility cause the delta of the ratio spread to "grow" in favor of the trader—the delta of the call ratio spread becomes more positive; the delta of the put ratio spread becomes more negative.

When considering a ratio spread, traders should look for situations that favor the above scenario. Some typical market conditions conducive to slow, limited, directional movement with the possibility of declining implied volatility are the following:

- Contratrend moves
  - The oversold bounce
  - The overbought correction
- Trend decelerations
  - Rally into congestion and resistance
  - Decline into congestion and support

- Special situations
  — Postmeltdown
  — Postmeltup
- Volatility skew plays
  — Implied volatility differential

Contratrend Moves

When the market is trending, it will occasionally pause and pull back as it corrects from temporary overbought or oversold conditions. These contratrend moves tend to be muted because they usually are accompanied by lower volumes as they trade back into support or resistance levels that contain the magnitude of the move. As the market retraces, time will pass and implied volatility may decline as movement in the underlying price contracts; these factors play into the strengths of the ratio spread. If the trend suddenly resumes, the risk is limited to the amount, if any, invested in the spread. **Figures 7.23** and **7.24** are examples of contratrend moves.

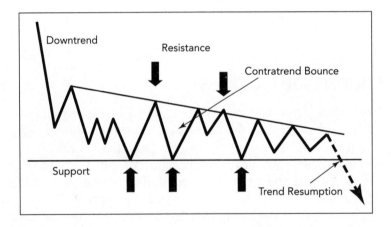

Figure 7.23 Oversold Bounce

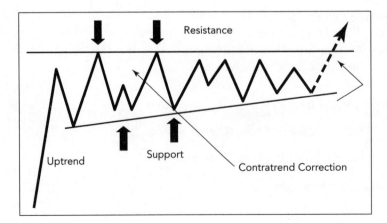

Figure 7.24 Overbought Correction

Figure 7.23 is an example of a bullish contratrend move known as an *oversold bounce;* Figure 7.24 is an example of a bearish contratrend move known as an *overbought correction.*

Trend Deceleration

When the market is trending, occasionally it will enter areas of previous price congestion. Price movement usually slows when this occurs because past inventory levels are approached and momentum traders look to take profits. Once again, slowing price movement, the passage of time, and declining implied volatility can occur in these zones, making them attractive for ratio spread strategies. **Figures 7.25** and **7.26** below are examples of reentry into previous areas of price congestion. Figure 7.25 is an example of a bullish rally into a previous congestion zone; Figure 7.26 is an example of a bearish decline into a previous congestion zone.

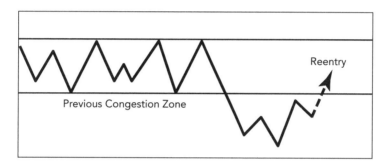

Figure 7.25 Rally into Congestion Zone

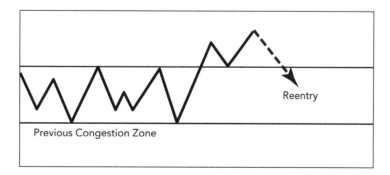

Figure 7.26 Decline into Congestion Zone

Special Situations

Meltdowns and meltups usually are news driven—either bad news or good news—and the underlying stock explodes to the downside or the upside with implied volatility increasing sharply. Bottom picking in meltdowns or top picking in meltups can be a dangerous business; these types of contrarian plays are risky because traders are going against a very powerful trend. But if they get it right, it can be a very lucrative trade. If a correction does occur, it usually is muted because price moves contratrend. Implied volatility usually backs off when this occurs and, again, this plays into the strengths of the ratio spread. In addition, if the trend resumes, risk is limited to initial investment.

Volatility Skew Plays

Occasionally market forces will create large implied volatility differentials between strike prices, which make "buy-low-volatility-strike, sell-high-volatility-strike" ratio spread strategies attractive. One could purchase an option at the lower implied volatility and sell a ratioed amount of options at the higher volatility. If the volatility normalizes, the trade may become profitable.

Warning: *Implied volatility differentials in and of themselves usually are not sufficient reason to initiate a ratio spread. These trades should be incorporated into market views that are optimal for ratio spreads—limited underlying movement, passage of time, and declining implied volatility.*

STRATEGY SELECTION

Once a trader determines that conditions favorable to a ratio spread exist, she needs to evaluate the following factors:

- Direction of the trend
- Support and resistance levels
- Congestion areas or zones
- Projected time of slow movement and/or declining volatility

Direction of Trend

Obviously, direction is important because ratio spreads do have a directional bias. Call ratio spreads are used to trade a market with a bullish bias, and put ratio spreads are used to trade a market with a bearish bias. The market's trend bias must be incorporated into strike selection.

Support and Resistance Levels

Support and resistance levels need to be defined for two reasons. They identify areas where price movement is likely to decelerate; this is important for strike selection. Support and resistance levels are also important because they are used to identify breakout levels for risk management, as will be seen in the following section, "Trade Management."

Congestion Areas or Zones

As with support and resistance levels, congestion areas or zones identify price levels at which the market is likely to decelerate and mark time as the market works its way through previously important price levels. When the market leaves these zones, it is likely that price movement will accelerate, which is an important factor in risk management.

Projected Time of Slow Movement and/or Declining Volatility

It is important for the trader to have a forecast of how long the slowed price movement and/or declining volatility phase will last, to select the expiration cycle of his ratio spread.

- **Strike Selection**

A forecast/knowledge of support and resistance levels and congestion zones is needed for strike selection. Selecting strikes for a ratio spread is similar to selecting strikes for a one-winged butterfly position. The difference is that, unlike the long at-the-money butterfly, the ratio spread usually has a directional bias. As with the long butterfly, the point of maximum profitability for the position is at the short strike of the structure, which should be located at one's price target. It is important that this level be backstopped by a support or resistance level or congestion zone to slow or stop the price movement of the underlying as it approaches the short strike. If the underlying moves through the short strike—upward in the case of the call ratio spread and downward in the case of the put ratio spread—there is open-ended risk.

For example, in **Figure 7.27** the underlying is moving sideways in a range between 97.50 (support) and 102.50 (resistance). In this case, establishing a 97.50/102.50 1-to-2 call ratio spread when the underlying is near support would seem to be an appropriate strike selection. In **Figure 7.28** the underlying is declining from 105.00 toward strong 95.00 support. In this case, establishing a 95.00/105.00 1-to-2 put ratio spread when the underlying is near resistance would seem to be an appropriate strike selection.

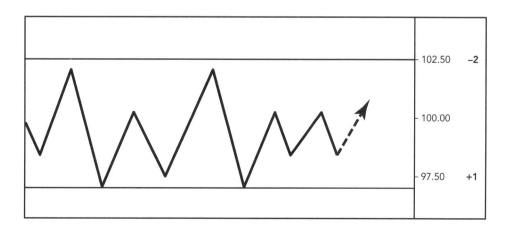

Figure 7.27 Call Ratio Spread Strike Selection

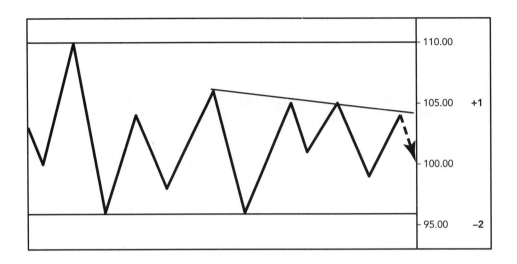

Figure 7.28 Put Ratio Spread Strike Selection

- **Expiry Selection**

To select the expiration month, a forecast of projected time of slow price movement and/or declining implied volatility is necessary. If a trader estimates that this behavior will persist for one month, then she would want to use options with an expiration cycle that mirrors the forecast. When in doubt, the trader should use the expiration cycle that expires before the projected end of the slow period.

TRADE MANAGEMENT

Ratio spreads have a high-risk profile. Again, like the one-winged butterfly, there is not an outside "wing option" that kicks in to limit risk if the short strikes are penetrated. Risk is open-ended, and for that reason, ratio spreads must be managed with an iron fist. Important questions to consider:

- Should the trader even consider ratio spreads?
- What is the most efficient way to take profits?
- What if the short strikes are threatened?
- What if the market moves down or up through the long strike?
- How should the trader manage risk or take losses?

Should the Trader Even Consider Ratio Spreads?

Ratio spreads have open-ended risk. Not only is there risk that the market will move through the short strikes and leave the trader long in a falling market or short in a rising market, there is also the danger of *event risk*.

Event risk occurs when a large, market-moving event causes the underlying in which the trader has a ratio spread to gap through her short strikes, leaving no chance to exit the trade or manage risk and exposing the trader to large losses. If her capital base is modest, or she can't live with the idea of overnight risk, then this spread is not for her. The trader needs to retreat to the long butterfly or condor strategy to trade decelerating price movement and/or declining implied volatility situations.

What Is the Most Efficient Way to Take Profits?

Ratio spreads will punish the greedy and undisciplined trader. As with the long butterfly and condor, the properly positioned ratio spread has positive time decay and the value of the position theoretically will increase in value every day. The temptation to try to get "one more day" of time decay out of this position can be a trader's undoing. This type of greedy behavior with a long butterfly or condor is not the end of the world, because they are limited-risk positions. The ratio spread, however, is not a limited-risk position, and getting greedy when red flags are flying can lead to disaster. It is vitally important to have an ironclad risk management plan in place—and to stick to it. "He who fights and runs away, will live to fight another day" is the proper mindset for ratio spreaders. Here are some important tips:

- **Take Partial Profits**

Take partial profits occasionally by scaling out of the trade. For example, if an investor's position consists of ten call ratio spreads (say, long 10 at-the-money calls and short 20 out-of-the-money calls), he should not be afraid to take some money off the table from time to time. He can slowly scale out of the position as it goes in his favor. This action takes profits and limits remaining risk.

- **Watch Market Action**

Remember the reason the investor got into this trade in the first place: He had a market forecast of weak directional price action over a period of time and/or declining implied volatility. If the underlying stock or index in which he has his position starts to behave as though this trend may end, he should get out.

What If the Short Strikes Are Threatened?

When the underlying price moves toward the short strike of a ratio spread it is a two-edged sword. It is moving toward the area of maximum profitability, but it is also moving toward the area of maximum—and unlimited—risk. This can be unnerving for the trader as the stakes begin to rise. When this occurs, there are some evasive maneuvers that can be employed. The spread can be "capped" and turned into a limited-risk butterfly—at additional cost of course—or the short strike can be "rolled" away from the underlying price to give the trader more breathing room.

These rolls can be on a one-to-one basis, which again will add additional cost, or on a ratioed basis, which may add additional costs and will add additional ultimate risk.

Example 1

An investor has on a 100/105 1-to-2 call ratio spread, and the underlying has moved up near 105.00, which is also an important resistance level. This movement is what he had forecast, and he expects the underlying price to continue to hover around the 105.00 area, but the risk is making him nervous. He decides to purchase an additional call at the 110 strike and convert his call ratio spread into a long butterfly that will still profit from the underlying hovering around 105.00, but will limit risk to the upside if the underlying price continues higher. **Figures 7.29** and **7.30** illustrate this procedure.

Calls	Strike	Puts
+1	100	
−2	105	

Figure 7.29 Existing 1-to-2 100/105 Call Ratio Spread

Calls	Strike	Puts
+1	100	
−2	105	
+1	110	

Figure 7.30 Purchase of an Additional 110 Call to Convert to a Long Butterfly

The result in Figure 7.30 is a long 100/105/110 call butterfly. The long call butterfly will still profit from the underlying price hovering around the 105.00 level, but upside risk is now capped—at the additional cost of the 100 call.

Example 2

The investor has on a 95/100 1-to-2 put ratio spread, and the underlying has moved down near 95.00, which is also an important support level. This movement is what he had forecast, but it happened a little faster than he expected. He still believes that the 95.00 support level will hold, but the risk is making him nervous. He decides to "roll" his short 95 puts down to the 90 strike to give himself a little extra breathing room. **Figures 7.31, 7.32,** and **7.33** illustrate this procedure.

Calls	Strike	Puts
	95	−2
	100	+1

Figure 7.31 Existing 95/100 1-to-2 Put Ratio Spread

Calls	Strike	Puts
	90	−2
	95	−2 +2
	100	+1

Figure 7.32 Rolling Short 95 Puts Down to the 90 Strike

Calls	Strike	Puts
	90	−2
	95	
	100	+1

Figure 7.33 Resulting 90/100 1-to-2 Put Ratio Spread

The result in Figure 7.33 is a 90/100 1-to-2 put ratio spread. Purchasing the 90/95 put spread rolls the position into a 90/100 1-to-2 put ratio spread. This rolls the area of risk down below the 90.00 area, giving the position extra breathing room and profit potential. Of course, this adds to the cost of the position, which raises the upside risk if the underlying were to rally.

Example 3

An investor has on a 100/105 1-to-2 call ratio spread, and the underlying has moved up near 105.00, which is also an important resistance level.

This movement is what he had forecast, but the risk is making him nervous. He decides to roll his short options to a higher strike, but he doesn't want to invest any additional money, so he decides to use another ratio spread. **Figures 7.34, 7.35,** and **7.36** illustrate this procedure.

Calls	Strike	Puts
+1	100	
−2	105	

Figure 7.34 Existing 100/105 1-to-2 Call Ratio Spread

Calls		Strike	Puts
	+1	100	
+2	−2	105	
	−4	110	

Figure 7.35 Rolling Short 105 Calls Up to the 110 Strike

Calls	Strike	Puts
+1	100	
	105	
−4	110	

Figure 7.36 Resulting 100/110 1-to-4 Call Ratio Spread

The result in Figure 7.36 is a 100/110 1-to-4 call ratio spread. By executing two 105/110 1-to-2 call ratio spreads, the trader has rolled the short 105 calls up to the 110 level, giving the position breathing room and additional profit potential and moving the area of risk higher. Because the roll was executed with a ratio spread, the additional cost is minimal. However, the ratio has now increased from 1 to 2 to 1 to 4, so the ultimate risk to the upside has been doubled.

What If the Market Moves Down or Up Through the Long Strike?

If the underlying price moves against the forecast direction, risk is limited to the initial cost of the ratio spread, if any. The trader will need to evaluate whether the amount of the initial investment is significant enough to warrant using a stop-loss. If the ratio spread was executed for a credit, there actually will be profit potential in an adverse market movement. Because time generally works in favor of a ratio spread, there may be a case for keeping the position even if the market moves opposite the forecast direction.

For example, suppose the trader had forecast a slow, upward directional move into a strong resistance level with declining implied volatility, and had executed a 1-to-2 call ratio spread for "even money" (neither a debit nor credit). Then, opposite of his forecast, the underlying starts to decline. Because there is no risk in the position to the downside, he can continue to hold for a possible rebound and fulfillment of his original forecast at a later date. If this occurs, some time will have passed, and all else being equal, the spread will perform even better. See **Figure 7.37** for an illustration.

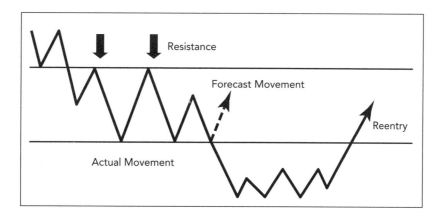

Figure 7.37 Incorrect Forecast Reinitiated

How Should the Trader Manage Risk or Take Losses?

His forecast was for a slow, directional move toward a target area. Hopefully, the target area is capped by a resistance level or a congestion zone above the current underlying price (in the case of an upward move) or floored by a support or congestion zone below the current underlying price (in the case of a downward move). As mentioned in "Investment Objectives," these boundaries are very important not only for structuring the ratio spread, but for risk management purposes as well. If they are penetrated, or if the underlying price begins to move with a greater velocity and in greater magnitudes than the trader had forecast, it is time for him to look for the exit because his forecast is incorrect.

Support and resistance levels are wonderful tools for risk management because they provide "lines in the sand" that, if crossed, are a call to action. The position will either need to be modified, as in the section above about short strikes, or exited completely. The investor cannot play mind games with this type of position and must act immediately, as shown in **Figure 7.38**.

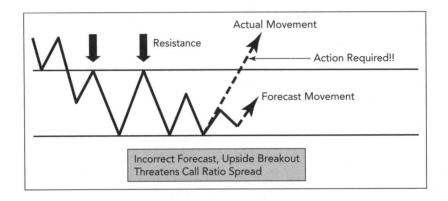

Figure 7.38 Breakout of Trading Range to the Upside

Figure 7.38 shows that the underlying price has moved sharply through the resistance level the trader was counting on to cap upward movement. Obviously, his forecast is incorrect, resistance has been breached, and he must take action. The position must be modified or exited.

In **Figure 7.39**, the underlying price has moved sharply through the support level the trader was counting on to act as a floor for downward movement. Obviously, his forecast is incorrect, support has been broken, and he must take action. The position must be modified or exited.

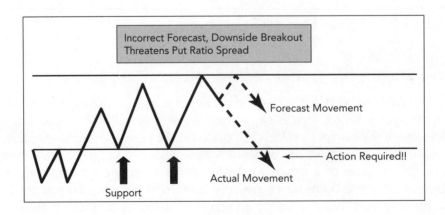

Figure 7.39 Breakout of Trading Range to the Downside

CHAPTER 7 EXERCISE

1. Because ratio spreads are net short of options, will they generally be long or short vega and positive or negative theta?

2. If one is projecting a mild correction where the underlying stock will trade lower for a time, which would be used: a call ratio spread or a put ratio spread?

3. A call ratio spread can be viewed as a _____ _____ _____ with an extra short call(s) at the upper strike or a _____ _____ _____ with a short call at the upper strike.

4. A put ratio spread can be viewed as a _____ _____ _____ with an extra short put(s) at the lower strike or a _____ _____ _____ with a short put at the lower strike.

5. Calculate the delta of the 95/100 1-to-2 call ratio spread with the options having the following deltas:
   95 strike call delta = 0.50
   100 strike call delta = 0.35

6. With a ratio spread, the gamma quickly becomes (positive) (negative) as the underlying price moves to the short strike, or as implied volatility rises.

7. Declining volatility and time decay work to expand the value of a ratio spread. True or false?

8. Does a call ratio spread have limited or unlimited risk on the upside?

9. What is the formula to determine the maximum profit of a ratio put spread?

10. Is it a call or a put ratio spread that can be used to take advantage of a contratrend recovery or a bounce, where the market has been declining with rising implied volatility?

Chapter 7 Exercise Answer Key

1. Short, positive
2. Put ratio spread
3. Bull call spread, long call butterfly
4. Bear put spread, long put butterfly
5. $(0.50 \times 1) + (0.35 \times -2) = -0.20$
6. Negative
7. True

8. Unlimited
9. $K_2 - K_1$ + credit received or − debit incurred when initiating
   the position
10. Call

CHAPTER 7 QUIZ

1. When the underlying price moves toward the short strike of a
   ratio spread, one can choose to either roll the position away from
   the strike or turn it into a _____ spread to limit or eliminate
   risk.

2. If an investor increases his call ratio spread from a 1 to 2 to a 1 to 4,
   the risk to the upside will _____.

3. An investor has on the 85/90 ratio put spread. He purchases the
   80/85 put spread. This rolls the position into a _____.

4. The passage of time and declining implied volatility results in
   the delta of the put ratio spread becoming (more positive) (more
   negative).

5. If a trader anticipates a slow, upward directional move into a strong
   resistance level with declining implied volatility, he might choose to
   put on a 1-to-2 _____ _____ spread.

6. Support and resistance levels and _____ _____ are needed
   for strike selection.

7. Support and resistance levels need to be determined because they
   identify areas where price movement is likely to decelerate; they are
   used to identify _____ levels for risk management.

8. When initiating ratio spreads, in the case of large implied
   volatility differentials between strike prices, would one purchase
   an option with the lower or the higher implied volatility and
   would one sell a greater number of options with the lower or the
   higher volatility?

9. If one initiated a call ratio spread for a debit, what is one's maximum
   loss?

10. Because the call ratio spread is generally short vega, will the value
    of the spread rise or fall when implied volatility rises, and rise or fall
    when implied volatility falls?

Chapter 7 Quiz Answer Key

1. Butterfly
2. Double
3. 80/90 1-to-2 put ratio spread
4. Negative
5. Call ratio
6. Congestion zones
7. Breakout
8. Lower, higher
9. Unlimited on the upside; on the downside, limited to the amount of the debit
10. Fall, rise

8

Backspreads

CONCEPT REVIEW

Consolidation pattern: An area pattern that breaks out in the direction of the previous trend (also called a *continuation pattern*).

VIX: The ticker symbol for the Chicago Board Options Exchange's Volatility Index, which shows the market's expectation of thirty-day volatility. The VIX is viewed as a measure of market risk. It is constructed using the implied volatilities of a broad range of options from the Standard & Poor's 500 Index.

STRATEGY OVERVIEW

Backspreads, also known as *volatility spreads*, are the exact opposite of ratio spreads, and are used to capture high-magnitude, high-velocity directional moves occurring in a short time frame. Backspreads can be especially effective for trading breakouts from low-volatility trading ranges and continuation patterns as well as for high-velocity directional moves. The term *backspread* is used when referring to any structure that involves the purchase of multiple out-of-the-money options that is underwritten by the sale of an at-the-money or nearer-the-money option of the same class and expiration cycle. For example, buying two ABC June 150 calls and selling one ABC June 140 call is a call backspread; buying four XYZ July 90 puts and selling one XYZ July 100 put is a put backspread.

Like ratio spreads, backspreads can be constructed in various ratios of contracts purchased to contracts sold. The ratio is up to the trader and depends on pricing and the amount of "gearing" desired. The greater the ratio, the greater the gearing of the position, and the more profit potential (and loss) it will have. Common ratios used by backspreaders are 1 to 2 (two options purchased for every one sold), 1 to 3 (three options purchased for every one sold), and 1 to 4 (four options purchased for every one sold);

however, any ratio may be used as long as more options are purchased than sold. Depending on the ratio used, the strikes involved, the time to expiration, and the implied volatility levels, the spread could be executed for a debit, even money, or a credit.

Because backspreads are net long of options (there are always more long options in the position than short options), they carry the characteristics of long option positions and generally will have long gamma and long vega, and will, therefore, benefit from rising volatility and strong directional movement. For the same reason, they generally will have a negative theta, meaning that the value of the position will usually decline with the passage of time. For these reasons backspreads can be most effective when one is expecting a high-velocity, high-magnitude directional move with steady to rising implied volatility, occurring in a short time frame.

- *Call backspreads* could be used when one is forecasting a high-magnitude upward directional move that will be accompanied by rising volatility. Many factors could trigger this type of movement: bullish news about, for example, good earnings, takeovers, and new products; technical conditions such as bullish breakouts from consolidation or continuation patterns; or simply a strong bullish trend.

- *Put backspreads* could be used when one is forecasting a high-magnitude downward directional move that will be accompanied by rising volatility. Many factors could trigger this type of movement: bearish news about, for example, poor earnings, lawsuits, and scandals; technical conditions such as bearish breakouts from consolidation or continuation patterns; or simply a strong bearish trend.

STRATEGY COMPOSITION

Call Backspread

The call backspread (**Figure 8.1**) is a bullish position consisting of the purchase of multiple out-of-the-money call options financed by the sale of an at-the-money or nearer-the-money call of the same expiration cycle. This structure gives the position leverage to the upside as it is net long calls.

Components:	Short 1 June 100 call at \$3.80 Long 2 June 105 calls at \$2.15 = June 100/105 call backspread at \$0.50 (debit)
Maximum Profit:	Unlimited to the upside, above the breakeven (above \$110.50)
Maximum Loss:	$(K_2 - K_1) -$ credit, or $+$ debit (\$105.00 $-$ \$100.00 $+$ \$0.50 = \$5.50)
Breakeven:	[(Number of long calls $\times$ long call breakeven) $-$ (number of short calls $\times$ short call breakeven)] / (number of long calls $-$ number of short calls) [(2 $\times$ \$107.15) $-$ (1 $\times$ \$103.80)] / (2 $-$ 1) = \$110.50

Figures 8.2 and **8.3** illustrate the structure of some basic call backspreads.

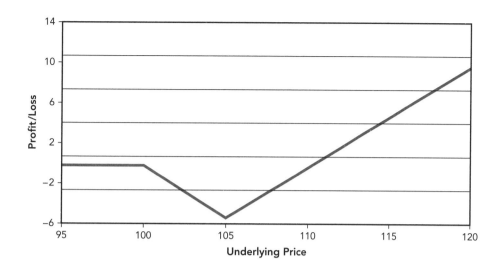

Figure 8.1 Call Backspread P&L Diagram

Calls	Strike	Puts
−1	100	
+2	105	

Figure 8.2 100/105 1-to-2 Call Backspread

Calls	Strike	Puts
−1	100	
+3	105	

Figure 8.3 100/105 1-to-3 Call Backspread

Put Backspread

The put backspread (**Figure 8.4**) is a bearish position consisting of the purchase of multiple out-of-the-money put options financed by the sale of an at-the-money or nearer-the-money put of the same expiration cycle. This structure gives the position leverage to the downside as it is net long puts.

Components: Long 2 Jan. 70 puts at $0.50
                   Short 1 Jan. 80 put at $1.50
                   = 70/80 put backspread at $0.50 (credit)

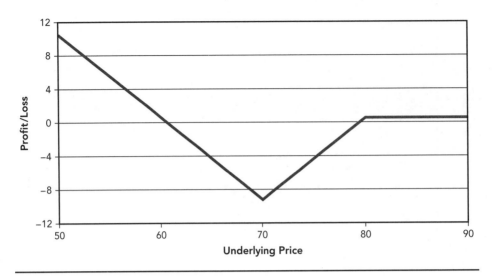

Figure 8.4 P&L Diagram

Maximum Profit: On the upside, limited to the credit received, if done for a credit ($1.50 − $1.00 = $0.50)
On the downside, anywhere below the break-even point ($59.50) down to zero

Maximum Loss: $K_2 − K_1$ − credit (if established for a credit)
($80.00 − $70.00 − $0.50 = $9.50)
$K_2 − K_1$ + debit (if established for a debit)

Breakeven: [(Number of long puts × long put breakeven) − (number of short puts × short put breakeven)]/(number of long calls − number of short calls)
[(2 × $69.50) − (1 × $78.50)]/(2 − 1) = $60.50

Figures 8.5 and **8.6** illustrate the structure of some basic put backspreads.

Calls	Strike	Puts
	70	+2
	80	−1

Figure 8.5 70/80 1-to-2 Put Backspread

Calls	Strike	Puts
	100	+3
	105	−1

Figure 8.6 100/105 1-to-3 Put Backspread

THE GREEKS OF BACKSPREADS

Like ratio spreads, backspreads are complex positions in terms of the Greeks. The existence of a long option position at one strike and a short option position at another strike makes the combined position very sensitive to changes in the underlying price, implied volatility, and time until expiration. We will examine the Greeks of basic 1-to-2 call and put backspreads.

The 1-to-2 Call Backspread

• Delta

The delta of a call backspread is dependent on the location of the underlying versus the strike, time to expiration, and implied volatility. Depending on those three factors, the delta can be long, neutral, or short at any particular underlying price. The delta of a complex position such as a backspread can be difficult to visualize without looking at graphs, but a good method for visualizing how the delta of a complex position responds to changing market conditions is to think of the delta of an option as the odds that the option will finish in-the-money. As options move into the money, their deltas increase (in absolute terms), so a position that is *net long units* (meaning there are more long options than short options) will generate an increasingly long delta on a large, upside underlying price move or an increasingly short delta on a large, downside underlying price move.

The delta of a call backspread is the sum of the position-adjusted deltas of its component options. For example, the delta of the 100/105 1-to-2 call backspread would be calculated as follows:

$$100 \text{ strike call delta} = 0.50$$

$$105 \text{ strike call delta} = 0.25$$

$$1\text{-to-2 call backspread delta} = (0.50 \times -1) + (0.25 \times 2) \text{ or } 0.00$$

The delta of the same spread with greater time until expiration or higher implied volatility might look something like this:

$$100 \text{ strike call delta} = 0.50$$

$$105 \text{ strike call delta} = 0.30$$

$$1\text{-to-2 call backspread delta} = (0.50 \times -1) + (0.30 \times 2) \text{ or } +0.10$$

The delta of the same spread with less time until expiration or lower implied volatility might look something like this:

$$100 \text{ strike call delta} = 0.50$$

$$105 \text{ strike call delta} = 0.10$$

$$1\text{-to-2 call backspread delta} = (0.50 \times -1) + (0.10 \times 2) \text{ or } -0.30$$

The preceding examples illustrate how the passage of time or declining implied volatility can work against the backspread. A position that is meant to take advantage of a strong bullish move above 105.00, such as the 100/105 1-to-2 call backspread, actually can generate a negative delta if the underlying is at or between the two strikes and enough time passes, or implied volatility declines. **Figure 8.7** illustrates the relationship of the delta of a call backspread to the time until expiration.

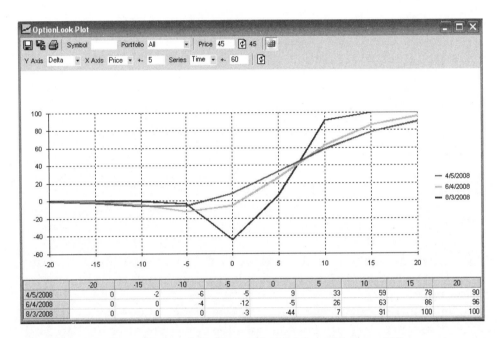

Figure 8.7   Call Backspread Delta vs. Underlying Price and Time
to Expiration: XYZ August 45/50 1-to-2 Call Backspread
Source: LiquidPoint, LLC

As Figure 8.7 shows, movement in the underlying price to the upside generally results in a rising delta as the two long calls at the higher strike outperform the one short call at the lower strike. If the underlying price moves to the downside, below the lower strike, the delta of the position will collapse toward zero. However, as time passes, the delta of the long out-of-the money call options begins to decrease faster than that of the short at- or near-the-money option. This causes the delta of the backspread to actually become negative in-between the strikes (see the August 3, 2008, data series in Figure 8.7). This is the danger zone for the backspread, and this is why timing is so important for the backspreader. If the trader is forecasting a large directional move and is trading it with a backspread, being off in the timing department can result in pain—even if he or she is correct about the ultimate direction and magnitude of the move. This same effect, but as a result of declining implied volatility, is shown in **Figure 8.8**. Notice the similarity in Figures 8.7 and 8.8 and recall that, as always, the effect of declining implied volatility on option positions mimics the effect of the passage of time.

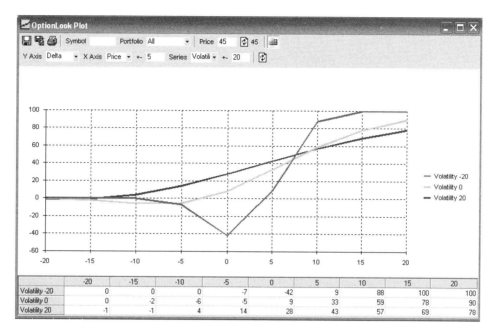

Figure 8.8 Call Backspread Delta vs. Underlying Price and Implied
Volatility: XYZ August 45/50 1-to-2 Call Backspread
Source: LiquidPoint, LLC

- **Gamma**

The gamma of a call backspread is the sum of the position-adjusted
gammas of its component options. For example, the gamma of the 100/105
1-to-2 call backspread is calculated as follows:

$$100 \text{ strike call gamma} = 0.08$$

$$105 \text{ strike call gamma} = 0.05$$

$$1\text{-to-2 call backspread gamma} = (0.08 \times -1) + (0.05 \times 2) \text{ or } 0.02$$

The gamma of the call backspread is highly sensitive to the location of
the underlying relative to the strikes. As with any spread made up of both
long and short options, the position will take on the gamma characteristics
of the underlying option position at the nearest strikes. Gamma quickly
becomes more positive as the underlying price rises toward the strike of
the long options or as implied volatility rises. **Figure 8.9** illustrates the relationship of the gamma of a call backspread to the underlying price and
time to expiration.

Figure 8.9 shows how the gamma of the call backspread depends on the
location of the underlying and time until expiration. Backspreads are structured to be generally long gamma, as can be seen with the April 6, 2008,
and the June 4, 2008, data series in the figure. Recall the relationship of the
gamma of an option to the time until expiration. As expiration approaches,
the gamma of an at-the-money option increases while the gamma of an in-
or out-of-the-money option decreases. For the backspread, this means that
when the expiration is approaching and the underlying price is closest to
the short option at the lower strike, the spread will have a negative gamma;

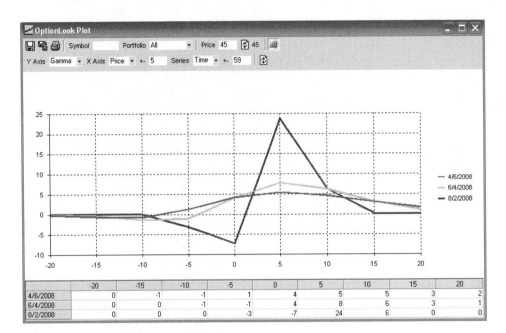

Figure 8.9 Call Backspread Gamma vs. Underlying Price and Time
to Expiration: XYZ August 45/50 1-to-2 Call Backspread
Source: LiquidPoint, LLC

when the underlying price is closer to the long options at the upper strike, the spread will have a large positive gamma. This can be seen with the August 2, 2008, data series in the same figure. The effect of the passage of time on the gamma of the call backspread is again mimicked by the effect of falling implied volatility, as illustrated by **Figure 8.10**.

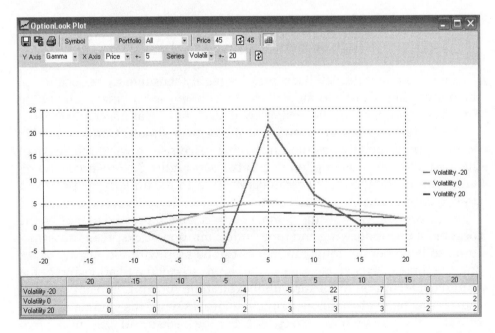

Figure 8.10 Call Backspread Gamma vs. Underlying Price and Implied
Volatility: XYZ August 45/50 1-to-2 Call Backspread
Source: LiquidPoint, LLC

• **Vega**

The vega of a call backspread is the sum of the position-adjusted vegas of its component options. For example, the vega of the 100/105 1-to-2 call backspread is calculated as follows:

$$100 \text{ strike call vega} = 0.15$$

$$105 \text{ strike call vega} = 0.10$$

$$1\text{-to-2 call backspread vega} = (0.15 \times -1) + (0.10 \times 2) \text{ or } 0.05$$

This means that for every 1 percent change in implied volatility, the price of the call backspread would change by approximately 0.05. Because the call backspread is generally long vega, the value of the spread will rise when implied volatility rises and fall when implied volatility falls. **Figure 8.11** illustrates the vega of the call backspread.

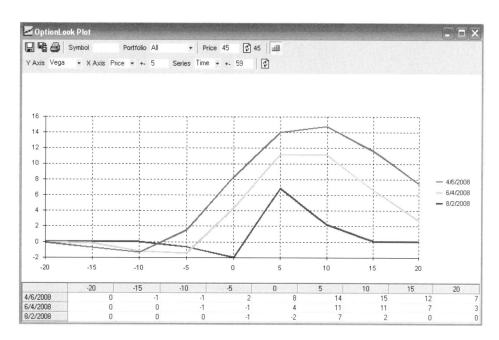

Figure 8.11: Call Backspread Vega vs. Underlying Price and Time
to Expiration: XYZ August 45/50 1-to-2 Call Backspread
Source: LiquidPoint, LLC

The vega of the spread is generally positive and becomes increasingly so when the underlying price is near the strike of the long calls. The exception can be when the underlying price is at or below the lower strike short call; then the vega of the call backspread could become negative. This is especially true as expiration approaches, as can be seen in the August 2, 2008, series in Figure 8.11.

Recall from Chapter 1 that vega increases with the time to expiration so that, all things being equal, the vega of an option with a greater amount of time left until expiration will be larger than that of an option with a lesser amount of time left until expiration. With regard to the call backspread, this means that the overall amount of positive vega generated by the position will decline as expiration approaches.

• Theta

The theta of the call backspread is the sum of the position-adjusted thetas of its component options. For example, the theta of the 100/105 1-to-2 call backspread would be calculated as follows:

$$100 \text{ strike call theta} = -0.06$$

$$105 \text{ strike call theta} = -0.04$$

$$1\text{-to-2 call backspread theta} = (-0.06 \times -1) + (-0.04 \times 2) \text{ or } -0.02$$

This means that the value of the call backspread would decrease by approximately 0.02 per calendar day (all else being equal). Because a call backspread generally has negative theta, the value of the spread will fall as time passes and option values decay. **Figure 8.12** illustrates the theta of a call backspread.

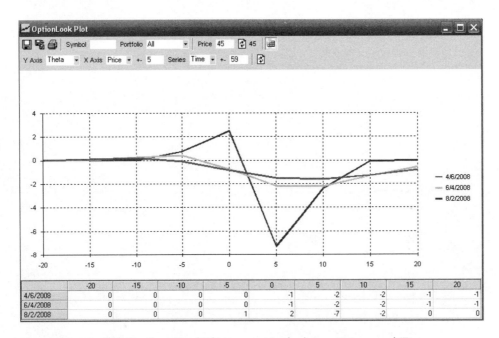

Figure 8.12 Call Backspread Theta vs. Underlying Price and Time
to Expiration: XYZ August 45/50 1-to-2 Call Backspread
Source: LiquidPoint, LLC

The preceding figure illustrates how the sensitivity of the position depends on the location of the underlying price and the time until expiration. The call backspread generally will have a negative theta because it is overall long options. When the underlying price is near the strike of the long options, the theta will be more negative; when the underlying price is nearer the strike of the short option, the theta will be less negative. Recall that the theta of an at-the-money option increases as the time to expiration decreases and the theta of an out-of-the-money option decreases as the time to expiration decreases, so the swings of negative to positive theta that occur as the underlying price shifts location between the long and short strikes becomes more dramatic. The theta of a call backspread could even become positive when the underlying is near the strike of the short option and expiration is approaching, as can be seen in the August 2, 2008, series in Figure 8.12.

The 1-to-2 Put Backspread

• Delta

As with the call backspread, the delta of a put backspread is dependent on the location of the underlying versus the strike, time to expiration, and implied volatility. The delta can be short, neutral, or long at any particular underlying price depending on those market factors. The delta of a put backspread is the sum of the position-adjusted deltas of its component options. For example the delta of the 100/105 1-to-2 put backspread would be calculated as follows:

$$100 \text{ strike put delta} = -0.25$$

$$105 \text{ strike put delta} = -0.50$$

$$1\text{-to-}2 \text{ put backspread delta} = (-0.25 \times 2) + (-0.50 \times -1) \text{ or } 0.00$$

The delta of the same spread with greater time until expiration or higher implied volatility might look something like this:

$$100 \text{ strike put delta} = -0.30$$

$$105 \text{ strike put delta} = -0.50$$

$$1\text{-to-}2 \text{ put backspread delta} = (-0.30 \times 2) + (-0.50 \times -1) \text{ or } -0.10$$

The delta of the same spread with less time until expiration or lower implied volatility might look something like this:

$$100 \text{ strike put delta} = -0.15$$

$$105 \text{ strike put delta} = -0.50$$

$$1\text{-to-}2 \text{ put backspread delta} = (-0.15 \times 2) + (-0.50 \times -1) \text{ or } +0.20$$

Figure 8.13 illustrates the relationship of the delta of a put backspread to the time until expiration.

As can be seen in Figure 8.13, the delta of the put backspread generally is negative, and becomes increasingly so with downward movement of the underlying price. However, as time passes (or implied volatility falls), the delta of the long out-of-the money options decreases (in absolute terms) faster than that of the short at- or near-the-money option. This causes the delta of the spread to become increasingly positive over time if the underlying price stays near the short strike or in between the strikes, as

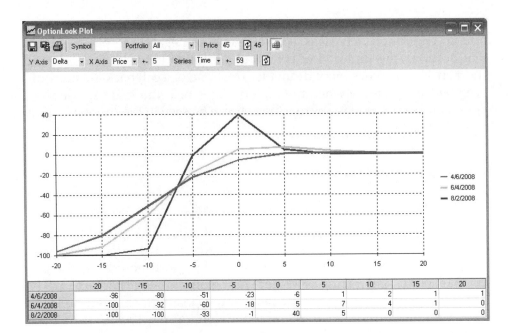

Figure 8.13 Put Backspread Delta vs. Underlying Price and Time
to Expiration: XYZ August 40/45 1-to-2 Put Backspread
Source: LiquidPoint, LLC

the August 2, 2008, data series in Figure 8.13 shows. This is the worst-case scenario for a put backspread. If the underlying falls far enough, the delta of the position will still flip to negative, but some pain will have to have been endured. The same effect, but as a result of declining implied volatility, can be observed in **Figure 8.14**.

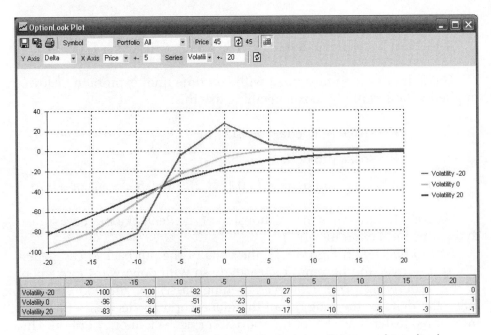

Figure 8.14 Put Backspread Delta vs. Underlying Price and Implied
Volatility: XYZ August 40/45 1-to-2 Put Backspread
Source: LiquidPoint, LLC

- **Gamma**

The gamma of a put backspread is the sum of the position-adjusted gammas of its component options. For example, the gamma of the 100/105 1-to-2 put backspread is calculated as follows:

$$100 \text{ strike put gamma} = 0.06$$

$$105 \text{ strike put gamma} = 0.10$$

$$1\text{-to-2 put backspread gamma} = (0.06 \times 2) + (0.10 \times -1) \text{ or } 0.02$$

As with the call backspread, the put backspread is highly sensitive to the location of the underlying relative to the strikes, and the position will take on the gamma characteristics of the underlying option position at the strikes nearest the underlying price. The gamma of a put backspread generally is positive because it is net long of options, and the gamma becomes increasingly positive as the underlying price falls toward the strike of the long options, or as implied volatility rises. **Figure 8.15** illustrates the relationship of the gamma of a put backspread to the underlying price and time to expiration.

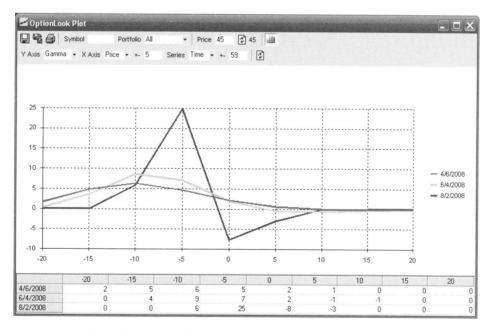

Figure 8.15 Put Backspread Gamma vs. Underlying Price and Time to Expiration: XYZ August 40/45 1-to-2 Put Backspread
Source: LiquidPoint, LLC

The preceding figure shows how the gamma of the put backspread depends on the location of the underlying and time until expiration. Recall that backspreads are structured to be generally long gamma, as can be seen in the April 6, 2008, and the June 4, 2008, data series in the figure. However, as expiration approaches, the gamma of an at-the-money option increases while the gamma of in- and out-of-the-money options decreases (in absolute terms). For the put backspread, this means that when expiration is approaching and the underlying price is closest to the short option at the upper strike, the spread will have a negative gamma; when the underlying price is closer to the long options at the lower strike, the spread will have a large positive gamma. This can be seen in the August 2, 2008, data series in Figure 8.15. The effect of the passage of time on the gamma of the put backspread is mimicked by the effect of falling implied volatility, as shown in **Figure 8.16**.

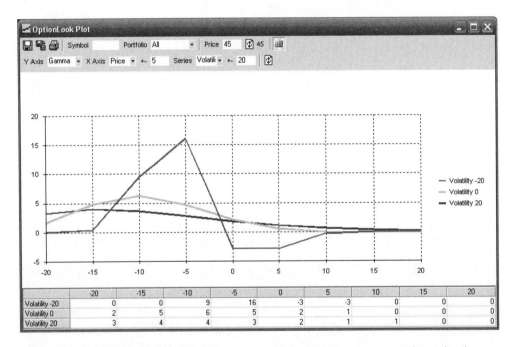

	-20	-15	-10	-5	0	5	10	15	20
Volatility -20	0	0	9	16	-3	-3	0	0	0
Volatility 0	2	5	6	5	2	1	0	0	0
Volatility 20	3	4	4	3	2	1	1	0	0

Figure 8.16 Put Backspread Gamma vs. Underlying Price and Implied Volatility: XYZ August 40/45 1-to-2 Put Backspread
Source: LiquidPoint, LLC

- **Vega**

The vega of a put backspread is the sum of the position-adjusted vegas of its component options. For example, the vega of the 100/105 1-to-2 put backspread is calculated as follows:

$$100 \text{ strike put vega} = 0.10$$

$$105 \text{ strike put vega} = 0.15$$

$$1\text{-to-2 put backspread vega} = (0.10 \times 2) + (0.15 \times -1) \text{ or } 0.05$$

This means that for every 1 percent change in implied volatility, the price of the put backspread would change by approximately 0.05. Because the put backspread generally is long vega, the value of the spread will rise when implied volatility rises and fall when implied volatility falls. **Figure 8.17** illustrates the vega of the put backspread.

The vega of the spread is generally positive and becomes increasingly so when the underlying price is near the strike of the long puts. The exception

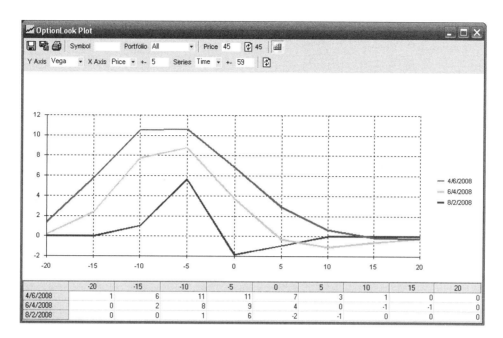

Figure 8.17 Put Backspread Vega vs. Underlying Price and Time
to Expiration: XYZ August 40/45 1-to-2 Put Backspread
Source: LiquidPoint, LLC

can occur when the underlying price is at or above the upper strike short put; then the vega of the put backspread could become negative. This is especially true as expiration approaches, as can be seen in the August 2, 2008, series in Figure 8.17.

Recall from Chapter 1 that vega increases with the time to expiration, so that, all things being equal, the vega of an option with a greater amount of time left until expiration will be larger than that of an option with a lesser amount of time left until expiration. With regard to the put backspread, this means that the overall amount of positive vega generated by the position will decline as expiration approaches.

- **Theta**

The theta of the put backspread is the sum of the position-adjusted thetas of its component options. For example, the theta of the 100/105 1-to-2 put backspread would be calculated as follows:

$$100 \text{ strike put theta} = -0.04$$

$$105 \text{ strike put theta} = -0.06$$

$$1\text{-to-2 put backspread theta} = (-0.04 \times 2) + (-0.06 \times -1) \text{ or } -0.02$$

This means that the value of the put backspread would decrease by approximately 0.02 per calendar day (all else being equal). Because a put backspread generally has negative theta, the value of the spread will fall as time passes and option values decay. **Figure 8.18** illustrates the theta of a put backspread.

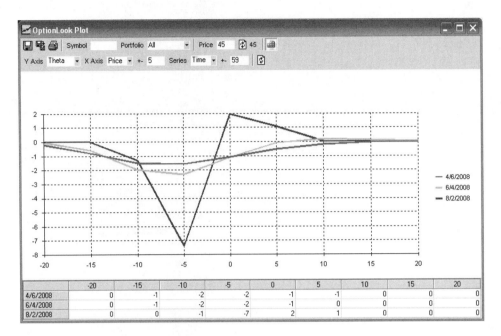

Figure 8.18 Put Backspread Theta vs. Underlying Price and Time to Expiration: XYZ August 40/45 1-to-2 Put Backspread
Source: LiquidPoint, LLC

The put backspread generally will have a negative theta because it is overall long options. When the underlying price is near the strike of the long puts, the theta will be more negative; when the underlying price is nearer the strike of the short put, the theta will be less negative. Recall that the theta of an at-the-money option increases as the time to expiration decreases, and the theta of an out-of-the-money option decreases as the time to expiration decreases, so the swings of negative to positive theta that occur as the underlying price shifts location between the long and short strikes become more dramatic. The theta of a put backspread with the underlying near the strike of the short put and expiration approaching could even become positive, as can be seen in the August 2, 2008, data series in Figure 8.18.

INVESTMENT OBJECTIVES

The backspread has an asymmetrical risk-reward profile that is exactly opposite that of the ratio spread. Backspreads have substantial profit potential on a large move in the direction of the long options strike (to zero for puts), have risk that is limited to the initial cost of the spread on a large move through the short option strike, and, in-between the strikes, have risk that is equal to the strike differential plus or minus the initial spread cost (if any). This makes the backspread a potentially powerful position for playing low-probability/high-reward scenarios and breakout scenarios, or for capturing strong directional trends. Because backspreads are net long options, they generally will have a positive vega, so steady-to-rising implied volatility is desirable. Backspreads also have negative theta, so the forecast move should take place in a short time frame.

When considering a backspread, traders should look for situations that favor the above scenarios. Some typical market conditions that might lead to high-magnitude, high-velocity movement in a short time frame with the possibility of rising implied volatility include the following:

- Breakouts
    — Consolidation patterns
    — Continuation patterns
    — Through resistance or support
- News
    — General market-moving news, good or bad
    — Company-specific news, good or bad
- Special situations
    — "Back door" if-then directional plays

Breakouts

Often the overall market or a specific underlying name will go through periods of price consolidation. These may be technical in nature (for example, the market is just taking a "breather") or occur during seasonal slow periods (for example, after earnings periods or holidays), or there might just be an overall lack of interest in a particular name or sector. When this happens, the price usually will consolidate and meander, waiting for some market-moving event to trigger the next phase of movement. Often these periods are accompanied by falling implied volatility due to lack of movement and lack of interest. Usually this phase ends and the underlying price "breaks out" of its pattern and begins moving again. If one is forecasting a directional breakout from a low volatility situation, a backspread can be a good way to capture profits. **Figures 8.19**, **8.20**, and **8.21** are examples of breakouts.

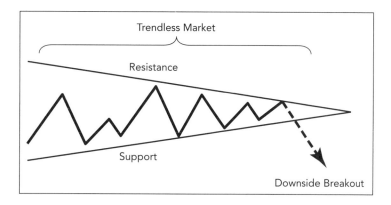

Figure 8.19 Consolidation Period Followed by Breakout

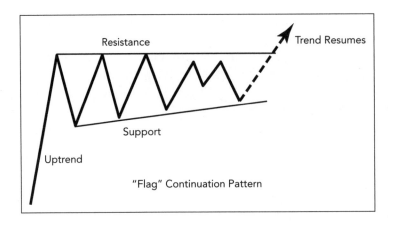

Figure 8.20 Continuation Pattern and Resumption of Trend

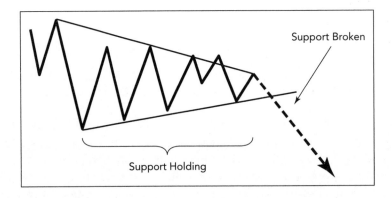

Figure 8.21 Breakdown Through Support

News

Economic news (for example, earnings, new products, hirings, and firings), whether affecting certain companies or sectors, or general economic news (for example, government reports, Federal Reserve Board actions, political developments, and events in other markets) also can trigger large directional moves. If the trader can properly interpret the news and forecast the direction in which the market or underlying is going to move, a backspread may be used to capture profits. One caveat, however, is that scheduled, highly anticipated releases of reports on the economy, earnings announcements, and so on, are almost always preceded by rising implied volatility, making structures that are net long options, such as backspreads, more expensive. Also, after the news is released, implied volatility usually sells off. Obviously, this is not good for a backspread, as it is generally long vega. However, if the magnitude of the directional move is large enough through the long strike, the gain in intrinsic value of the position will be greater than the losses due to implied volatility declines. In this situation the decision of whether or not to use a backspread depends on the trader's price forecast.

Special Situations

Many times the market or specific underlying issues will move directionally and sentiment will begin to become overly optimistic or pessimistic in the direction of the trend—overly bullish in an uptrend, overly bearish in a downtrend—and traders can begin to sense that market participants are getting overloaded in one direction or another. Bullish consensus figures, VIX readings, put/call ratios, media chatter, and so on can be good indicators that market participants are getting either too optimistic or pessimistic. In cases like this some "what-if" back door plays using backspreads could be employed. An example of the thought process behind a "what-if" back door play is the following:

> *Everybody and their brother is long this stock, and they keep pushing it higher. The talking heads babble about it all day long, and of course the analysts all love it. If this thing ever starts to move lower, the exit door is going to get awfully small. . . .*

This can be a great situation for some back door put backspreads, sprinkled like landmines in price zones that, if reached, would almost certainly be experiencing volatile conditions. If the market keeps moving in the current direction, no harm, but if it doesn't. . . .

Figure 8.22 depicts a euphoric, high-volume rally, which, if terminated, could result in some ugly downside price action. The trader anticipates that if the support lines are broken, the price will accelerate lower, and he places a back door put backspread just below each support level.

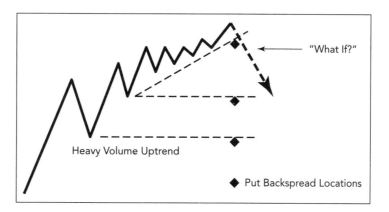

Figure 8.22 Back Door Backspreads

STRATEGY SELECTION

Once the trader determines that conditions favorable to a backspread exist, she needs to evaluate the following factors:

- Direction of trend
- Breakout and/or price acceleration levels
- Timing

Direction of Trend

Obviously, direction is important because backspreads have a directional bias. Call backspreads are used to trade a market with a bullish bias, and put backspreads are used to trade a market with a bearish bias. The market's trend bias must be incorporated into strike selection.

Breakout and/or Price Acceleration Levels

Breakout and/or price acceleration levels need to be defined. They identify areas where price movement is likely to accelerate, which is important to know for strike selection.

Timing

As we have learned, the passage of time and/or declining implied volatility is harmful to the backspread. One's forecast of market timing is important for two reasons: It helps in deciding whether to use a backspread, and if a backspread is to be used, what expiration cycle to select.

- **Strike Selection**

Breakout and price acceleration zones (usually below known support and above known resistance levels) are needed for strike selection. The backspread needs to be structured so that the long strike is positioned to capture price movement through the projected knowledge of breakout or acceleration zone, while the short strike is backstopped by support or resistance. As we have seen, what the backspreader needs to avoid is the underlying's price meandering near the short strike or in between the strikes. The backspreader would like the underlying price either to accelerate sharply through the long strike of the backspread or to back off. **Figure 8.23** illustrates the structuring of a call backspread.

In Figure 8.23, the trader's forecast is that penetration of resistance at 47.50 is likely to result in a high-velocity, high-magnitude price move toward 60.00. The call backspread is structured with the short call at the resistance level and long calls in the forecast price acceleration zone. A 47.50/50.00 1-to-2 call backspread or a 47.50/52.50 1-to-4 call backspread might be good choices in this situation.

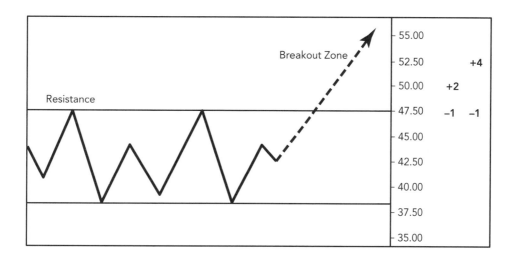

Figure 8.23 Call Backspread Strike Selection Possibilities

- **Expiry Selection**

The forecast breakout time is needed for selection of the expiration month. As we have seen, the passage of time is the enemy of the backspread, and being off in one's timing can be painful. This can be avoided somewhat by purchasing backspreads of longer-dated expirations, but longer-dated backspreads are more expensive than shorter-dated backspreads because they carry more extrinsic value. So if one is confident of one's timing forecast, the expiration date that corresponds to that forecast should be used; however, if timing might be an issue, one should "buy extra time" by purchasing a backspread in a further expiration that will give one a reasonable margin of error in timing.

TRADE MANAGEMENT

Backspreads, being net long options (there are more long options in the position than short options), are limited risk positions and therefore offer the trader a certain level of comfort. However, limited risk positions still have risk (sometimes significant), and it is important not to get sloppy or lazy with a backspread, because they are best suited for specific situations. As market conditions change they need to be reevaluated to determine whether a backspread is still the optimal strategy or adjustments may need to be made.

- Is the backspread appropriate?
- What is the most efficient way to take profits?
- How should the trader manage risk or take losses?

Is the Backspread Appropriate?

The forecast of a high-magnitude directional move does not necessarily indicate a backspread. Buying a backspread involves the overall purchase of options (one is buying more than selling) and, therefore, the purchase of volatility. If implied volatility levels are already high, this type of strategy might not be advisable. In addition, as we have seen, accuracy of timing is an issue. Backspreads have negative time decay. If one's timing forecast is a bit hazy or if the timing is unknown, a strategy that is not so sensitive to the passage of time might be more appropriate.

What Is the Most Efficient Way to Take Profits?

When one correctly forecasts a high-velocity move and has a backspread in place, profits might appear quickly, and they need to be managed or they might disappear just as quickly. Here are some important tips:

- **Take Partial Profits by Rolling**

Recall from Chapter 4 the procedures for "rolling" a long call or a long put position along with market movement and systematically extracting profit from the position while limiting risk and maintaining market exposure. As long as one's forecast continues to call for high-magnitude directional movement in the underlying, one can use this method. The following are several examples of "rolling the trade."

Example 1

An investor has on a 100/105 1-to-2 call backspread and the underlying has exploded up to 110.00. He has substantial profit in the position but believes the move is far from over. He would like to take some money off the table but stay in the position for a chance to capture additional upside movement. He decides to roll his long 105.00 calls up to the 110.00 strike. **Figure 8.24** illustrates this procedure.

Calls		Strike	Puts
−1		100	
+2	−2	105	
	+2	110	

Figure 8.24 Rolling Long Calls in the 100/105 1-to-2 Call Backspread

The result in the preceding figure is a 100/110 1-to-2 call backspread. The trader sold the 105/110 call vertical spread, extracted some profit, and rolled the long call options up to 110.00, which is now the current underlying price, and has left himself in position for further upside price appreciation.

Example 2

The investor has a 95/100 1-to-2 put backspread and, as forecast, the underlying has broken down through 95.00, which was an important support level. He has a good profit in the position, and now it looks as though the stock is really going to accelerate downward. He would like to "gear up" his position and raise his leverage by expanding the ratio but without investing additional money. He decides to execute a 87.50/95 1-to-4 put backspread for a credit, rolling his long puts down to 87.50 and doubling his exposure, while still extracting money from the trade. **Figures 8.25, 8.26**, and **8.27** illustrate this procedure.

Calls	Strike	Puts
	95	+2
	100	−1

Figure 8.25 Existing 95/100 1-to-2 Put Backspread

Calls	Strike	Puts	
	87.50	+4	
	90		
	95	+2	−2
	100	−1	

Figure 8.26 Rolling Long 95 Puts Down to the 87.50 Strike and Doubling the Ratio

Calls	Strike	Puts
	87.50	+4
	90	
	95	
	100	−1

Figure 8.27 Resulting 87.50/100 1-to-4 Put Backspread

The result in Figure 8.27 is a 87.50/100 1-to-4 put backspread. The investor executed the 87.50/95 1-to-4 put backspread for a credit, rolling his long puts down to the 87.50 strike and doubling the ratio, which positioned him for a potential explosive move to the downside.

• Watch Market Action

In addition to taking partial profits, don't stay too long at the party. If the underlying price movement begins to slow or runs into old support or resistance levels, or if implied volatility begins to drop, it may be a sign that the move or at least the current phase of the move is coming to an end. If the movement type begins to transition from high-magnitude, high-velocity to something else, one should get out of the backspread and switch to a different strategy.

How Should the Trader Manage Risk or Take Losses?

As always, the trader needs a game plan for taking profits, and his forecast should include price and timing targets. If the targets are met, he needs to evaluate the new situation and decide whether to continue with the trade by rolling, as in the previous examples, or to exit and take profits. The forecast should also include price and timing levels that will indicate when the trader is wrong and should exit the trade. With these types of trades, it is important to have both price and time stop-loss levels. If either is hit, the trader should exit the trade. For example, suppose his forecast was for an upside breakout out of a consolidation pattern this week. If by the close of business Friday the move has not taken place, he should exit the trade.

This type of discipline is necessary for managing backspreads because it is easy to fall in love with the potentially unlimited profit potential of a backspread and get into the mindset of "tomorrow, definitely tomorrow it's going to happen." Meanwhile, the time decay piles up, and as we have seen, there is a chance that even if the anticipated directional move were ultimately to occur it might actually work against the position. The trader must use price and time stop-losses. If his initial forecast is off in either department, he must exit the trade.

CHAPTER 8 EXERCISE

1. A call backspread could be employed when one is expecting a major upward move in the underlying, which is accompanied by a (rising) (falling) volatility.

2. The delta of the call backspread is dependent on the location of the underlying relative to the strike, the time to expiration, and the _____.

3. Backspreads have unlimited profit potential on a large move in the direction of which: the long or the short options strike?

4. Calculate the gamma of the following 90/95 put 1-to-2 backspread:

   90 strike put gamma = 0.07
   95 strike put gamma = 0.10

5. Is the vega of the backspread typically positive or negative, and does it become more so when the underlying price is near the strike of the long or the short options?

6. If support lines are broken, and one expects the price of the underlying to continue to fall, a (call) (put) backspread could be placed just (above) (below) each support level.

7. A backspread could be used to take advantage of a directional breakout from a (low-) (high-)volatility market situation.

8. The vega of the call backspread could become negative in some situations. True or false?

9. A call backspread can generate negative delta if the underlying is at or between the two strikes and implied volatility rises. True or false?

10. Is the passage of time helpful or harmful to the backspread?

Chapter 8 Exercise Answer Key

1. Rising
2. Implied volatility
3. Long
4. Put backspread gamma = $(0.07 \times 2) + (0.10 \times -1) = 0.04$
5. Positive, long
6. Put, below
7. Low
8. True, if the underlying price is at or below the lower strike short call.
9. False. Implied volatility levels would need to fall.
10. Harmful

CHAPTER 8 QUIZ

1. As time passes, the delta of the long out-of-the-money call options will (increase) (decrease) faster than that of the short at-the-money option.

2. Steady to rising _____ _____ is an optimal situation for a backspread.

3. In the case of a call backspread, if the expectation is that the penetration of resistance is 37 and has a likelihood of reaching 50, a 37/40 call backspread might be a good choice. True or false?

4. You have on the 1-to-2 110/115 call backspread. The underlying has rallied up to 120 level. You want to lock in some of the profits, but you think the stock will still experience price movement on the upside. You sell two of the 115/120 call vertical spreads rolling your long calls to the 120 strike. This will result in giving you more room on the upside for price appreciation. True or false?

5. Does the gamma quickly become more positive or negative as the underlying price rises toward the strike of the long options in the case of the call backspread?

6. Name the reason you need to define breakout and/or price acceleration levels.

7. An investor has on the 100/105 1-to-2 put backspread. The stock has penetrated 100, and he thinks that the stock is going to continue downward even further. Therefore, he wants to expand his ratio, without an outlay of additional capital. He could put on the 95/100 2-to-4 put backspread for even money, rolling the long puts down to 100. True or false?

8. As expiration nears, does the gamma of an at-the-money option increase or decrease, and does the gamma of an in- or out-of-the-money option increase or decrease?

9. The theta of a call backspread could become positive with the underlying nearing the strike of the short option and the expiration approaching. True or false?

10. If a put backspread had a theta of –0.05, would this mean that the value of the spread would increase or decrease by approximately 0.05 each calendar day?

Chapter 8 Quiz Answer Key

1. Decrease
2. Implied volatility
3. True
4. True
5. Positive
6. To help determine strike selection
7. True
8. Increase, decrease
9. True
10. Decrease

Appendix

FINAL EXAM PART I

For Questions 1–6 assume the market has sold off sharply over the last few trading days.

1. Would an investor expect implied volatilities to be lower or higher than they were before the sell-off?

2. If an investor was expecting a bounce from the current levels, which of the following might he consider employing?

   a. Bull call spread
   b. Call ratio spread
   c. Butterfly spread
   d. Condor spread
   e. All of the above

3. An investor was expecting the sell-off to continue, he might consider employing a long put, a bear spread, a call backspread, or a short call. True or false?

4. If the market did bounce, one would expect implied volatilities to be even higher. True or false?

5. Would one expect a twelve-day implied volatility to be higher or lower than a forty-day implied volatility?

6. If an investor had a bear spread in place before the sell-off, and his view was that the market was going to go sideways and volatility decline, he could add a bull spread to create a long butterfly or condor, or sell another put to create a put ratio spread. True or false?

For Questions 7–12, assume the market has rallied slowly into resistance over the last week and that implied volatilities are now low.

7. An investor has just received a sell signal in XYZ stock, and his indicators are signaling a large decline within the next twenty-four

to forty-eight hours. Which of the following strategies could be employed to take advantage of low volatility?

   a. Put backspread
   b. Long put
   c. Both *a* and *b*
   d. Call backspread

8. An investor implements a position based on the assumptions in Question 7. Three days pass and nothing happens, so he should consider exiting the trade. True or false?

9. DEF has rallied right to a key resistance level. An investor believes that DEF will either sell off sharply or break out to the upside from this level. Should he buy or sell a straddle or strangle?

10. XYZ's implied volatility is near historical lows. An investor believes it is about to break out sharply to the upside. Should he consider employing the put backspread or the call backspread to take advantage of the low volatility?

11. Assume an investor's position prior to a current rally was a call ratio spread. The market has drifted upward and implied volatilities have dropped, resulting in a profitable position. He believes the market will move sideways and implied volatilities will go lower. However, the unlimited-risk aspect of the ratio spread makes him nervous. What adjustment could he make to the position to allow him to capture his new market view while limiting his upside risk?

12. The term structure of implied volatility shows a sharp upward slope. If an investor thought the market was about to make a sharp move in either direction, would he consider a long at-the-money calendar spread or a short at-the-money calendar spread to take advantage of this?

For Questions 13–16 assume the market has been going sideways for some time and that implied volatilities are very low.

13. An investor buys the calendar spread, and the strike price is exactly the same as the underlying price. Specify the direction of the spread's delta, gamma, theta, and vega.

   Delta: positive, negative, or neutral

   Gamma: positive, negative, or neutral

   Theta: positive, negative, or neutral

   Vega: positive, negative, or neutral

14. An investor decides that the long calendar spread is the proper trade, but that the market has a slightly positive bias. Where should

he locate his long calendar spread relative to the current underlying price?

a. Above the current price
b. At the current price
c. Below the current price

15. An investor correctly predicted that the market would go sideways and implied volatility would collapse, and he has a profitable at-the-money long iron butterfly. Now he believes volatility has gotten too low, and he would like to have a long volatility position. If he covered the short straddle component, this would leave him with a

    _____.

16. An investor receives a sell signal indicating he can expect a sharp move down within twenty-four to forty-eight hours. He decides he wants to buy puts. What maturity level would be optimal, long-dated or short-dated?

17. An investor wants to put on a bull spread. The call spread market is $3.55–$3.65, while the put spread market is $1.35–$1.40. The box is valued at $4.95. Should he buy the call spread or sell the put spread?

18. An investor wants to initiate a bear spread. The call spread is $1.40–$1.50, while the put spread is $3.50–$3.60. The box value is $4.90. Should he sell the call spread or buy the put spread?

19. If an investor had on the long XYZ Dec. 40/45/50/55 call condor, his maximum profit would be $5.00 + the premium paid to initiate the position. True or false?

20. A covered call is a long stock and a short call. It has the same risk/reward profile as a synthetic _____.

21. Can a long jelly roll be viewed as a long or a short call time spread, and a long or a short put time spread?

For Questions 22–25 consider the following position:

Long 1 March 300/310 call vertical at $7.00

Short 1 March 320/330 call vertical at $3.50

22. What position is this?

23. Risk is limited to _____.

24. Loss begins above _____ and below _____.

25. The maximum profit is _____.

For Questions 26–28 determine whether the strategies are bullish, bearish, and/or neutral in terms of directional bias.

26. +Oct. 50 call, −Nov. 50 call (underlying at 45)

27. +95 put, −90 put

28. Short the 30/35/40 butterfly (underlying at 35)

29. The short 60/65/70 call butterfly is a combination of the _____ spread and the _____ spread.

30. If an investor buys the at-the-money time spread, and the underlying stock moves significantly in either direction, would the spread increase or decrease in value?

31. _____ is the slope of the difference between the implied volatilities of different strike prices for a given expiration.

32. Does the gamma of at-the-money options increase or decrease as expiration approaches, and does the gamma of in-the-money and out-of-the-money options increase or decrease as expiration approaches?

33. Which of the following would help a trader who is long strangles?

   a. The underlying market moves up sharply.
   b. Implied volatility begins to fall.
   c. The market moves down sharply.
   d. The underlying market trades in a small range between the strikes.

34. What are the risks when implementing the following ratio spread?

   XYZ stock is trading at $27.75

   Buy 1 Sept. 25 call at $3.75

   Sell 3 Sept. 30 calls at $1.25 each

   a. Stock stays between $25.00 and $30.00.
   b. Stock climbs over $35.00.
   c. Stock drops to $25.00.
   d. Implied volatility increases.

35. Buying a straddle is often done in anticipation of which: an increase or a decrease in implied volatility?

36. A motive for putting on a backspread is the anticipation of a

   a. Stable market
   b. Gapping market
   c. Grinding trend
   d. Sideways market

37. Where would a loss occur if an investor were selling the following butterfly?

XYZ is trading at $34.75
Sell 1 May 30 call at $5.125
Buy 2 May 35 calls at $0.75 each
Sell 1 May 40 call at $0.125

a. $37
b. $34
c. $33
d. $35

38. When an investor buys an at-the-money time spread, the position is:

a. Long vega, short gamma
b. Long gamma, short vega
c. Long vega, long gamma
d. Short vega, short gamma

39. If a long time spread widens on a down move, it could mean:

a. Implied volatility increased.
b. The delta of the spread is remaining constant.
c. Theta increased.
d. Vega decreased.

40. The value of the 40/45 call vertical is $2.75, and the value of the 45/50 call vertical is $1.875. What is the value of the 40/45/50 call butterfly?

41. If an investor bought stock at $104.00 and sold a 100 strike call against it for $5.50, what is the break-even point (assume thirty days to expiration)?

42. An investor has on the 110/120 collar. What spreads does he need to buy and to sell in order to roll the position to the next expiration cycle?

43. An investor could roll the 90/95 reverse-collar by buying the 95/100 vertical call spread. True or false?

44. An investor is long a 75/80 call spread and would like to roll it up to the 80/85 call vertical. To accomplish this roll, he should sell the 75/80/85 call butterfly. True or false?

45. Combining a long time spread with a short time spread creates a _____.

46. If an investor has the 70/75/80 iron butterfly position on, what does she need to do to convert it to a bear spread?

47. An investor has on a long butterfly position and wants additional range of coverage. He can purchase an additional butterfly and turn his position into a _____.

48. If support levels are broken and an investor anticipates that the stock is going to continue to fall, he could initiate a put backspread just below each support level. True or false?

49. A call ratio spread can be viewed as a _____ with an extra short call at the upper strike.

50. An upward sloping *term structure* refers to a situation in which long-dated implied volatilities are much lower than shorter-dated implied volatilities. True or false?

Final Exam Answer Key

1. Higher
2. e
3. A call backspread would be incorrect, as a put backspread would be a possibility.
4. False. Implied volatilities would be lower.
5. Higher
6. True
7. c
8. True
9. Buy
10. Call backspread
11. Buy a further out-of-the-money call to create a long butterfly.
12. Short at-the-money calendar spread
13. Delta: neutral
    Gamma: negative
    Theta: positive
    Vega: positive
14. Above the current price
15. Long strangle
16. Short dated
17. Sell the put spread. (If the call spread ask price + the put spread bid price is greater than the box value, sell the put spread—$3.65 + $1.35 > $4.95, so sell the put spread at $1.35.)
18. Sell the call spread. (If the call spread bid + the put spread ask is greater than the box value, sell the call spread—$1.40 + $3.60 > $4.95, so sell the call spread at $1.40.)
19. False: $5.00 − the premium paid
20. Short put
21. Long, short
22. Long condor
23. $3.50 (amount paid for the condor)
24. $326.50, $303.50
25. $6.50

26. Bearish
27. Bearish
28. Bullish or bearish
29. Vertical bull, vertical bear
30. Decrease
31. Volatility skew
32. Increase, decrease
33. a, c
34. b, d
35. Increase
36. b
37. b, d
38. a
39. a, c
40. $0.875
41. $98.50 ($104 − $5.50)
42. Buy the 110 put calendar spread; sell the 120 call calendar spread.
43. False; he needs to sell the vertical call spread.
44. True
45. Jelly roll
46. Close out the 70/75 bull put spread.
47. Long condor
48. True
49. Bull call spread
50. False. It occurs when short-dated implied volatilities are lower than longer-dated volatilities.

FINAL EXAM PART II

(Each question is worth 2 points)

Scenario 1

You have purchased 100 shares of XYZ stock at $45.50. You do not antici-
pate much movement over the next 30 days and elect to short the 47.50 call
at $1.50.

1. Explain two ways that the position can make money.

2. Explain how the position can lose money.

3. What is the position known as, and can it be considered a synthetic?

4. The stock rallies to $48.50, breaking key resistance in the process, and
    you do not want to be called away on your long stock. The 47.50 call
    is now priced at $2.00 and the 50 call is priced at $0.75. What action
    can you take to protect your position?

5. Describe the new risk-reward properties of the action taken in
    Question 4.

Scenario 2

You are looking at a market index currently trading at 1365. After doing your
market analysis, you believe that the market can move lower to the 1300–1325
area by expiration. There is a confluence of technical indicators showing that
1300 is solid support. The two trades you are considering are purchasing the
1350 put at $23.00 or purchasing the 1300–1350 put spread at $15.00.

1. Based on your thesis, which trade would you prefer to initiate?

2. The stock moves down as anticipated to 1300. What are two ways
    that you can "get out" of this position?

3. Describe the Greeks of boxes.

4. Assume you elected to "box" this trade. What are some risks associ-
    ated with boxes?

5. Break down all the synthetic positions in a long box.

Scenario 3

You have been long ABC stock in your family trust for many years. It has
appreciated tremendously, and you figure that just as you have insurance

on your home and car, you should implement an insurance plan on your investment in case a catastrophic event occurs.

1. What can you do to protect your investment in ABC stock without too much capital outlay, and what is the strategy called?

2. ABC stock is currently at $125.00. The six-month 100 put is trading at $3.00 and the six-month 135 call is trading at $6.50. Use these two options to construct your strategy and discuss the risk, reward, and break-even points.

3. The stock drops below $100.00. You are quite pleased that the 100 put is now providing protection. However, you do not want to exercise the long 100 put and thus trigger a sale. What action can you take to avoid this?

4. Describe the Greeks with this strategy.

5. What is a similar strategy that can be implemented if a trader is short stock instead of long stock?

Scenario 4

You are a volatility trader. You seek to trade stocks that have a tremendous amount of movement in either direction.

1. What basic strategies would you look to implement?

2. A pharmaceutical company is subject to approval of what could be the next "wonder" drug. The stock has moved up in anticipation of approval, but approval would mean even more movement to the upside. If approval is not granted, you anticipate that the stock will correct. In any case a large move is on the horizon. The stock is at $100.00. The 100 call is trading at $20.00, and the 100 put is trading at $19.00. What strategy can you use? Discuss the risk, reward, and breakeven.

3. Approval for the drug is granted and the stock moves from $100.00 to $120.00 on the day of the announcement. You are extremely excited that your hard work has paid off. Unfortunately, the 100 straddle that you purchased is trading at $40.00, only $1.00 more than you paid for it. What has happened?

4. You liquidate your straddle. You believe the stock should move sideways now, but you want to give it a little room. The 100 put is trading at $5.00 and the 140 call is at $4.50 with the stock at $120.00. What can you trade? Discuss the risk, reward, breakeven, and exposure to vega.

5. New developments are coming to light that could begin to move the stock. You don't want to take off the position but are getting more

concerned that volatility will begin to increase. The stock is still at $120.00. You want to take advantage of movement without the risk of having an intensive vega play like the 100 straddle you previously held. What can you do and what is that package called?

Scenario 5

Range-bound markets are your favorite. The idea of making money while the stock sits and not having unlimited loss exposure excites you.

1. What kinds of limited-risk strategies can be used in range-bound markets?

2. DEF stock is at $55.00. Use the following prices:

Calls	Strike	Puts
+3.50	52.5	+0.50
+1.75	55	+1.35
+0.75	57.5	+3.00

   What are the risk, reward, and break-even points if you were to purchase the 52.5/55/57.5 put butterfly?

3. Where do you want the stock to be to realize your maximum gain?

4. You don't quite think that you are going to hit the bull's-eye, and the stock could actually be in the small zone of 55–58. Can you trade another put butterfly that will increase the odds of making a profit, and what is that new position called?

5. If you are long the 52.5/55/57.5 put butterfly and then sell the 52.5/55/57.5 call butterfly, what is your position?

Answer Key

Scenario 1

1. The position can make money if the stock remains unchanged at $45.50. The 47.50 call would expire out-of-the-money and you would retain the entire premium of $1.50. The stock could also rally up to $47.50, in which case you would have a $2.00 gain on the stock in addition to the $1.50 collected from the expiring call. This would be a total of $3.50, which represents the maximum reward for this strategy. In addition, a decline in volatility would reduce the option premium of the 47.50 call; depending on the price of the stock, this could also make money.

2. This position is only partially hedged by the 47.50 call. The stock can drop by the amount of the call premium collected before the position begins to lose money. This is at $44.00 ($45.50 − $1.50), which represents the breakeven. If the stock drops any further, there is no more protection and you will lose dollar for dollar. In addition, a rise in volatility would increase the premium of the short call and depending on the stock price could also cause the position to lose money.

3. This position is known as a covered call. This is actually a misnomer. The only party covered is your brokerage/clearing firm. They consider it a "covered" because you already have long stock in your account in case the call is assigned. It can also be referred to as a buy-write or covered-write. The position is synthetically known as a short put. Short options have unlimited risk (stock price to zero in this case). Covered calls are much riskier then they are perceived to be because the stock is not protected all the way down to zero, only a portion of it.

4. The best way to protect your position is to roll up the 47.50 call. You can do this by purchasing the 47.50/50 call spread for $1.25. At this point you are now short the 50 call at $0.25 credit. Remember that you took in a $1.50 credit initially for the 47.50 call. You now have made $3.00 on the appreciation of the stock and could still collect a credit if the 50 call remains out-of-the-money at expiration.

5. The new position allows the stock to move up to $50.00 without having to worry about being assigned. You are still holding a $0.25 credit, so the stock could move lower by this amount before you begin to give back profits. The breakeven of the new position is at $48.25. The maximum reward is $1.75 (50.00 − 48.50 + 0.25), which occurs at $50.00. Again, this is a synthetic short put, so there is risk if the stock drops all the way to zero.

Scenario 2

1. The 1300–1350 put spread for $15.00 is the better choice here. If the index drops to 1325, which is the top of the predicted zone, both the put spread and the 1350 put will be worth $25.00 at expiration. The put spread costs $15.00 versus $23.00 for the 1350 put. If the index drops to 1300, then both trades will be worth $50.00. This will be a profit of $35.00 for the put spread and $27.00 for the 1350 put. Breakeven is 1335 for the put spread versus 1327 for the 1350 put.

2. The simplest way to get out of this position is by selling the 1300–1350 put spread. This may not be the best choice, however. If the index declines you will be dealing with in-the-money puts that have high deltas. Market makers will widen out the bid-ask spreads to compensate themselves for the higher delta risk. Thus, it might be more difficult to execute the put spread is when dealing with wider

bid-ask spreads. The calls, on the other hand, will be out-of-the-money and have smaller deltas and thus tighter bid-ask spreads. It would be easier to execute the 1300–1350 call spread. Purchasing this would "box" the trade and lock in profits, although increase commission costs.

3. Boxes do not have any delta, gamma, theta, or vega risk. They are considered "flat" positions. They may have exercise risk.

4. Since we know the value of a box at expiration with certainty, the value of that box today is the present value of the difference between strikes (European style expiration). Boxes do have rho risk. Changes in interest rates will change the value of the box. Additional risks include pin risk at expiration and possible assignment risk if the box is American style.

5. A long box consists of a long call spread and a long put spread. It also is a long combo at the lower strike and a short combo at the higher strike. It can be viewed as a reversal at the lower strike and a conversion at the higher strike with the stock canceling itself out. It can also be viewed as a long gut and a short strangle. Knowing all the synthetic relationships can help a trader lock in profits and reduce risk.

Scenario 3

1. A put with strike price below the current stock price can be purchased and a call with a strike price above the current stock price can be sold. This will provide downside protection, and the sale of the call will reduce the cost of the insurance. Depending on the strikes selected this can be implemented for a debit, for even money, or for a credit. This strategy is called a collar.

2. Using these options, you can construct the collar for $3.50 credit. If the stock remains unchanged you will keep the entire premium of the collar, thus generating income in a sideways market. The maximum reward is at 135, where the stock gains $10.00 and you still keep the entire premium of the collar for a total gain of $13.50. On the downside there is protection if the stock drops down to $121.50, because you have collected $3.50 from the collar. There is a zone where you will lose until the stock drops below the put strike and then begins to protect dollar for dollar on the downside.

3. The 100 put will have to be rolled down. This can be achieved by selling put spreads and collecting a credit. The credit you collect is like cashing in the insurance policy without giving up the full insurance.

4. The Greeks can be very tricky with collars. The important thing to know is whether you are approaching a long option or a short option

and whether it is a call or put. Knowing the basic properties of the Greeks, you can then figure out how they change. When the stock is anywhere between the strikes, you will have a net positive delta because of the long stock. If the stock drops below the put strike the long put will approach -100 deltas, taking the position down to zero deltas and fully hedging the position. On the upside, the short call will approach negative deltas, taking the position to zero deltas, thus eliminating any more potential gains. Gamma, theta, and vega will increase in absolute terms as you approach a strike and then decrease as you move away.

5. A reverse-collar can be implemented by shorting the downside put and buying the upside call. Because of how the equity skew is priced, this can almost always be achieved for credits and could offer good risk-reward parameters for traders who short stock.

Scenario 4

1. A trader that seeks volatility will be looking to trade strategies that have a great deal of exposure to vega. Two very vega-sensitive strategies involve straddles and strangles.

2. The 100 straddle can be obtained by purchasing the 100 call and the 100 put for a \$39.00 debit. This strategy's maximum risk is the debit paid, \$39.00. The reward may be considered unlimited if the stock continues to rally. There are two break-even points: the strike plus the debit, 139, and the strike minus the debit, 61.

3. The volatility of the options collapsed after the announcement. This is very typical. As people are placing their "bets" by purchasing puts and calls, market makers are increasing the premiums. When the announcement happens, people begin to cash in their winning "tickets" or unload their losing trades. This reduces the volatility and reduces option prices. This is the case here. Even though the movement that was anticipated occurred, the volatility was crushed and the position made very little money.

4. Shorting the 100/140 strangle would be appropriate. The strangle would collect \$9.50, which is your maximum reward. The break-even points are $100 - 9.50 = 90.50$ and $140 + 9.50 = 149.50$. This gives the stock some room to move without incurring losses. Since you are short options, the maximum risk is unlimited and the vega is negative. You want volatility to decrease.

5. Purchasing the 120 straddle while still holding the short 100/140 strangle would place you in the iron butterfly. This will result in profit if the stock moves up or down, away from the 120 strike, and gives you less exposure to vega in case you are wrong about the stock movement and volatility continues to decline.

Scenario 5

1. Butterflies, condors, and their iron equivalents are limited-risk strategies that can be used during sideways or consolidating markets.

2. The put fly can be purchased for $0.80. This is the maximum loss. This is a 2.50-point butterfly, so the maximum gain is $1.70. The break-even points are the lowest strike plus debit, or 53.30, and the highest strike minus debit, or 56.70.

3. With all butterflies, your maximum gain is realized at the middle strike.

4. Purchasing the 55/57.5/60 put butterfly will turn your position into the 52.5/55/57.5/60 put condor, which realizes its maximum profit if the stock falls in the 55/57.5 zone, thus increasing your odds of a profit.

5. You are short the 52.5/55 box and long the 55/57.5 box.

Index

About the Authors

Anthony J. Saliba has been a pioneer and active participant in the derivatives markets for more than twenty-five years. His derivatives activities have spanned derivatives trading, training, and developing electronic trading systems and solutions. He began his career trading equity options as an independent market maker at the Chicago Board Options Exchange (CBOE) in 1979. Over the next decade, he gained extensive experience in trading currencies, equities, and S&P 500 and S&P 100 contracts. In each of these markets, he emerged as a respected presence and quickly acquired a reputation as one of the top traders. His trading accomplishments, most notably his success during the crash of '87, earned him a place in the national bestseller *Market Wizards: Interviews with Top Traders*, by Jack Schwager.

Due to his innovative trading ideas, Saliba has become an internationally recognized consultant on the emergence and function of electronic markets and trading systems. He is often quoted in industry publications, including the *Wall Street Journal*, the *Financial Times*, and www.theStreet.com, and is frequently invited to speak at industry forums. He has founded numerous industry-related companies, including Saliba Partners, LLC (1984–1999), a proprietary options trading firm that included a Designated Primary Market Maker (DPM) floor operation on the Chicago Board Options Exchange; International Trading Institute, Ltd. (1989), a derivatives consulting and training firm providing advanced options trading education to large institutional market participants; First Traders Analytical Solutions, LLC (1992), a provider of front- and middle-office trading, pricing, and risk-management systems; LiquidPoint, LLC (1999), a broker-dealer offering options execution/facilitation and enhanced liquidity and potential price improvement for many large Wall Street firms; and Saliba Portfolio Management, LLC (2002), a portfolio management firm providing state-of-the-art investment enhancement techniques through the use of derivatives. In July 2007, Saliba's firm, LiquidPoint, LLC, became part of BNY ConvergEx Group, a leading global agency brokerage and investment technology firm. Saliba is a director of BNY ConvergEx Group and continues to serve as president and CEO of LiquidPoint.

Joseph C. Corona has been actively involved in trading options for more than twenty-five years. During this time he traded on the floors of the Chicago Board Options Exchange, the Chicago Board of Trade, the Chicago

Mercantile Exchange, and the London International Financial Futures and Options Exchange, as well as in the over-the-counter markets and the major electronic venues. During the course of his career he has traded equity, equity index, fixed income, currency, energy, and commodities options both as a market maker and proprietary trader. In addition, he has extensive experience in the training and management of derivatives traders and has built and managed trading desks in the United States, Europe, and Asia.

Corona has also been an adjunct instructor at International Trading Institute since 1990, delivering courses in advanced options trading and risk analysis techniques to hundreds of traders and trading desks in North, South, and Central America; Europe; and Asia. He also contributes to various financial markets websites and is a frequent speaker at industry conferences.

Karen E. Johnson joined Saliba in 1992 and has been actively involved in the start-up and/or management of a number of Saliba-affiliated companies, including Saliba Partners, First Traders Analytical Solutions, LiquidPoint, SalibaCo, LLC, International Trading Institute, and Saliba Portfolio Management. Her focus has been in the areas of business and product development, operations management, and sales.

Johnson is the former president of International Trading Institute and currently serves on its board of directors. Throughout her sixteen years with the Saliba companies, she has spent much of her time working with global financial institutions developing curricula and training programs for both established markets and such emerging marketplaces as Mexico, Panama, Colombia, Korea, Malaysia, and Poland.

Her previous publishing experience includes developing the concept and managing the writing and publication of *The Options Workbook: Fundamental Spread Concepts and Strategies*, by Anthony J. Saliba and the staff of International Trading Institute. Currently in its third edition, it has proven to be an excellent educational tool for the novice investor or trader.

About International Trading Institute

Anthony J. Saliba's awareness of the need for derivatives education in the marketplace inspired him to start International Trading Institute (ITI) in 1989. ITI offers hands-on options trading workshops delivered by professional traders. The hallmark of the ITI curriculum is the fostering of rigor and discipline in trading and risk management. ITI is an internationally renowned firm that has trained more than five thousand students from over thirty countries in the past nineteen years. Clientele include many large global financial institutions such as Citibank, DeutscheBank, UBS, and Credit Suisse. We invite you to visit our website, www.itichicago .com, for more information about our workshops or for additional option strategy lessons and commentary.

About Bloomberg

Bloomberg L.P., founded in 1981, is a global information services, news, and media company. Headquartered in New York, the company has sales and news operations worldwide.

Serving customers on six continents, Bloomberg, through its wholly-owned subsidiary Bloomberg Finance L.P., holds a unique position within the financial services industry by providing an unparalleled range of features in a single package known as the Bloomberg Professional® service. By addressing the demand for investment performance and efficiency through an exceptional combination of information, analytic, electronic trading, and straight-through-processing tools, Bloomberg has built a worldwide customer base of corporations, issuers, financial intermediaries, and institutional investors.

Bloomberg News, founded in 1990, provides stories and columns on business, general news, politics, and sports to leading newspapers and magazines throughout the world. Bloomberg Television, a 24-hour business and financial news network, is produced and distributed globally in seven languages. Bloomberg Radio is an international radio network anchored by flagship station Bloomberg 1130 (WBBR-AM) in New York.

In addition to the Bloomberg Press line of books, Bloomberg publishes *Bloomberg Markets* magazine. To learn more about Bloomberg, call a sales representative at:

London: +44-20-7330-7500
New York: +1-212-318-2000
Tokyo: +81-3-3201-8900

SUBSCRIBE TO *BLOOMBERG MARKETS* & GET A FREE ISSUE

The magazine for and about people who move markets.

• Free issue plus 12 more for $19.95
• Save more with two years for $29.95

To subscribe to *BLOOMBERG MARKETS*, go to:
www.bloomberg.com/news/marketsmag/